STUCK ON THE DRAWING BOARD

STUCK ON THE DRAWING BOARD

UNBUILT BRITISH
COMMERCIAL AIRCRAFT
SINCE 1945

RICHARD PAYNE

TEMPUS

Dedication

This book is dedicated to my mother and father for all the assistance that they have given me in its preparation, and also to both my nans who sadly passed away before my book could be realised.

First published 2004
Reprinted 2006

Tempus Publishing Ltd
The Mill, Brimscombe Port
Stroud, Gloucestershire GL5 2QG
www.tempus-publishing.com

British Library Cataloguing in Publication Data.
A catalogue record for this book is available from the British Library.

ISBN 0 7524 3172 2

Typesetting and origination by Tempus Publishing.
Printed and bound in Great Britain.

Contents

Acknowledgements

Having spent the best part of over six years researching this book, there are many people who have devoted a lot of time and effort in assisting me. To anybody I have missed, please accept my apologies.

Aviation Traders

Avro Heritage Centre

BAE SYSTEMS

B–N Group

Bombardier Aerospace

Boulton Paul Association

Bristol Aero Collection

British Airways Archives

Brough Heritage

FHL

GKN Aerospace Services

GKN Westland

Handley Page Archives

Hunting

Imperial War Museum

Midland Air Museum

Museum of Berkshire Aviation

North West Heritage

RAF Museum Hendon

Southampton Hall of Aviation

Ulster Aviation Society

Westland Helicopters

Richard Micklefield

George Jenks

Pamela and Barry Guess, Mike Fielding
   Airbus Mike Fish
   Prestwick Ian Adams
   Woodford Dan Gurney

Sheila Dewart and Mark Wilson

Olivia Johnson

Cyril Plimmer

John Battersby and Oliver Dearden

Keith Hayward

Steve Gillard

R.J. Harris

David Cheek

A.J. Roden

A. Fraser-Mitchell

Anna Blundell-Williams

Yvonne Oliver

Diane James

Jean and Ken Fostekew

Brian Tomlinson

Peter Elliott

D. Upward

Paul McMaster

Fred Ballam and David Gibbings

Peter Amos (Folland & Miles)
Bill Harrison (Fairey)
Brian Kerry (AT(E)L)
Derek King
Eric Myall
Brian Robinson (AT(E)L)
Ray Wheeler (Saunders Roe)

John Wilson
Tony Butler
Colin Cruddas (Flight Refuelling)
De Havilland Heritage Museum
Grahame Gates (Miles)
David Gearing (Hunting)
Alan Greenhalgh (Beagle & Avro)

Special thanks must also be made to Mike Hooks, Mike Eacock and Ray Williams for kindly supplying a number of illustrations and photographs; to the kind generosity, time and hospitality of Mr & Mrs Derek Brown and to Mr Nigel Price who also devoted a lot of time and effort as well as feeding me in the process.

I would also like especially to thank the staff at the Brooklands Museum, including Julian Temple, Jack Fuller and Albert Kitchenside, for allowing me endless access to the archives and providing much valuable assistance.

As a source for further reference, the Public Records Office at Kew is invaluable, and among the many files that were consulted the most relevant were AVIA 54, 63 & 65, BT 217 & 245, DR1 and DSIR 23 & 27.

Finally, I would like to thank my mother and father for their patience, in putting up with piles of old archive material, reading my manuscript and checking for grammatical errors, as well as acting as chauffeur, and in many cases general gofers – a big thank you to the both of them. Without them I could never have done this – and they now probably know as much about unbuilt aircraft as I do.

Preface

An interest in anything that never actually happened is unusual, so how did my interest in unbuilt British transport projects occur?

Over twenty years ago, for Christmas I was bought two excellent books; Derek Wood's *Project Cancelled* and Charles Gardner's *British Aircraft Corporation*. During the festive season these books were read and reread. Suddenly I was greeted by projects that I had never heard of, let alone seen pictures of before – a whole new world of aerospace had been opened up to me, full of delights such as the BAC Three-Eleven, Vickers V1000, Bristol 200 and many, many more.

Since that time I have scoured air fairs, bookshops, anywhere I might find more information – magazines, brochures, anything on those projects for which nothing or very little survives. I have been lucky that so many people have been able to share my enthusiasm, rooting through attics for long put away memories of their working lives, or sifting through boxes of archives in museums.

So to those people, I hope that this book means as much as it does to me, to show just how much work has been done by those in the British Aircraft Industry, and yet who today have so little to show for their endeavours. Many opportunities presented themselves over the years for Britain to remain a major force in the Aerospace field. Sadly, it seems those days are now long gone – so it is perhaps fitting that with the last Avro RJ having taken to the skies (and with it the last of a long line of British transports) we can take time to reflect on some of those wondrous projects that design offices spent so many hours working on.

Chapter 1

Success and Failure

The commercial activities of the British Aircraft Industry since the end of the Second World War are a paradox. On the one hand they have consistently produced aircraft that have broken new grounds, both in technology – the Comet, Viscount, Britannia and Concorde, and in environmental consideration – the 146. Yet, in the majority of cases, the industry appears to have failed to capitalise on this and convert these firsts into profitable and large production runs. It seems that, commercially at least, British invention and being ahead of the competition has nearly always meant coming off second best. All the successes that should have been enjoyed by hundreds, if not thousands, of successful British transports – especially jets – rolling off British production lines, built by British workers and earning valuable foreign currency, seem to have been reaped by those in the Americas and Europe.

Since 1945 the British Industry as a whole have been beset by problems caused by a multitude of factors. Some, admittedly, have been of its own doing, but many are the result of incessant government interference with stop-go-stop policies and numerous reports, such as the infamous Sandy's White Paper of 1957, and the Plowden Report of 1965. Neither of these made comforting reading to either the leaders of industry or to its workers, who saw that in the first instance, there would be practically no future in military aircraft design and production, and in the second, the ending of government funding for indigenous British transport aircraft. Is it therefore any wonder that many of the world's airlines shied away from buying British during these difficult and turbulent times, when there was no guarantee that their products would still be in production a few years hence.

Notwithstanding this, was the indifference shown by one of the state airlines, namely BOAC (British Overseas Airways Corporation), towards the home industry, especially from the mid-fifties onwards. This resulted in the taxpayer being asked to fund the airline's future purchases, but with the airline refusing to reciprocate by buying British aircraft supported by British taxpayers. It was therefore fortunate during this difficult period that sister carrier BEA (British European Airways) maintained its support for the home industry – in turn transforming the Viscount into a major success and supporting, if not ever being able to operate, both the BAC Two-Eleven and Three-Eleven jetliners. Of course BEA also made mistakes – its biggest being the panic decision to scale back the potentially world-beating original de Havilland 121 design after a dip in passenger traffic and, instead, ordering what eventually became the underpowered, reduced range and much smaller Trident.

It is, of course, easy to be retrospective with regards to policies of the time, but the failure of both the government and BOAC to support the Vickers V1000 and its civil VC7 derivative, was probably the most costly error of all. Amazingly, BOAC, who in 1955 saw no

BAC Three-Eleven
Possibly the most important transport aircraft ever considered in Britain, the BAC Three-Eleven, shown in BEA
colours, could have heralded a new dawn for the British Aircraft Industry. (Copyright BAE SYSTEMS – via
Brooklands Museum Trust)

requirement for a new long-range jetliner, suddenly, just twelve months later, with
government blessing, were allowed to order US Boeing jets. This set a precedent for the
airline's future purchases, a policy that has been maintained to this day by its successor British
Airways – bar the Airbus narrow body order a few years ago.

It is worth remembering that prior to the Second World War, attempts had been made to
recapture ground already lost to the German and American industries with two new large
British aircraft specifications, 14/38 for a long-haul transport, and 15/38 a short-medium-
haul aircraft. These projects had been the result of a committee set up in November 1937
under Lord Cadman, who had reported on the lack of British contractors to embark on
modern commercial transports. As a result of this failure to remain with the game, any new
British project would now be competing against the DC2 and DC3. In an effort to assist
manufacturers, the government was willing to provide financial assistance towards the cost of
production tooling and development of a prototype. The Short S32 was chosen for 14/38 and
the Fairey FC1 (Fairey Commercial) for 15/38, against proposals from Bristol, General (GAL
40) and Folland. By 1939 production on the prototype FC1 was well advanced with a wooden
mock-up having been built at Hayes, while three S32 fuselages were under construction.
However, the outbreak of the Second World War led to all resources and manufacture
naturally being directed towards bomber and fighter aircraft design and production. As a result
of these changed priorities, development of the new airliners was unable to be continued. The
FC1 was cancelled on 17 October, and the S32 on 13 November 1939.

The advent of war naturally stifled commercial aircraft design and production in Britain.
Both of the above projects would certainly have provided competition to the new DC4 and

BAe 146-300
Had it been launched in 1984, BAe's original stretched 146-300, which could accommodate between 120 and 130 passengers, and had increased power and additional wingtips, may well have captured some of the large orders that went to the competing Fokker 100. (Copyright BAE SYSTEMS)

Constellation emerging from American factories, but to what degree of success, is, of course, pure conjecture. It was not until around 1941 that confidence allowed even consideration being given to the future requirements of the airline industry on the war's conclusion, which, in the event, was to be a further four years in the future.

What is especially evident in the twenty-five years that followed the war's cessation is how the fortunes of the industries were so intrinsically dependent on the state carriers: BOAC, BEA and for a short time BSAAC (British South American Airways Corporation). All airliner policy, bar some small private ventures, was so directed towards meeting the requirements of the two state carriers, especially specification wise, that little attention was directed towards the all important export market. That this occurred at a time when maintaining production in British factories and earning valuable foreign currency should have been a priority, showed how insular future planning was at that time. By the early sixties the American jetliner industry had succeeded in achieving a near-virtual monopoly on supplying the world's major airlines (bar orders for the French Caravelle). The only exception to this was in the Soviet Union and Britain, whose industries continued to produce designs so tailored towards their own state airlines that there was little chance of expanding production and development through lucrative overseas orders.

That the majority of aircraft design and production immediately after the war was dedicated to BOAC and BEA (plus BSAAC for a short while) was due to the air transport system that operated in Britain at that time. From 12 April 1947, BOAC became the sole operator of intercontinental services, except for BSAAC services to South America, with the newly set up British European Airways Corporation flying all European and internal scheduled services (although private airlines were later able to operate routes under BEA Associate Agreements). This date signalled the end of privately operated scheduled services in Britain for a number of years. As a consequence of this, all future airliner production would be directed by the two main carriers, firstly under the Brabazon Committee, and then under such specifications as the Medium-Range and Long-Range Empire aircraft and replacements for the Rapide, DC3 and Viscount.

This stranglehold by the state carriers on British manufacturers was only broken when the newly formed second force airline British United Airways was formed in 1960, by the merger of the Airwork Group and Hunting-Clan. When the new carrier placed the launch order in May 1961 for ten BAC One-Elevens, it became the first major British airliner launched without sponsorship by a state carrier.

Interestingly, this aircraft was to become the cornerstone of British commercial aircraft manufacture throughout the sixties and seventies, proving invaluable to its maker BAC, and becoming the bestselling jet transport produced in the UK until the 146 series overtook it in the nineties. It too, could have had even greater success had fate, in the hands of Rolls-Royce in 1971 and British Airways in 1978, not precluded its development even further. This resulted in British Aerospace finalising a deal for future production of the type to be undertaken under licence in Romania, initially from kits supplied from UK production lines.

Aerospace has always been, and continues to be, a pawn in the hands of politicians. On the one hand they applaud the achievements of the industry and the enormous contribution it makes to UK plc, yet this acclaim has, on many occasions, failed to be backed by hard cash at times when it was so important. The foremost instances of this have been the failure to support the V1000/VC7, full UK partnership on the original A300 and the BAC Three-Eleven.

Almost in spite of this negativity, amazingly, since 1945 over 5,000 UK-designed transports have been produced. Yet, of these, only the Viscount, Dove, Jetstream 31, 1-11, 125, Islander, 748 and 146 series can really be considered a success. The majority of the fifty or so different designs that actually reached production failed to be built in significant numbers and some, such as the Brabazon, Princess, Rotodyne and Accountant, were only flown in single figures.

Vickers Valiant and V1000
Models of the Vickers Valiant bomber and Vickers V1000 military transport show the family resemblance between the two. The cancellation of the V1000 and its commercial sister aircraft, the VC7, was to many minds the start of the decline of the British Aircraft Industry. (Copyright BAE SYSTEMS – via Brooklands Museum Trust)

*Avro Atlantic
Based around the Avro
Vulcan Bomber, the four
turbojet-powered Type 722
Atlantic was designed as a
Transatlantic airliner, with
seating for up to 113
passengers. (Copyright BAE
SYSTEMS − via Tony
Butler)*

Of those that promised so much, de Havilland's Comet failed because structurally it was ahead of its time. The major investigations that followed the tragic crashes ensured that all future British and foreign aircraft should never experience the failures that the Comet airframe suffered. The much-praised VC10 was initially too late for the big jet market and then suffered the indignity of its own sponsoring airline wishing to cancel its order for an aircraft that had been designed specifically for its own use. This negativity did much damage to BAC's sales campaigns and caused the cancellation of at least one export order.

The One-Eleven, a potentially world-beating design, firstly suffered through the loss of the prototype aircraft when encountering a deep stall problem, and secondly, the failure of being developed further into the larger and more powerful series 600. This meant that as passenger numbers grew, potential major customers were not offered a growth aircraft which could have competed against the 737 and DC9. Concorde, although a technological 'tour de force', saw its future abridged by the economic crisis of the mid-seventies, combined with the suddenly more vocal US environmental pressure which came to light after the cancellation of their own SST.

What is certainly true is that the post-war years saw far too many British companies embarking on both commercial and military projects. There were just not enough contracts to be distributed between, what amounted to at the war's cessation, around twenty-seven different design and production teams. The opportunity which therefore presented itself in the immediate post-war period should have seen some major consolidation in the industry.

When reorganisation did belatedly arrive in 1960, the result was to be two main aircraft companies, Hawker Siddeley Aviation and the British Aircraft Corporation (BAC), each formed by the takeover or merger of most of the airframe companies. Westland at Yeovil absorbed all British helicopter activity, which then encompassed Bristol Helicopters, Fairey and Saunders Roe. Meanwhile, the majority government-owned Short Brothers & Harland remained outside of the new big groups and continued to be treated as a special case. Of the remaining companies, Handley Page soldiered on for a short time as the last of the original independents, despite having held talks with Hawker Siddeley. In the light aircraft field Beagle Aircraft (British Executive and General Aircraft Ltd) was formed, taking over Auster and F.G. Miles. Today all that remains is BAE SYSTEMS (a shadow of the former nationalised British Aerospace Corporation), AgustaWestland, B-N Group (formerly Britten-Norman) and Bombardier (Shorts), together with the UK factories at Filton and Broughton of Airbus UK.

When in 1977 the nationalisation of the industries saw the creation of the British Aerospace Corporation (BAe), an opportunity arose for what would become one final major investment in new transports. One of the major decisions was for BAe to rejoin the Airbus programme, albeit in a much reduced capacity to that originally conceived, while the 146 feederliner was relaunched and a new variant of the Jetstream re-entered production. However, at the same time one final opportunity arose to produce a new 150-seater jet.

The decision at the time not to proceed with a British-based programme, either the BAe (BAC) X-Eleven or European JET meant that France and the Toulouse factory has become the main centre for all future European mainline transports, including the new Airbus A380, although the former EADS factory at Hamburg does have final assembly of the A318, A319 and A321 series. This, amazingly, was a situation that was foretold, and worried industrialists over a decade beforehand, but it is now evident that little was done to avoid it.

The closure of the BAE SYSTEMS RJX programme as announced at the end of 2001 firstly brought to an end indigenous airliner manufacture in Britain, but secondly, and with added poignancy, meant that this 146 derivative will probably be the last UK-designed transport. It is therefore highly unlikely in the present climate that any major new British commercial designs will emerge from the design offices of BAE SYSTEMS, AgustaWestland or Bombardier – Shorts.

It is interesting to conjecture just what the economic state of the country would now be had some of the projects shown and described in the following chapters ever been realised. Certainly the cancellation of the VC7 and Three-Eleven severely impaired the future success of an indigenous transport industry, from which it was never able to recover fully. The decision to withdraw from the original Airbus A300 reduced future British influence over this important programme, which became further evident when Britain rejoined the programme in 1979, playing second fiddle to both Aerospatiale and Deutsche Airbus. In the new Airbus Integrated Co. – which is now basically a subsidiary of EADS who own 80 per cent – BAE SYSTEMS is purely the minor shareholder with the remaining balance, and for how long will this share be maintained?

When the aircraft designers could at last turn their attentions away from the war effort, one could certainly not accuse the projects that emanated from their drawing boards as lacking vision. Since 1945, over 500 commercial aircraft designs have emerged from companies both big and small, many of these purely design office studies rather than meeting a hard specification. Among those projects that remained stillborn included mammoth 1,000-seater jet flying boats, variable geometry supersonic airliners and vertical take-off and landing transports.

What the future state of the British Industries may have been had some of the projects mentioned gone ahead, we will never know. This once great and proud industry is now but a shadow of its former self with none of its great leaders to guide it. The heart and policy of the largest British aircraft company, BAE SYSTEMS, now appears to lie little with actually designing and building aircraft, and more with systems integration, with much of the company now based in the USA. We can, however, at least take a glimpse into those studies that promised so much.

Sadly, many of the details of project studies have now been lost, destroyed in purges at factories or even more tragically burnt when former design centres were bulldozed. However, through the efforts of heritage centres, museums and personal records, many have been saved for posterity; these are the projects that forever remained stuck on the drawing board.

Chapter 2

The Brabazon Committee

The onset of war naturally led to a near cessation of thoughts on transport aircraft design. There was also a long-held belief, although never acknowledged, that with agreement with the United States, Britain dropped all her research into the production of heavy transport aircraft. Whether this was true or not, the six-year-war period did cause a near stagnation in that sector of industry. When the war concluded, the US was already well advanced with its big and efficient Douglas DC4 and Lockheed Constellation airliners, both of which would make great impressions on the world's airways.

However, Britain did not completely abandon all thoughts of transport aircraft development. In 1941 a committee was formed on civil aviation to consider transport variants of military aircraft and among the aircraft reviewed were the Short Shetland and Stirling. Around the same time Sir Ralph Sorley (Air Ministry) and Sir Roy Fedden (formerly chief engineer and designer at Bristol Aeroplane) were shown some of the work being carried out on civil designs while on a tour of the US Aerospace industry.

Reporting on their return, the British government announced its intention to investigate the development of future civil transport designs. Following this, a more challenging inter-departmental committee was appointed by the Ministry of Aircraft Production and the Secretary of State for Air: its remit to 'advise on the design and production of transport aircraft'. The objective of this committee was to recommend the development of a number of designs, which, more importantly, would not directly be in competition with those aircraft already established in the market i.e. those from the USA. These aircraft would be required to demonstrate a significant advance in design, 'jumping a generation', and be able to steal a march on their US competitors.

In effect, it can be seen that British Civil Aircraft manufacture can be considered to have started afresh from the war's cessation.

The Brabazon Committees

The Committee set up by the Minister of Aircraft Production, Col. Llewellyn, asked an early aviation pioneer, Lord Brabazon of Tara, his predecessor, to act as chairman. This committee, originally called the Transport Aircraft Committee, began working on 23 December 1942. Its remit was to prepare an 'outline specification for several aircraft types needed for post-war air transport' and, also to consider which military aircraft could best be converted into transport aircraft. This, it was felt, was essential in order to maintain the industry in the short term, both in design and production when the war finished, ensuring that American transports were not bought, allied with the foreign currency problems that would be caused by this. As is usual, the committee took the name of its chairman and, from then onwards became known as the now-famous Brabazon Committee.

The members of the committee were to be taken from the Air Ministry, Ministry of Aircraft Production and Ministry of Production. These were Lt-Col. Sir Francis Shelmerdine (an ex-director of civil aviation), N.E. Rowe (Director of Technical Development at the Ministry of Aircraft Production), Sir Henry Self, W.P. Hildred, K.T. Spencer and J.H. Riddoch as secretary.

The committee reported to the cabinet on 9 February 1943 and proposed four types of military aircraft that could be converted to commercial transports for the interim. These were the Short Sunderland, a variant of the Handley Page Halifax with a new larger fuselage (which became the Hermes in civil form), the Lancaster-derived Avro York (already flying as a prototype) and the Short Shetland. The report also continued with plans for five completely new commercial landplanes which were numbered from one to five and would give valuable production work after the war.

The original five types were as follows:

> **Type 1** – a pressurised long-range airliner capable of travelling non-stop from London to New York to be powered by six or eight engines with a cruising speed of 275mph. The most ambitious of all the proposals, it was estimated that this major project would take more than five years to reach production.
>
> **Type 2** – An unpressurised DC3 replacement able to carry twenty passengers on Empire and European feeder services at more than 200mph.
>
> **Type 3** – A four-engined Empire route airliner to replace the York.
>
> **Type 4** – A North Atlantic jet propelled mailplane cruising at more than 400mph.
>
> **Type 5** – A small feederliner able to carry up to twelve passengers for colonial and domestic UK routes.

The report stressed the need for work to begin on at least four of the five types as soon as possible. Failure to do so, they said, could result in the types as finally produced already being obsolete. The committee also went to great lengths to stress the need for the industries to continue after the war, and the importance of an associated air transport structure being in place to operate these new aircraft types.

A second committee was established, again chaired by Lord Brabazon, to 'consider the types recommended in relation to traffic needs and economics and to prepare a list of requirements for each type in sufficient detail to provide a working basis for design and development and to recommend accordingly'. Among the members of this new committee were Capt. Geoffrey de Havilland and A.C. Campbell Orde, who represented the aircraft and airline industries respectively. The first report was issued in August 1943 and mostly concerned the importance of the Type 1, with its non-stop, all-year North Atlantic service.

The second interim report, published in November 1943, proposed that the Type 3 Specification be split into two, with the original design becoming the Type 3A while a new Medium/Long-Range Empire/European aircraft able to carry between forty and sixty passengers became the Type 3B. The Type 5 Specification was also split, with the Type 5A being a new fourteen-seater, and the Type 5B taking on the old Type 5 Specification for an eight-seater transport. The report also called for the conversion of the Lancaster IV for commercial use (this requiring a pressurised fuselage and improved wing), the aircraft as proposed by the Air Ministry becoming the Avro Tudor (Avro 687, later superseded by the Avro 688).

The publication of the third interim report in July 1944 saw a fundamental change, as the Type 4 Specification had now evolved from a mailplane into a passenger-carrying jetliner for Empire and European routes. Meanwhile, the Type 5A was now being recommended with four engines and the 3B was being proposed for long-haul European, South African and Empire services.

The fourth interim report was published in November 1944, by which time the Type 1 had become known as the Bristol 167, with possible proposals for a stretched variant for short-haul services. With the 167 now having further potential in addition to one stop and non-stop Transatlantic services and, with the availability of the Tudor, the need for the Type 3A was less pressing. A new Type 3 Specification was therefore issued, replacing Types 3A and 3B for a pressurised twenty-five-passenger berthed aircraft for medium/long-haul Empire services.

By the time the fifth interim report was published in November 1945, the committee had already recommended the development of a Type 2B turboprop medium-haul airliner (the original Type 2 becoming the 2A) for which two separately designed prototypes were to be ordered.

In view of the leading role Britain was playing in the development of turbine aircraft engines through the work of two engineers Dr A.A. Griffith at the RAE and Sir Frank Whittle, it was not surprising that the Committee recommended that the use of these new engines would give an important competitive advantage over the established American designs that were piston-powered. In fact, since 1943, increasing attention had been devoted to propeller turbines, and the first engine of this type in the world to fly, the Rolls-Royce Trent, did so in a Gloster Meteor on 20 September 1945.

With a valuable amount of design and production work expected from these new specifications, it is not surprising that nearly all of Britain's major transport manufacturers presented designs for at least one of the new Types required, although some of those submitted were unsolicited.

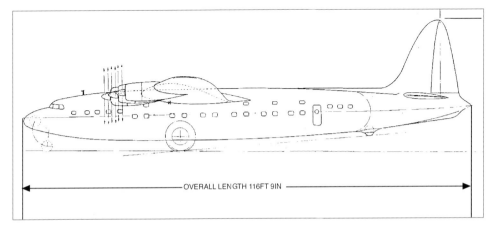

OVERALL LENGTH 116FT 9IN

Short 'Transatlantic Express'
An unsolicited proposal from Shorts for the Brabazon 1 Specification, the 'Transatlantic Express' high-wing monoplane was powered by six Bristol Centaurus 12 engines. (Courtesy of Bombardier Aerospace)

Type 1 (Specification 2/44)

The specification for the Type 1 Brabazon project was issued as 2/44 for a 'Civil Transport for the North Atlantic service'. This was cancelled by Specification 2/44/2 on 15 August 1946. The type was the only one for which a public announcement was made about its construction, this being made on 11 March 1943. The Type 1 under contract 2/44/2 was for the construction of a prototype aircraft which could operate non-stop services between London and New York from prepared runways. The aircraft should be able to operate over a range of 3,000 nautical miles with power being provided by eight Bristol Centaurus engines buried within the wing with the possibility of access during flight. These would drive 4 co-axial propellers of the fully feathering type and, of which at least two of the inboard propellers should have reversible pitch propellers. Accommodation was to be provided for fifty sleeping passengers and 100 day passengers, together with a crew of two pilots, five stewards and a radio officer, engineer and navigator.

Such a project was a mammoth task for British industry to undertake and, as such, was given top priority in relation to design and prototype construction, with the first production aircraft envisaged in five years. The contract was only issued to Bristol Aircraft, who had already been working on a massive 100-ton bomber.

The resultant design, the Bristol 167 Brabazon, took five years before making its inaugural flight on 4 September 1949 and has been well documented with regards to its infamous career. It remains the largest landplane ever built in Britain, necessitating the demolition of part of a village close to the Bristol Filton factory. However, by the time of its first flight it was already

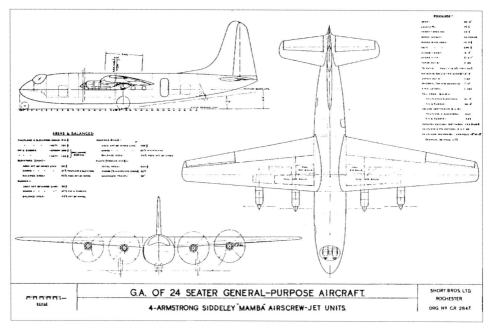

Short S.A5/S.43/General Purpose Transport
Originally proposed in both high- and low-wing layouts, the S.A5 or general purpose transport was Shorts
proposal to meet the Brabazon 2 Specifications. (Courtesy of Bombardier Aerospace)

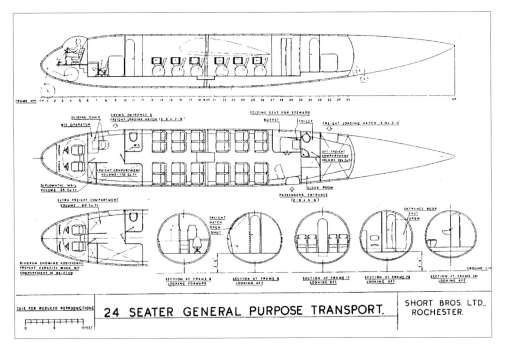

Short S.A5/S.43/General Purpose Transport
Interior layout of the S.A5/General Purpose Transport, showing accommodation at four abreast for up to twenty-four passengers. (Courtesy of Bombardier Aerospace)

out of date – the Brabazon 4 jetliner (de Havilland Comet) had flown some five weeks earlier and the writing was already on the wall for slow cruise ship luxury airliners. 'Speed not luxury' was the new 'in' phrase – the faster the better. Production of the Brabazon 2 powered by the Proteus turboprop continued for a short time, while the sister aircraft continued test flying up to its 164th and final flight which was made on the 20th September 1952. The order to cancel the programme was not made until 17 July 1953, with work on scrapping both aircraft beginning in October of that year.

The Bristol 167 was the only solicited proposal for the Brabazon 1 Specification, the contract not being open to competitive tender, it having been deemed a waste of resources for the specification to be issued to industry and, thereby dissipating the all important design effort during the war. Two other British manufacturers, namely Shorts and Miles, did put forward unsolicited proposals for the requirement without having seen the official specification.

Shorts

Short Type 1 Proposal – 'Transatlantic Express'

The Short proposal for the Type 1 originally came at the instigation of BOAC when they submitted a sketch of a much smaller aircraft than the 167 with an AUW of 175,000lb. The design was of a high-wing monoplane powered by six Bristol Centaurus 12 engines mounted in conventional nacelles on the wing, with a cruising speed of 259mph and a cruising height

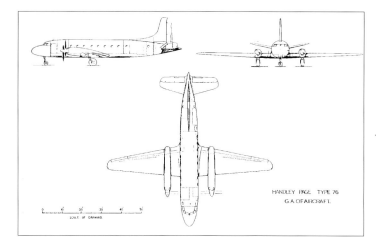

HANDLEY PAGE   TYPE 76
G.A. OF AIRCRAFT

Handley Page HP.76
The first of a trio of designs
from Handley Page to meet
the Brabazon 2B
Specification, the HP.76
was powered by Armstrong
Siddeley Mamba coupled
twin turboprops driving
contra-rotating propellers.
(RAF Museum Hendon)

of 20,000ft. Seating capacity was for up to twenty-four day passengers with alternative night-time accommodation provided for twenty-four beds, two per compartment, each with folding washbasins.

Length 116ft 9in, Span 184ft, Height 33ft, Wing Area 3,073sq.ft

Short Tailless Type 1 Proposal

A second proposal for a large long-range pusher aircraft was studied with Prof. G.T.R. Hill, who had pioneered tailless aircraft. The design powered by five Rolls-Royce Griffon or Centaurus engines was based around Hill's Pterodactyl VIII study. The interior of what was basically a 'flying wing' airliner featured a quilted pressurised cabin in the centre of the plane which was formed by intersecting spherical shells. The cabin would have been spacious but was ahead of its time. Freight and fuel would be carried in the swept wings. With an all-up weight of 185,000lb, a cruising speed of 287mph could be attained with a cruising altitude of 20,000ft.

Span 176ft, Wing Area 5,300sq.ft

The Ministry of Aircraft Production could not, however, see itself at the time giving a contract to Shorts for a civil prototype, as it had just recently lost the services of its chief designer Arthur Gouge, and it was felt that their resources were already stretched for the war effort.

Miles

X11

Miles' project was based around the company's X configuration, which saw the engines being buried within the wing as had featured in earlier design studies including the X7 and X10. The fifty-seater X11 featured a cruising speed of 350mph and a range of 3,450 miles powered by eight Rolls-Royce P.I.26 engines of 2,300hp coupled in pairs and buried in the laminar flow high wing, which was blended into the fuselage. With an all-up weight of 165,000lb and payload of 24,000lb the design was the smallest of the Type 1 proposals.

Length 110ft, Span 150ft, Wing Area 2,350sq.ft

Type 2

The Type 2 was to be a short-haul twin-engined aircraft of all-metal construction. It was intended to replace the DC3 for short- and medium- range routes within the British Commonwealth, and it was thought that it would take 3 1/2 years to reach production. The type was eventually to be met by two separate requirements – the Type 2A powered by two piston engines, and the Type 2B by four turboprops.

Type 2A (Specifciation 25/43)

Airspeed AS.57 Ambassador

The first of the Brabazon Committee's contracts, 25/43, was issued on 15 September 1944 to Airspeed Aircraft for construction of a high-wing prototype twin-engined Centaurus transport to operate over short- and medium-range routes and be able to accommodate up to thirty-nine passengers. A cruising speed of 200mph was to be achieved over short stage lengths. The aircraft proved to be a success, but time had overtaken the project; by the time it had made its maiden flight from Christchurch on 10 July 1947, the Brabazon Committee had already recommended development of the turboprop Type 2B. The resultant design, the Vickers VC2, coupled with the Rolls-Royce Dart turboprop engine, proved a winner and, despite being popular with passengers, the only customer for the Ambassador remained BEA, who took twenty aircraft.

Westland Projects

The Westland Co. undertook a number of studies of projects for a Type 2A airliner which included a thirty-seater powered by two Rolls-Royce or Armstrong Siddeley engines of 1000hp, with an all-up weight of 18,500lb.
Span 61ft

Type 2B (Specification 8/46)

Specification 8/46 for the new Type 2B was for an aircraft able to operate over short- and medium-range routes, to accommodate up to thirty-two passengers, powered by four gas turbine engines and for the possible carriage of mixed cargo. A cruising speed of no less than 240 knots was envisaged, with a still air range of 700 miles at a height of 20,000ft. The specification eventually emerged into two separate aircraft: the Vickers VC2 and the Armstrong Whitworth AW.55.

Vickers VC2 Viceroy (Type 609)

This groundbreaking Dart-powered aircraft, for which a contract was issued to Vickers in August 1946, made its first flight on 16 July 1948. A number of early studies featured alternative powerplants to the Dart including a four-engined Armstrong Siddeley Mamba and a twin Napier E128D Double Naiads variant. After a slow and worrying beginning, the design, quickly renamed Viscount, was stretched for BEA into the series 700 (forty to fifty-three seats) and then series 800 (standard accommodation up to sixty-five passengers). It went on to become one of the mainstays of the world's leading airlines during the fifties. With a production run of 444, it has remained the most successful mainline British transport aircraft. Competing alongside the VC2 for the Type 2B order were designs from Shorts and Blackburn.

Blackburn B-55

The original Blackburn submission to meet Type 2 appears to have been the Blackburn B-55, a 1946 design for a low-wing monoplane. Two variants were proposed: the Type 1, powered by four Rolls-Royce Dart engines with seating for twenty-four passengers at four abreast, with an AUW of 38,500lb, and the Type 2, powered by four Armstrong Siddeley Mambas with three abreast seating for twenty-four passengers and an AUW of 35,200lb.
(Type 1) Length 73ft 6in, Span 88ft, Height 26ft 6in, Wing Area 980sq.ft
(Type 2) Span 82ft, Wing Area 845sq.ft

Short S.A5/S43

Also shown in records as the twenty-four-seater General Purpose Aircraft, the S.A5 was one of the last designs to come from the Shorts Rochester design team before moving to Belfast. Originally studied in both high and low-wing configurations, a low-wing design was chosen with a tailplane mounted on the rear fuselage. Power was to be provided by four Armstrong Siddeley Mamba engines with an AUW of 40,000lb and seating for twenty-four passengers at four abreast, with freight holds at both the front and rear.
Length 72ft 6in, Span 90ft, Height 25ft 9in

Alongside the decision to order the VC2 was a stand-by option should the Dart powerplant fail. A contract was issued to Armstrong Whitworth Aircraft on 24 June 1947 for the AW.55 project.

Specification C16/46

Armstrong Whitworth AW.55 Apollo

Designed to Specification C16/46, the Apollo was to be powered by four Armstrong Siddeley Mamba turboprops. The failure of the Apollo lay with the choice of engine which had many shortcomings, mainly in efficiency. After making its first flight on 10 April 1949, both prototype aircraft were only to serve with the A & AEE (Aeroplane and Armament Experimental Establishment) and the RAE (Royal Aircraft Establishment). Armstrong Whitworth's strong military work and the lead set by the Viscount did not lead to the company devoting too much effort to trying to create a saleable aircraft by development and the project was soon dropped. One interesting development that was studied for a short time was the Mk2 variant, powered by four Rolls-Royce Derwent jet engines. The Viscount had already made a similar study and had been flown powered by two Rolls-Royce Tay engines. However, unlike with the Viscount, the Apollo Mk2 remained purely a design study.

Alongside the AW.55 were a number of designs submitted by Blackburn, Handley Page and Shorts, with a design study unidentified, but probably based on the S.A5. In early documentation reference is also made of the Miles M.56 transport competing against the AW.55, while Westland were also shown as submitting a design.

Blackburn B-65

This July 1946 study was powered by two Armstrong Siddeley Mamba engines and could accommodate up to twenty passengers with an AUW of 26,000lb.
Length 78ft 6in, Span 104ft, Wing Area 943sq.ft

Handley Page HP.76

Handley Page chose not to submit proposals for the original Type 2 Specification when originally put forward under Specification 25/43 as they were already heavily involved in production of the Halifax bomber. However, the company later put forward a design against Specification 16/46, the HP.76. This low-wing pressurised thirty-four-seater featured sophisticated high lift slotted flaps for short take-off and slow landing, and spoiler type ailerons. Initial power came from Rolls-Royce Tweed twinned turboprops. However, in 1945, Rolls-Royce abandoned the Tweed engine, so the design was reworked with Armstrong Siddeley Mamba coupled twin turboprops driving six-bladed contra rotating propellers. The small nacelle design gave exceptionally low drag. The 9ft diameter fuselage of monocoque construction was increased to 10ft 6in, allowing for twenty-four passengers to be carried at four abreast in a passenger cabin 27ft 9in long and 6ft 6in high. With a payload of 7,500lb, a range of 1,065 miles was forecast, the all-up weight was put at 35,000lb and a cruising speed of 298mph was anticipated.
Length 76ft, Span 83ft, Height 22ft 10in, Wing Area 860sq.ft

Handley Page HP.76
An artist's impression of the HP.76 in flight. (RAF Museum Hendon)

Handley Page HP.77

The Type 77 that followed the HP.76 was proposed in March 1946 and was basically identical in size, except that it was powered by two Bristol Theseus engines driving contra rotating propellers. The extra power afforded by the new engines increased the maximum cruising speed to 337mph and up to twenty-four passengers could be carried.

Handley Page HP.78

One final attempt for a Type 2 airliner was made by Handley Page in early 1946. The HP.78 was powered by four Armstrong Siddeley Mamba's located in separate nacelles driving four 9ft 4in propellers. Seating was provided for up to forty passengers at four abreast, it had a cruising speed of 296mph, with a payload of 7,500lb projected over a range of 910 miles, with an estimated AUW put at 34,000lb. Other differences to the HP.76 included the forward end of the fuselage where it now finished in the form of a hemisphere with the nose wheel undercarriage mounted ahead of this and there was also a slightly revised wing layout, while later proposals had an increase in wing span.
Span 100ft

Type 3 Specification 6/45

The Type 3 remained the only specification drawn up by the Brabazon Committee which never reached production, despite undergoing a number of gestations. In its second interim report the specification had been split into two: the 3A and 3B. At the same time, the Avro 687 (Tudor) was being proposed as an interim aircraft based on the Lancaster IV, to be superseded by the Avro 688 (Tudor I) – a new design. Seeing that versions of this aircraft could do much of the work specified for the 3B, this specification was abandoned.

With the Type 3A now less urgent, a new specification was drawn up under a revised Type 3 for medium-/long-haul Empire routes capable of operating over stages of 1,000 nautical

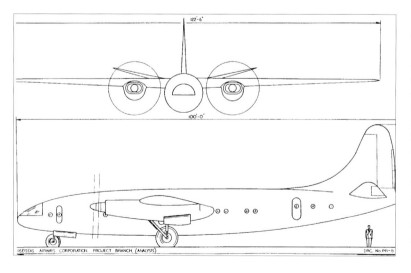

Avro 693 To meet the Brabazon 3 Specification, the Avro 693 was originally proposed to be powered by either paired Rolls-Royce Clydes or Armstrong Siddeley Python turboprops. (BAE SYSTEMS – via British Airways Archives)

miles, for routes such as London–Australia and possibly the Atlantic. Accommodation within the pressurised fuselage would be for up to twenty night or forty day passengers, with power provided by four turbine engines driving fully feathered propellers. It was envisaged that the aircraft would cruise at 350mph. The company that responded most actively to this requirement were A.V. Roe (Avro) with their Type 693.

Avro 693

Avro's original projects against the Type 3 Specification were the Avro 690 and 692 (or Avro XXII and XXIII), both powered by six Rolls-Royce Merlin 100 engines. These were superseded by the Avro 693 in 1945, which began life powered by four paired Rolls-Royce Clyde turboprops with contra rotating propellers. This paired option was then dropped for safety reasons by the time an order was placed for two prototype 693s in April 1946. But the project evolved with proposals for Armstrong Siddeley Python turboprops, and then, finally, four Rolls-Royce AJ.65 (later Avon) tubojets.

The 693 was a large airliner and, by December 1946, the design featured a fuselage some 110ft long with a high wing of 135ft span, and wing area of around 2,700sq.ft. It was larger than the other jetliner proposed by the Brabazon Committee, the Type 4 project that became the Comet, and could carry forty day or twenty night passengers. The four Rolls-Royce AJ.65 engines, each of 6,500lb static thrust, were integrated within the wing, with the tailplane mounted midway on the fin. A cruising speed of 438mph at 40,000ft was envisaged. It would have a range of 3,513 miles with a 7,500lb payload. A decision was made to go ahead with the 693 in November 1946 but, as the project progressed, it became clear that BOAC would have no need for two jetliners. With the airline backing the DH106 (Type 4), it could not justify introducing two completely new and advanced jetliners into its fleet. On 1 January 1947, the carrier announced that it was not going to order yet another British jet but it was not until July 1947 that the prototype orders for the 693 were cancelled and the type became the only one of the Brabazon Committee designs not to be built.

Avro 693 (Dec 1946 Spec.) Length 110ft, Span 135ft, Height 27ft 6in, Wing Area 2,700sq.ft

Although Avro were contracted for the Type 3 Specification, Armstrong Whitworth (for which no information has proved available) also tendered a project, while Airspeed and Miles undertook studies meeting a similar specification. Airspeed's design (no project number) had potential for flight refuelling and was powered by four Bristol Hercules engines. This could accommodate up to forty passengers in day configuration or twenty in bunks. Miles undertook two studies, the X14 and X15, both with the company's X-wing configuration, which could operate over the London–Gander–New York or London–Melbourne with stops. The X14 was powered by four Bristol Centaurus engines, and the X15 by six Napier Sabre engines.

Type 4 (Specification 20/44 – Replaced by 22/46)

The Type 4 Specification was originally proposed as a North Atlantic jet mailplane which would be capable of cruising at more than 400mph (644kph), carrying no less than 1 ton of mail. However, by the time of the Brabazon Committee's third interim report, it had been decided that it was not yet possible for a jet aircraft to be able to operate a one-stop North

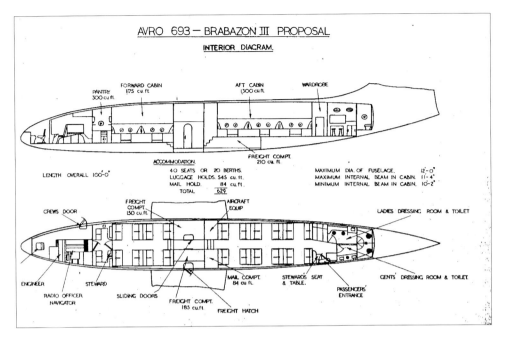

Avro 693
Interior layout of the turboprop Avro 693, showing accommodation for forty passengers, as proposed for BOAC.
(BAE SYSTEMS – via British Airways Archives)

Atlantic route. Consequently, the specification was adjusted to become a passenger-carrying aircraft for European and Empire routes, powered by two or more jet engines with a gross weight of around 30,000lb. Accommodation was to be provided for up to fourteen passengers, with a cruising speed of 450mph and a range of 700–800 miles.

De Havilland 106 Comet

The Comet must be one of the most documented aircraft in history from its pioneering beginnings as the world's first dedicated jetliner, to the catastrophic crashes of 1953/54, the aircraft's subsequent grounding and then the emergence of a new generation: the Comet 4, which pioneered non-stop transatlantic jet services in 1958.

Interesting early proposals from de Havilland for a jet transport had included adapting the DH95 Flamingo with a pair of Goblin engines. Other projects saw an enlarged all-metal Vampire, designs with canards powered by three Goblin engines to studies with highly swept wings and four Ghost engines, either with or without a tailplane. In 1945 it had been decided to proceed with a tailless design but, by the end of 1945, a more conventional layout was decided upon, which eventually became the familiar graceful DH106 Comet shape. The Comet should have become the major player in the three-pronged attack that the British Industries could have made to the world's airliners, encompassing the Viscount and Britannia. Tragically, the crashes of 1953 and 1954 proved disastrous and, by the time the Comet 4 re-emerged in 1958, the Americans had already caught up, and the type never achieved the sales that were originally envisaged.

It has been noted that Westland also submitted a design against this requirement, and a drawing of a thirty-seater low-wing, twinjet powered by Rolls-Royce AJ.65 turbojets may have been such a project.

Type 5

The Type V was originally proposed as a piston-engined feederliner for minor UK domestic and colonial routes, able to accommodate between eight and twelve passengers. It was envisaged that the aircraft would have a cruising speed of 175mph, with a still air range of 1,000 miles. The original specification was split by the Brabazon Committee's second interim report when the first Type 5 became the Type 5B, an eight-seater twin, while a new fourteen-seater Type 5A was proposed.

Type 5A Specification (18/44)

It had originally been conceived that the 5A would be a twin-engined aircraft. This was later amended to four engines (possibly Gipsy Queens). It would have a still air range of 750 miles and a cruising speed of 175mph. The all-metal aircraft would also have the ability to take-off and land from small airstrips.

Miles M.60 Marathon

The original Specification 18/44 was awarded to Miles Aircraft for the M.60 Marathon, and three prototypes were ordered in October 1944. This was superseded by 18/44 (Issue 2) of 8 August 1946, with the main change being the deletion of the requirement for the aircraft

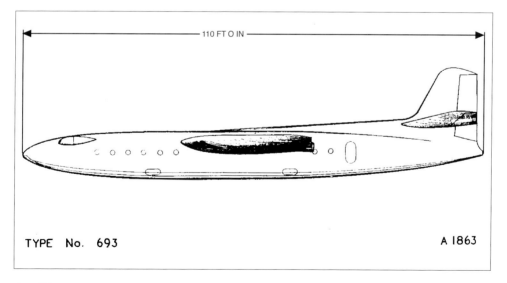

Avro 693
Side view of the Avro 693, for which two prototypes were ordered, powered by four Rolls-Royce AJ.5 turbojets integrated within the wing. (BAE SYSTEMS)

to be pressurised. Making its first flight on 19 May 1946, the aircraft was sadly not successful, with only forty aircraft being built, and never operated by its intended customer, BEA. A later development was the sole M.69, powered by two Armstrong Siddeley Mamba engines, which made its first flight in July 1949.

De Havilland Flamingo II

An early proposal put forward by de Havilland was for a development of the pre-war Flamingo. With the jigs for the aircraft still in storage at Hatfield, the Flamingo II would have been powered by either Pratt & Whitney Twin Wasps or uprated Bristol Perseus engines. There was also talk that possible production may have been undertaken by Westland. The developed Flamingo featured a fuselage stretched by 2ft at the rear and 6in at the nose, with the incorporation of a single fin and rudder. These changes saw the gross weight of the aircraft increase to 19,500lb, and would have seen an increase over the original DH95 in range of 300 miles, with a cruising speed of 240mph. In the event, it was decided that a new aircraft would be a better proposition.

Percival P41/P42

Percival put forward two designs for the Brabazon 5A Specification, the P41 and P42 in 1944. Both designs featured high-wing layouts to seat up to twenty passengers. The P41 was powered by two Perseus engines, while the four-engined P42 featured four Leonides of 2,020hp or alternatively, Gipsy engines. The P42 had a gross weight of 18,524lb and a cruising speed of 187mph.
(P41) Length 55ft 8in, Span 67ft 6in, Height 18ft
(P42) Length 69ft, Span 55ft 6in

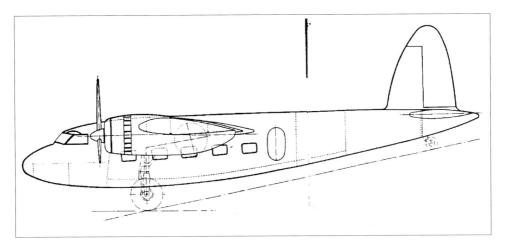

De Havilland Flamingo II
The major change to the pre-war de Havilland Flamingo, when proposed to meet the Brabazon 5A Specification, was the use of a single fin and rudder, coupled with a fuselage stretched by 2½ft. The 'new' design was designated the Flamingo II. (BAE SYSTEMS – via British Airways Archives)

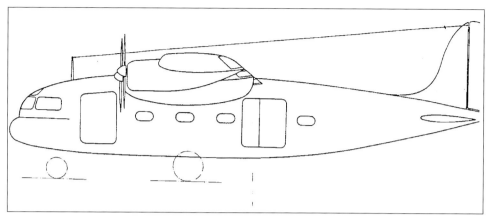

Percival P42
Side view of the Percival P42 for the Brabazon 5A Specification, powered by four Alvis Leonides. Its sister aircraft, the P41, was a twin Perseus design. (BAE SYSTEMS)

Other designs submitted to the Type 5A Specification came from Armstrong Whitworth (of which no information has come to light) and Westland, who proposed a ten-/twelve-seater powered by two turbojets.

Type 5B (Specification 26/43)

Specification 26/43 was for a small all-metal twin-engined aircraft powered by de Havilland Gipsy engines with fully feathered propellers for use on short stages of up to 750 miles within the Empire. Accommodation was to be provided for eight passengers, with mail/freight carrying also a consideration. Specification 26/43 (Issue 2) of 17 February 1945 superseded the above, and included the provision for carrying ten passengers without a toilet.

De Havilland 104 Dove

The de Havilland Dove DH104 was selected as the winning design and flew from Hatfield on 25 September 1945. The aircraft was to become one of the most successful of all British commercial types, with a production run of around 526 aircraft, including those operated by the RAF as a communications aircraft.

Designs to meet this specification were also proposed by Westland for a twin-engined aircraft with a wing span of 50ft, wing area of 330sq.ft and all-up weight of 9,860lb, while Airspeed proposed a derivative of the AS.64.

The Brabazon Committee attempted to push Britain's industries into a new era and, with the Viscount and Comet, this was certainly achieved. Had the latter's career not been tragically abbreviated there is no knowing how successful the Comet and its developments, as well as future projects, would have been. That many of the customers who would have bought the de Havilland jet would have remained faithful to the company is probably true, as can be seen with Douglas, Boeing and now Airbus, but the success of later designs can be purely conjecture.

Chapter 3

New Aircraft for BOAC

Medium-Range Empire Aircraft (Specification 2/47)

With BOAC responsible for all international routes from Britain, excluding those to Europe operated by BEA and to South America by BSAAC, all large medium- and long-range airliner development was tailored towards the requirements of the state carrier. Although the Brabazon Committee had produced specifications for many of the future aircraft requirements, it was found that there were a number of deficiencies, so further 'supplementary' designs were required. One of the most important of these was to be the Medium-Range Empire (MRE) Transport.

The MRE supplementary design basically fulfilled the original Brabazon Type 3A Specification, for which the Avro 693 had originally been chosen, and had undergone much gestation before finally being cancelled in 1947. The potential prize of such a lucrative contract was to occupy many of the major commercial design teams after BOAC issued a requirement in December 1946. The resultant Specification – 2/47 – was issued as a replacement for BOAC's Constellations. The new aircraft was to be powered by four air-cooled engines and would accommodate between thirty-two and thirty-six passengers and accompanying freight. It was to operate over the medium-range sectors of BOAC's Empire routes to places like India and Pakistan. Initially, it was also decided that it must have the capability to operate from grass airstrips with a maximum operating weight of 100,000lb. The initial powerplant was to be the Bristol Centaurus, however the chosen design was required to be able to convert to receiving either the Napier Nomad or the Bristol Proteus. As well as the companies listed below, there was also a proposal from Lockheed, the Project X, a Constellation development powered by Bristol Centaurus engines.

Armstrong Whitworth AW.57

A low-wing airliner, similar in design to the Apollo, the AW.57 was powered by four Centaurus 57 engines with contra rotating propellers. Special features included gust alleviation by 'floating' ailerons and a system for automatic power assistance of rudder operation at large rudder angles. An all-up weight of 90,000lb was envisaged, with accommodation for thirty-two passengers at four abreast.
Length 99ft, Span 125ft, Height 30ft, Wing Area 1,900sq.ft

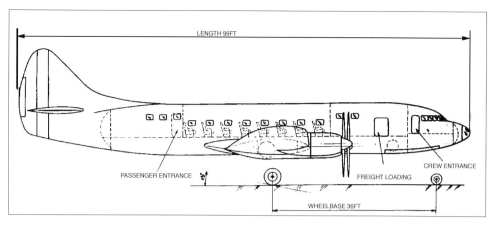

Armstrong Whitworth AW.57
Side view of the Armstrong Whitworth AW.57, looking very similar to an enlarged AW.55 Apollo, and powered by four Bristol Centaurus 57 engines. (BAE SYSTEMS – via British Airways Archives)

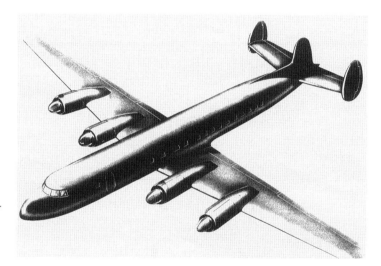

Avro 697
An artist's impression of the Avro 697, a contender for the Medium-Range Empire Aircraft. (BAE SYSTEMS)

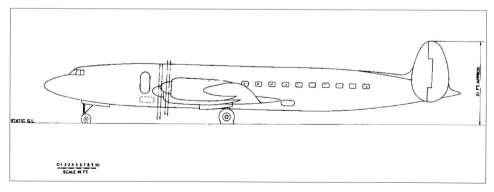

Avro 697
The Avro 697, developed from the Avro Tudor II for Specification 2/47. (BAE SYSTEMS)

Avro 697

The Avro 697 of June 1947 was a development of the Tudor II, being a low-wing triple-fin design, powered by four engines with contra rotating propellers, and able to travel at an average speed of 325mph. Accommodation was provided for a maximum of forty-eight passengers in a day layout over a range of 2,100 miles. However, the basic day layout was for thirty-two passengers (11,000lb payload), who could be carried over a range of up to 3,140 miles at 250mph, or 2,600miles at 325mph, cruising at 20,000ft. Freight compartments were provided in the main fuselage and in both forward and aft underfloor holds. Maximum take-off weight was 100,000lb.
Length 109ft, Span 126ft, Height 21ft 9in, Wing Area 1,606sq.ft

Blackburn B-70

Designed in January 1947, the B-70 was a low-wing monoplane with single fin looking, in body, very similar to the Lockheed Constellation which it was due to replace, with a Dolphin-like curved fuselage. Submitted to the MOA on 23 April 1947, power would have been provided by four radial Centaurus engines with an all-up weight of 91,500lb. Accommodation was provided for thirty-two passengers at four abreast with a lounge and bar in the rear of fuselage, and cargo holds at both the front and rear of the aircraft, plus additional underfloor compartments.
Length 114ft 4in, Span 120ft, Wing Area 1,500sq.ft

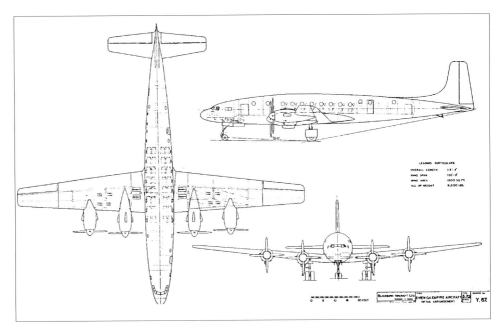

Blackburn B-70
Blackburn's B-70 Empire aircraft was similar in design to the Lockheed Constellation. (BAE SYSTEMS – via British Airways Archives)

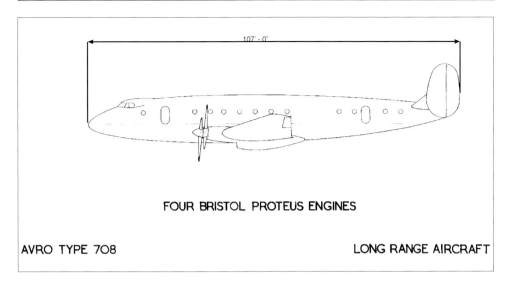

107' - 0"

FOUR BRISTOL PROTEUS ENGINES

AVRO TYPE 708   LONG RANGE AIRCRAFT

Avro 708
One of three proposals submitted by Avro under the 708 legend, the P2 was powered by four coupled Bristol Proteus
engines. (BAE SYSTEMS)

Bristol – Project Y And Type 175

Bristol undertook two studies to meet the MRE Specification, Project Y and Type 175. Project Y was complimentary to Lockheed's Project X design, except that it was based around the conversion of several Lockheed Constellations to the strengthened series 749, which would then have been re-engined with Bristol Centaurus engines. The company also investigated building new aircraft at Filton under licence at a later date. Bristol's main submission, however, lay with the Type 175, an all-new low-wing design, initially powered by four Centaurus engines, providing seating for thirty-six passengers with an all-up weight of 94,000lb.

Handley Page 83/84/85/86

Handley Page initially proposed three Hermes developments for the MRE, all encompassing a new high-lift double-slotted trailing-edge flap, used so that additional drag penalty would not be incurred while cruising, enabling the necessary take-off and landing performance to be met. The HP.83 was powered by four Bristol Centaurus 663 piston engines, and the HP.84 by four single Bristol Proteus engines. Meanwhile, the HP.85 had a single-spar wing and was powered by two coupled Proteus turboprops. None of these proposals met with much success, so as a last minute addition in June 1947, the HP.86 was proposed. This combined the HP.83's four Bristol Centaurus engines with the single-spar wing of the HP.85.
(HP.86) Length 95ft 10in, Span 140ft, Height 33ft, Wing Area 1,950sq.ft

The joint MoS, MCA and BOAC Committee, which met on 14 July 1947, decided that the Bristol 175 (later named Britannia) best met the 2/47 Specification. The Bristol design was chosen because of the company's wider experience, with the Blackburn study coming a close second. It was felt that the Armstrong Whitworth design was not advanced enough and had inferior take-off performance, due to the engines, which would also have given the design relatively poor 'Nairobi' performance. BOAC was also not keen on contra-rotating propellers. The Handley Page and Avro projects were deemed unacceptable as they were developments of existing aircraft. The Avro 697 was considered too heavy, while the HP.83 was handicapped by low permissible landing weights. Project Y was ruled out due to the high dollar expenditure being unjustified.

Three Bristol 175 prototype aircraft were ordered on behalf of BOAC by the Ministry of Supply on 5 July 1948. All were to be powered by Centaurus engines, with provision for the second and third to be converted to Proteus power. However, after BOAC ordered twenty-five aircraft on 28 July 1949, it decided that both the prototypes and production aircraft would be Proteus-powered, and one prototype was therefore duly cancelled. As events turned out, the Britannia, which at that time looked like becoming yet another British world beater alongside the Viscount and Comet, was to endure a lengthy gestation. By the time all the problems had been ironed out and it received its certificate of airworthiness on 30 December 1955, the big fast American jets had arrived. Major orders, including one from Qantas, were thus unfulfilled and only eighty-five Britannias were built, including a number at Shorts in Belfast.

The Long-Range Empire (LRE) Aircraft (Specification 5/48)

With the medium-range aircraft now taken care of, attention turned towards a new long-range airliner. Under Specification 5/48, the new aircraft would accommodate no fewer than thirty day/night passengers, and be powered by four engines. Among the powerplant options were the Nomad, Clyde, Python and Proteus. Design speed was to be between 300 and 350mph, and it would be able to carry a payload of 9,000lb over a range of 4,500 miles.

Six companies were originally invited to tender for the LRE (Long-Range Empire) aircraft, which was to supersede the Brabazon 3 project and act as insurance against the Comet. The specification was put forward to the ICAR Committee in a joint paper by the Ministry of Supply and Ministry of Civil Aviation in July 1947. Airspeed, Blackburn, English Electric, Fairey, A.V. Roe (Avro) and Shorts were all invited to tender. As the scheme progressed, however, both Airspeed and English Electric withdrew. The remaining companies put forward a number of project studies against the specification which was issued in October 1947, while Bristol also supplied information with a derivative of the 175 Britannia.

Avro 708

A.V. Roe put forward three different variants of their project 708, a low-wing twin-finned design. The 708(N) featured four Nomad engines in tandem and the 708(P1), four individual tractor Proteus engines, both with 14ft diameter propellers. The 708(P2) was powered by four coupled twin tractor Proteus engines with a propeller diameter of 16ft. All studies featured the same fuselage length of 107ft, while the 708(P1) and 708(P2) had an increased wing span of some 8ft, and a corresponding increase in wing area. The initial proposal, the 708(N) had an all-up weight of 106,000lb and, featured a double-bubble fuselage 11ft 4in wide and 13ft high. Speed was quoted at 315mph while the range, with a payload of 9,000lb, was 4,500 miles. The later designs featured increases in AUW to 117,000lb. The Tudor II derivative, Avro 709, was also considered against specification.

708(N) – Length 107ft, Span 132ft
708(P1) and 708(P2) – Span 140ft, Height 26ft 10in, Wing Area 1,765sq.ft
708(P1) and 708(P2) – Wing Area 1,950sq.ft

Blackburn B-73

Blackburn submitted three proposals for the LRE. Although each was given the designation of B-73, the three studies had many differences.

B-73A

A double-bubble fuselage design with accommodation on two decks, the B-73A was powered by four Bristol Proteus engines of 3,670ehp. The all-up weight was put at 142,000lb and accommodation was provided for forty-eight day/night passengers in a fuselage some 11ft 7in wide and 16ft 7in high. A 17,500lb payload could be carried at 325mph over 4,500 miles. In all day configuration, up to 100 passengers could be carried.

Length 114ft 9in, Span 161ft, Height 38ft, Wing Area 2,000sq.ft

B-73B

A single-deck circular fuselage variant of the B-73, the 'B' was also powered by Bristol Proteus engines and could carry forty day/night passengers, or a maximum of seventy-two day passengers. The all-up weight was reduced to 130,000lb, with a reduction in wing span and corresponding wing area.

Length 115ft 8in, Span 147ft, Height 34ft 6in, Wing Area 1,800sq.ft

B-73C

A further single-deck design, the B-73C was powered by four Napier Nomad engines of 3,125ehp, with seating for thirty-two day/night passengers. The circular fuselage diameter was increased to 13ft 3in, although the less powerful Nomad engines enabled a payload of only 12,100lb to be carried for the 4,500mile range. The B-73C had an AUW of 125,000lb.

Length 104ft 8in, Span 153ft, Wing Area 1,800sq.ft

Fairey Queen Series

The Fairey Co. studied three separate aircraft to meet the LRE Specification under the Queen series. All the proposals featured a common mid-wing layout and were powered by four engines. The double-deck design of faired double-bubble cross-section was 12ft 5in wide and 15ft 3in high. The major differences between the three studies were in engine choice, fuselage length and wing span.

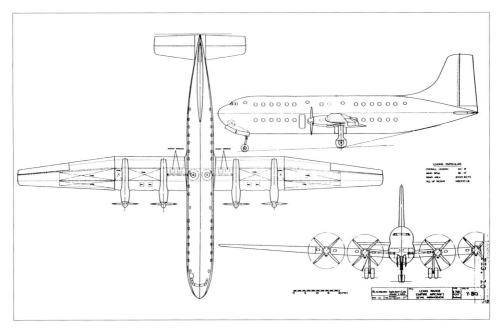

Blackburn B-73
The Blackburn B-73A double-deck proposal for the Long-Range Empire aircraft could accommodate up to 100 passengers. (BAE SYSTEMS)

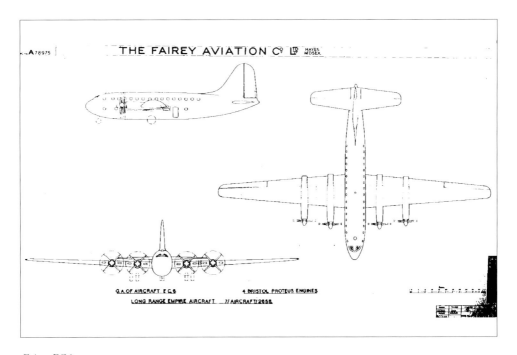

Fairey FC6
The smallest of the Fairey Queen Series proposed for the LRE Specification, the FC6 was powered by four Bristol Proteus engines. (Westland Helicopters – via RAF Museum Hendon)

FC4

A super luxury Proteus-powered airliner of 3,670ehp, the FC4, was the largest of the Fairey Queen series, providing accommodation for twenty-four day/night berths or fifty-six day passengers, and had an all-up weight of 130,000lb. Slower than the other competitors, the Queen series could travel at 300mph and was only able to take a payload of 7,500lb over the 4,500 mile range.
Length 118ft, Span 163ft, Height 34ft 8in, Wing Area 2,200sq.ft

FC5

With an all-up weight of 120,000lb and powered by Nomad engines of 3,125ehp, the FC5 featured the same wing span as the FC4, but a reduced length fuselage. Provision was again provided for twenty-four day/night passengers, or fifty-eight day passengers. A slightly increased payload of 8,000lb could be carried over the specified 4,500 mile range.
Length 114ft, Span 163ft, Height 34ft 8in, Wing Area 2,200sq.ft

FC6

The FC6 reverted to the Proteus engine, and was considerably shorter than either the FC4 or FC5, with a slightly reduced wing span. Accommodation was provided in standard luxury

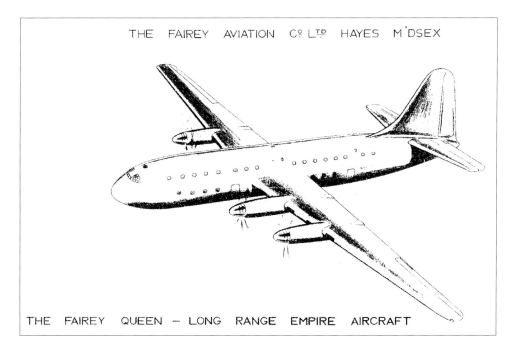

Fairey Queen Series
The Fairey Queen Series covered the FC4 (illustrated), FC5 and FC6, all of which were double-deck designs of varying fuselage and wing length. (Westland Helicopters – via RAF Museum Hendon)

as against super luxury for twenty-eight day/night passengers, or fifty-eight day passengers. A maximum payload of 8,500lb could be carried over a range of 4,500 miles.
Length 99ft 9in, Span 158ft 6in, Height 34ft 8in, Wing Area 2,050sq.ft

Shorts Projects

Short S.A8 Landplane

Shorts first proposal to the LRE was based around a landplane development of their proposed S.A8 flying boat which was first mooted in September 1946, before Specification 5/48 had been issued. This design featured a low-wing layout with double-bubble fuselage providing accommodation on two decks. It was powered by four Napier Nomad compound engines.
Length 118ft 6in, Span 156ft, Height 39ft, Wing Area 2,130sq.ft

Short LRE1

A low-wing design put forward from the Rochester factory in March 1948, the LRE1 could accommodate up to thirty day passengers or a maximum of forty-four in a circular fuselage of 12ft diameter. Again powered by four Napier Nomad engines of 3,125ehp, the design had an all-up weight of 118,000lb. A maximum cruise speed of 330mph was projected, with the capability to carry a payload of 9,200lb for 4,500 miles.
Length 100ft, Span 138ft 6in, Height 28ft 6in, Wing Area 1,658sq.ft

Commonwealth

Shorts final submission from November 1948 came from its Belfast factory. Externally similar to the LRE1, the Commonwealth was again a low-wing design with a circular fuselage. Accommodation was on a single-deck of 11ft 3in diameter, with provision for up to forty-four day passengers, thirty day passengers, plus ten dining room seats or twenty day/night passengers. Powerplant options were either four Nomad or Centaurus engines with propellers of a diameter of 14ft or 15ft for Nomad or Centaurus respectively. The design had a maximum take-off weight of 118,00lb and a gross wing area of 1,790sq.ft with a cruising speed of between 307 and 337 mph envisaged. A maximum still air range of 6,000 statute miles was planned.
Length 100ft, Span 146ft 6in, Height 31in, Wing Area 1,790sq.ft

The LRE never came to fruition in its original form and none of the above designs ever proceeded, although BOAC did eventually get a new long-range transport powered by jet engines.

Vickers Projects For BOAC

V1000 and VC7

In 1951 a new specification was issued for a fast long-range strategic transport for the RAF. This was to replace the RAF's existing Handley Page Hastings aircraft. It would be capable

Vickers V1000
An artist's impression of the V1000 military transport in flight. (BAE SYSTEMS – via Brooklands Museum Trust)

of flying service personnel and freight to any part of the world to accompany the new V-bombers then under development. One of the conditions for the new aircraft was that it must be based on an existing airframe. Under the Ministry of Supply, a working party was set up in June 1951 and, in November of that year, it reported on the proposals as drawn up by the invited aircraft companies.

Of the five companies that presented proposals, de Havilland naturally proposed a stretched development of their Comet jet airliner, while the other four contenders were developments of their respective company's bombers. This led to all the projects being powered by Rolls-Royce's new Conway by-pass engine and based on the Handley Page Victor, Avro Vulcan, Vickers Valiant and Short S.A4 Sperrin. The major change to these designs were new fuselages allied to the existing wing, landing gear and tail units. Additionally, Bristol and Saunders Roe put forward variants of their Britannia and Duchess respectively, but both were ruled out early on.

Alongside the RAF specification for a personnel transport was an opportunity for a joint military/civil transport, with a proposal for a large long-range commercial variant for BOAC. As the studies progressed it became clear that the Shorts fuselage diameter was too small at only 9ft 6in, and had capacity problems, having accommodation for only fifty passengers, while having deficiencies in range. The Avro study featured a double-bubble fuselage which it was felt would restrict weight on take-off and require longer runways. The conclusions of the study were that the best designs were those from de Havilland and Vickers.

The winner of the contract was Vickers–Armstrong, whose original study was heavily dependent on the Valiant bomber Type 716. However, by the time a contract was placed on 2 October 1952 to meet Specification C132d issued under OR315, the resultant aircraft bore very little resemblance to its bomber ancestry. The contract for one prototype V1000 aircraft, XD662, followed in March 1953.

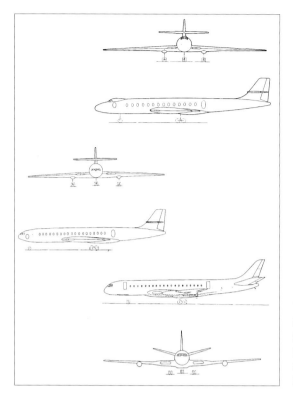

Vickers V1000
Evolution of the V1000 from a Valiant-based
transport (top) to the final definitive design
(bottom) with the tailplane now mounted on
the rear fuselage. (BAE SYSTEMS – via
Brooklands Museum Trust)

Following this, a production order for six aircraft was placed in June 1954, when it was envisaged that the total RAF requirement would be for twelve aircraft. The important VC7 commercial development was envisaged for both the North Atlantic and Empire routes, and would have been the first of the big jetliners. The original design with developed Avon engines had first been proposed as a Comet II replacement but by 1954 was being put forward against the Comet 3 replacement, its chief competitors being the Avro Atlantic, Bristol 187 and Handley Page 97 (Pacific). Thus, out of the RAF specification had developed a joint large transport programme that could encompass both military and civil requirements, and for which BOAC had been consulted throughout the course of discussions.

As a much larger airliner than the Comet, there was greater complexity in its design and, naturally, this led to the development programme beginning to stretch out. To meet both civil and military requirements, the RAF had been forced to accept a bigger aircraft than originally anticipated, with a larger wing to enable carriage of the maximum fuel to meet BOAC's needs. The basic V1000 was to be a low-wing design with the Rolls-Royce engines mounted similarly to the Valiant within the highly swept inner wing. The wingtips, as on the proceeding VC10, were of the Küchemann variety, and the fuselage tail cone was built integrally with the fin, the tailplane being mounted midway on the rear fuselage. Featuring a 12ft 6in diameter fuselage, accommodation could be provided for up 100 passengers at six abreast.

The programme appeared to be going well, with prototype construction of XD662 under way at Vickers Wisley test flight factory, when it was found that the all-up weight had increased by some 18,000lb to 248,000lb. This should not have proved a problem as all that was required was an uprating of the Conway engines. However, for some strange reason

BOAC now appeared to think that the engine would be incapable of providing the extra power required, especially for direct London to New York services, and began to cool towards the VC7. A meeting of the TARC in September 1955 did the V1000 no favours, as it saw no civil requirement for the aircraft. Instead, the committee advocated developments of the Britannia and Comet while putting forward design studies for a new high subsonic aircraft to be available by 1964, and also for a Supersonic Transport.

At this time it was still projected that the first V1000 would make its maiden flight in June 1956, with the first production aircraft flying in January 1959, and entry into airline service in late 1959/60. In the meantime, Vickers were already looking at different engine options which included developed Conway's Rco 5, RB125s or even developed Bristol BOL7s, as well as underwing engines, either in individual nacelles or two engines in a combined nacelle. Then came the final nail in the coffin; the RAF had been told to cut back on expenditure – and one of its most expensive projects was of course the V1000. Added to this, politics was now coming into play. This was especially the case with regards to assistance towards the floundering government-owned Shorts, who had seen a major loss of work on the Comet and Swift jet fighter. There was also the need for further support for the already flying and slow-selling Britannia turboprop – which was now encountering many problems in trying to enable it to enter service. The writing was on the wall for the V1000.

Attempts were made to keep BOAC interested in the VC7 variant, but the airline would have none of it. The airline argued that the extra weight increase had penalised the aircraft's performance. With the RAF unable to buy and BOAC unwilling, the V1000 and its civil sister, the VC7, were dead. Ironically, less than a year later, BOAC were allowed to order Boeing 707s powered by developed Rolls-Royce Conway engines – who, they had argued just a year earlier, would not be capable of providing the extra thrust for the VC7.

Vickers V1000
The Vickers V1000 under construction at Wisley, prior to cancellation in November 1955. (BAE SYSTEMS – via Brooklands Museum Trust)

It was not just BOAC who were originally interested in the VC7. Early design studies had seen BEA making encouraging noises towards the aircraft back in 1952. Trans-Canada Airlines, who had successfully introduced the Viscount in April 1955, had also shown great interest in the VC7, to such a degree that they had even tried to persuade the British government to continue with the programme. However, with no domestic orders there was little chance of this happening.

On 11 November 1955 when the cancellation decision was announced, the prototype at Wisley was 80 per cent completed and nearly £4 million pounds had been spent. The cancellation was a decision that was to have repercussions for many years to come, and was the point from which British airliner development never truly recovered.

It was not just Vickers who suffered from this calamitous cancellation. It has been pointed out many times since, that the whole of the British Aircraft Industry lost its way. This one decision allowed the American industry to enter and operate a near monopoly in the large long-range jetliner market for almost forty years thereafter, before competition finally emerged with the European Airbus A340.

VC7 Length 146ft, Span 140ft, Height 38ft 6in, Wing Area 3,263sq.ft

Future Large Civil Aircraft – Pure Jet for 1964

Farcically, on 7 February 1956, just weeks after cancelling the VC7, the Ministry of Supply issued a letter to suppliers, requesting proposals for a new long-range high-speed aircraft, capable of carrying a 30,000lb payload, powered by Rolls-Royce Conway engines. Vickers naturally dusted down their VC7 to see if it could meet the requirement, looking at both podded and buried engine variants, but this was to no avail, even though the project met most of BOAC's new requirements.

The Ministry initially sent out invitations for the new study to Avro, de Havilland, Bristol, Armstrong Whitworth and Handley Page. Later, Fairey, Saunders Roe, Vickers–Armstrong, Folland, Boulton Paul, Shorts, English Electric, Hawker and Gloster were invited to put forward proposals. Avro, who had been proposing the Atlantic airliner based on the Vulcan bomber originally as a Comet 3 replacement in 1954, against the Vickers 1000 and Bristol 187, decided to study a joint effort with sister company, Avro Canada, but this project appears not to have been taken too seriously. Of the other companies invited, the only serious projects put forward came from Armstrong Whitworth, Bristol, de Havilland, Handley Page and Vickers.

Armstrong Whitworth AW. 174

A low-wing Transatlantic and Commonwealth airliner was proposed in June 1956. The 174 was a swept-wing design with the tailplane mounted on the rear fuselage with four podded engines mounted underwing in pairs. Proposed powerplants included the Bristol Olympus 531 or Rolls-Royce Conway 20. An all-up weight of 240,000lb was quoted, and accommodation provided for 110 passengers. There were, however, worries about the engine position as, although podded engines were considered a good idea, there were worries that being low slung they could cause serious damage in the event of a belly landing.

Length 140ft 6in, Span 134ft, Height 38ft 6in, Wing Area 2,900sq.ft

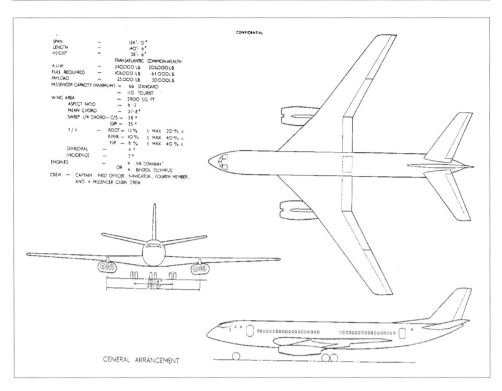

Armstrong Whitworth AW.174
The Armstrong Whitworth AW.174, proposed for BOAC's pure jet fleet for the sixties, would have been powered by either four Bristol Olympus or four Rolls-Royce Conway engines. (BAE SYSTEMS – via Ray Williams)

Bristol Britannia 600/Type 187

The 187 was one of a number of proposals put forward by Bristol for a follow-on Britannia. Other schemes had included variants of the Britannia to be powered by the new Bristol Orion engine. Of these, the series 400 featured a modified wing, the 420 a fuselage stretch to accommodate 133 passengers, the 430 a new thin wing and larger fuselage to seat 152, while the series 520 incorporated the 430 wing with developed Orion engines.

The new low-wing Bristol 187 (also called the Britannia 600), although considered to be based on the Britannia, was really a new aircraft with major alterations to the fuselage, and had a new wing. The project underwent a number of designs. An early variant from 1953 featured a fuselage of slightly wider circular diameter than the Britannia, with a new T-tail and swept fin, longer fuselage and shorter wing span, with 9½ per cent thickness on chord. Up to 102 tourist passengers could be accommodated at 40in-pitch with capacity for 1,220 cu.ft of freight. Power would be provided by the new Bristol BE25 turboprops of 4,500shp.

As time progressed the design evolved into a double-bubble fuselage with an external diameter of 12ft 6in. The powerplant remained four Bristol Orion 2 engines with the seating capacity increased to 170 passengers at six abreast, and capable of travelling from London–New York non-stop, with a payload of 32,700lb at 410 knots, and an AUW of 215,000lb. Boundary layer control was planned for the future, and a cruising speed of 435

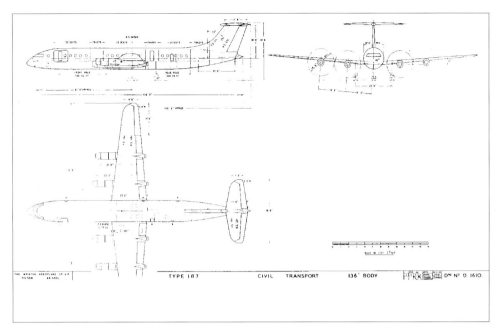

Bristol 187
An early scheme of the Bristol 187, a Britannia follow-on design with T-tail. (BAE SYSTEMS)

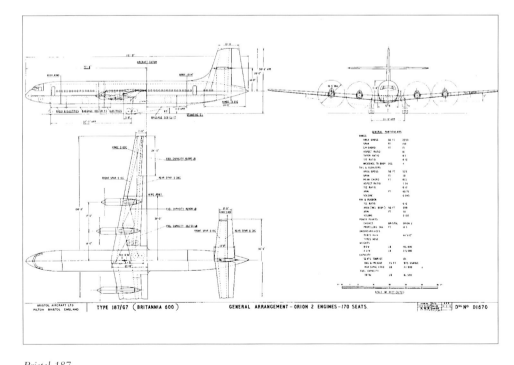

Bristol 187
A later proposal for the Bristol 187, also called the Britannia 600, featured a double-bubble fuselage and could accommodate up to 170 passengers. (BAE SYSTEMS – via British Airways Archives)

knots was forecast. In mixed traffic configuration, 105 passengers could be carried, with twenty-four first-class seats at four abreast at a 53in-pitch. There were eighty-one tourist seats at five and six abreast with an eight-seater lounge in the rear of the cabin.

Bristol themselves would have needed assistance to build the aircraft and proposed using the facilities of Shorts, who, had the project gone ahead, would probably have built one of the prototypes. The company had also held talks with Armstrong Whitworth, Fairey and English Electric. Development costs were estimated to be between £14 to 30 million. The government were expected to provide about half of this, with sales of up to 100 aircraft envisaged until 1965, with BOAC taking about twenty-five. Production plans called for deliveries of thirty aircraft per year, with a break even achieved on seventy-five sales. Shorts were to assume responsibility for the wing and tailplane, with a first flight planned for early 1959 and entry into service with BOAC planned for autumn 1962. There was, however, scepticism with regards to building yet another large turboprop long-range airliner, even though BOAC showed early interest and, with the Britannia not selling in great numbers and Bristol requiring government assistance, the project was put into abeyance.
Length 141ft, Span 150ft, Height 39ft 6in, Wing Area 2,250sq.ft

Bristol/Convair/Canadair Joint Project

With Bristol thinking they could not handle a project the size of the 187, discussions were also held with General Dynamics (Convair) and Canadair during 1955/56 over the development of the 187. The new study was to be powered by four Bristol BE25 series 2 engines and would accommodate up to 150 passengers at six abreast on two decks, within a fuselage diameter of 13ft 8in. The mid-wing monoplane would have a range of 5,300 statute miles (4,600 nautical miles) and would operate the Transatlantic non-stop with a 25,000lb payload. The proposed all-up weight was put at 205,000lb.

It was envisaged that the maiden flight would take place in January 1960, with entry into service by April 1962. BOAC were interested in the proposals early on, as they featured a double-bubble fuselage. However, the government was not so keen, especially as it appeared that Bristol and the UK would have ended up giving a lot of technical knowledge to their American rivals. Design and production would have been split with Convair at San Diego having design responsibility, including production drawing, wing design and system and fuselage detail. Bristol would have been responsible for fuselage layout, stressing and general structure, manufacturing the fuselage and tail while there would have been two final assembly lines, one at Filton and the other at San Diego. The Bristol BE25 would also have been built under licence in America.

De Havilland Comet 5

De Havilland's original proposal for a new jet for BOAC was centred on a development of the Comet 4. It was the Comet 5, which BOAC at first appeared to favour. A number of studies were made under the Comet 5 moniker. One of these centred around a stretched Comet 4 with an AUW of 226,000lb, powered by four Rolls-Royce Conway 10 engines of 16,000lb thrust. These were mounted, as with earlier Comets, in the wing which now had a sweep back on ¼ chord of 30 degrees, and also featured a swept fin looking not unlike the

V1000/VC7. Seating was provided for up to 105 passengers in tourist-class, and the maximum cruising speed was 563 mph at 30,000ft. Development costs of the project were put at £8 to 10 million, and the company wanted orders for at least thirty aircraft to proceed. The first aircraft would have been available for delivery in 1962/63, with BOAC looking at ordering around twenty aircraft.
Fuselage Length 131ft, Wing Span 137ft, Wing Area 2,750sq.ft

De Havilland DH118

Replacing the Comet 5 was the 118 Comet development, accommodating up to 147 passengers in a six-abreast layout at 34in pitch. The 118 was powered by four 17,000lb Rolls-Royce Conway engines mounted in pods beneath the wings, and would have been capable of non-stop Transatlantic operations. An all-up weight of 240,000lb was proposed, and the aircraft would have been able to operate from existing airfields. The 118 Comet development was taken very seriously by both BOAC and the government in the mid-fifties. In a strange act, BOAC, who had been advocating the use of big turboprop airliners, and saw no need for the VC7, had at the same time been discussing a follow-on Comet development with de Havilland. Indeed, by November 1956, it was announced that BOAC and the Ministry of Transport and Civil Aviation were seriously discussing the 118, which would not have been available until 1962/63. However, by February 1957, the 118 had been dropped as de Havilland turned its attentions towards an all-new aircraft, firstly for BEA (DH119), then a joint study to meet the requirements of both BEA and BOAC (DH120), before settling on meeting purely BEA's specification, which became the 121 Trident.
Fuselage Length 137ft 6in, Span 137ft

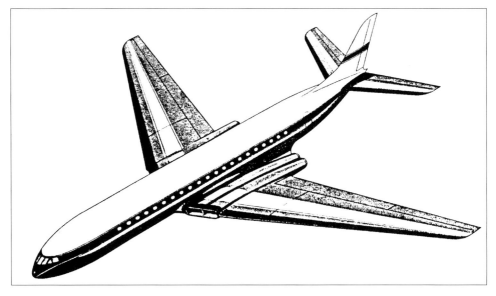

De Havilland Comet 5
An artist's impression of the Comet 5, which featured a new swept fin and was powered by four Rolls-Royce Conway engines. (BAE SYSTEMS – via de Havilland Heritage Museum)

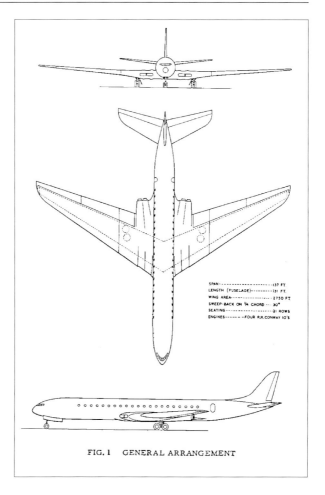

SPAN---------------------------137 FT.
LENGTH (FUSELAGE)----------131 FT.
WING AREA--------------------2750 FT.
SWEEP-BACK ON ¼ CHORD --- 30°
SEATING ----------------------21 ROWS
ENGINES------ - -FOUR R.R.CONWAY 10'S

De Havilland Comet 5
General arrangement drawing of the de
Havilland Comet 5 which, it was
hoped, would continue production of the
pioneering transport into the sixties to
meet BOAC's requirements. (BAE
SYSTEMS – via de Havilland
Heritage Museum)

FIG. 1   GENERAL ARRANGEMENT

Handley Page 97

The HP.97, which had its origins in 1951, had initially been proposed to BOAC in 1952 when the specification for a new long-range transport had first surfaced. Developed from the HP.80, Handley Page had offered the HP.96 for military transport and the HP.97 (also briefly called the Pacific) for civil use, but at that time the airline and government had chosen Vickers to manufacture the V1000/VC7. When BOAC's requirement resurfaced, Handley Page chose to resubmit the HP.97, which could be used as a passenger/freighter. Based around the Victor design, the HP.97 utilised the V-bombers wings, powerplant (Rolls-Royce Conway – Victor B2) and tail unit, combined with a new double-deck double-bubble fuselage 12ft wide and 15ft 6in high, with an estimated all-up weight of 190,000lb. In a ninety-six-seater, four-abreast arrangement, the upper deck would provide the seating accommodation, with a circular staircase leading to the lower deck where ladies and mens dressing rooms and toilets would be located. Provision on this deck was also made for a large lounge and galley. In another layout, twenty first-class seats were provided at the front of the upper deck cabin, separated from the tourist-class where seventy-five passengers could be accommodated at six abreast, next to a lounge and bar. The lower deck would provide accommodation for a

further forty-two passengers at five abreast, the decks again being accessed by a circular staircase. Provision was also made for front and rear baggage holds. The design had a proposed maximum all-up weight of 210,000lb and a range of 4,800 nautical miles. It was scheduled to make its maiden flight in 1958, and be available for BOAC for 1960.
Length 126ft 3in, Span 125ft 6in, Height 33ft, Wing Area 2,680sq.ft

Handley Page 102 And 108

The HP.102, proposed in 1955, was a tapered straight-winged laminar-flow-controlled airliner capable of operating over the same stages as the Boeing 707, carrying a payload of 25,000lb. Accommodation was provided for up to 120 tourist-class or eighty first-class passengers, with an AUW of between 120–150,000lb, and a range of 4,070 miles. It could travel at 435 knots.

The HP.108 design, which superseded the HP.102 in 1956, also featured the low tapered unswept wing layout, with four Rolls-Royce Avon RA28 or RA29 engines of 10,000lb static thrust mounted in underslung twin nacelles, and there was a straight fin very reminiscent of the Comet design. To assist the design and save drag, small chord ailerons and elevators would be utilised, while the rudder was to be of a very small chord. To reduce speed on landing, blow-up flaps were also proposed. Accommodation was provided for up to 120 passengers with an all-up weight of 210,000lb and cruising speed of 435mph. Further designs of the HP.108 included slightly swept wings of 28½ degrees.
HP.108 Wing Span 150ft, Wing Area 3,000sq.ft

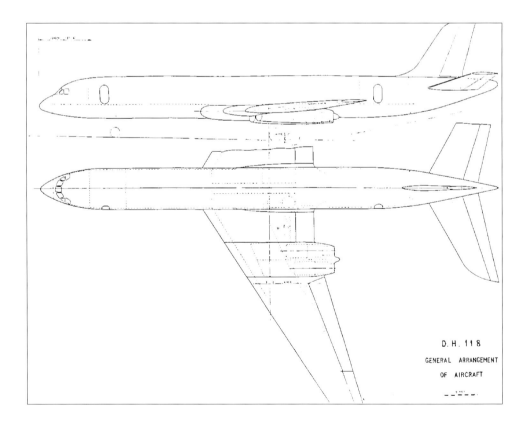

D.H. 118

GENERAL ARRANGEMENT

OF AIRCRAFT

Above: *Handley Page HP.97*
A model of the Handley Page HP.97
long-range transport, derived from the
Victor bomber. (Mike Hooks)

Right: *Handley Page HP.97*
The Handley Page HP.97 featured a
double-bubble fuselage, with
accommodation provided over two decks.
(Handley Page Association)

Opposite: *De Havilland 118*
Derived from the Comet 5, the de
Havilland 118, powered by four Rolls-
Royce Conway engines mounted
underneath the wing, was, for a while, a
serious contender for BOAC's new jet
order. (BAE SYSTEMS – via British
Airways Archives)

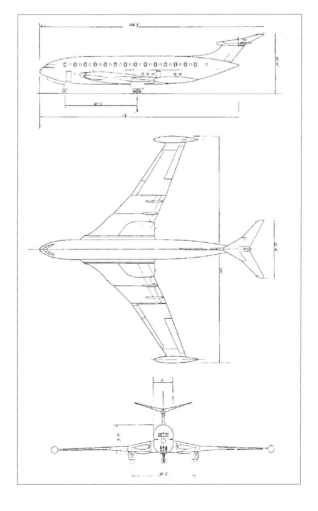

Handley Page 111C – Treble One

Handley Page's last attempt to produce a large long-range airliner for BOAC surfaced in May 1958 as the HP.111C (Treble One) which had an all-up weight of 260,000lb. Like the HP.97, the 111C was based around the Victor bomber, however the new design now featured a circular fuselage which was proposed for a number of roles – general freighter with rear loading, specialised freighter, freight/passenger or passenger aircraft. In the latter role as proposed to BOAC, accommodation was provided for 147 passengers on the upper deck and an additional fifty seats on the lower deck, with a cargo hold ahead of the wing, or 153 passengers on the upper deck with freight on the lower deck. The maximum passenger load could be carried across the Atlantic with one stop, or alternatively 133 passengers could be carried non-stop from London–New York. Four Rolls-Royce Conway 42 engines were mounted in pairs in the trailing edge of each inner wing, although Handley Page also proposed that Pratt & Whitney JT3-D3 engines could also be offered. The wing structure was to be essentially the same as that of the Victor, except for the section across the fuselage, engine and undercarriage bays, wing tips and trailing edge boxes. A cabin mock-up was built at Cricklewood, which was viewed by BOAC. Meanwhile, the military transport variant, the HP.111, had been selected by the Air Staff to meet the requirement for its large military transport. However, politics were to yet again prevail; the RAF were told that they could not have the aircraft they wanted but instead the order must go to Shorts in order to maintain employment in Northern Ireland with their Belfast project. The loss of the military order

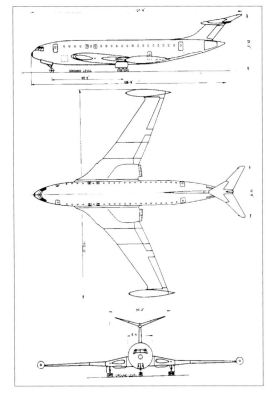

Handley Page HP.111C
The Handley Page HP.111C was the result of further development of the Victor bomber into a transport. It was similar to the earlier HP.97, except that the double-bubble fuselage was replaced by a circular fuselage. (Handley Page Association)

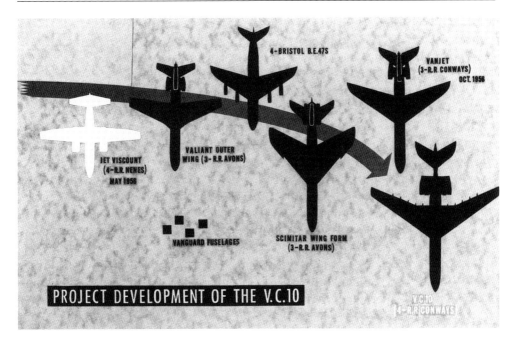

Vickers VC10 Development
Evolution of the VC10 from early Jet Viscount designs through Vanguard-based fuselages, married to various wing
planforms and engines, before emerging as the Conway-powered rear-engined VC10. (BAE SYSTEMS – via
Brooklands Museum Trust)

ended any hopes of production of a civil variant and, also effectively took Handley Page out
of large airliner design and production.
Length 137ft 8in, Span 130ft (Including Tip Tanks), Height 35ft 3in, Wing Area 2,827sq.ft

Vickers VC10

The VC10 designation was applied to a number of projects in the mid- to late fifties. Earlier
studies had centred on meeting the specification issued by BEA for a new short-/medium-
range jet, which took on various designations at Vickers, including the Vanjet and medium-
range Jet, as well as various schemes of VC10. All of these made use of the Vanguard fuselage,
which was mated to various wing planforms including the Scimitar and Valiant. Later
however, the design was changed to meet BOAC's pure jet requirement, and emerged as a
completely new airliner, not based around Vanguard components or jigs. These featured three
and then later four, rear mounted Conway engines, enabling an uncluttered wing, giving
good airfield performance.

   With BOAC being told that there was no possibility of reviving the VC7/V1000, early
government proposals were for the airline to take thirty Comet 5s plus ten Boeing 707s.
Meanwhile, the airline's DC7s would be sold and an additional ten Britannia 310s would be
ordered, plus sixty Bristol Orion engines for the later series Britannia. As already mentioned,
the airline was especially keen on the DH118, which replaced the Comet 5. However, de
Havilland said that they would only proceed with the new programme if thirty aircraft were to

Vickers Super VC10
The original Super VC10, as proposed and ordered by BOAC in June 1960, could accommodate up to 212
passengers in a fuselage stretched by 28ft over the standard VC10. (BAE SYSTEMS)

be ordered as a break even of seventy aircraft was projected. With BOAC looking at ordering
only twenty DH118s, de Havilland were reluctant to commit themselves to the project.

In the event, the 118 was not proceeded with, and the AW.174 and Handley Page projects
were discounted. BOAC therefore elected to order the all-new Vickers VC10 with a Letter
of Intent for thirty-five aircraft being placed in May 1957, and a full contract signed for on
14 January 1958, with an additional twenty options. In 1959, Vickers proposed the VC10
Super 200 (Super VC10) development – which would have been the largest jet at that time
– to seat up to 212 passengers, with an all-up weight of 347,000lb. This aircraft, which was
stretched by some 28ft, was designed for the high density Transatlantic routes, and would have
been powered by four Rolls-Royce Conway 42/2 engines. BOAC placed an order for ten of
these enormous aircraft in June 1960, with a first flight scheduled for early 1964, and
deliveries planned for the beginning of 1965. However, by 1961 the airline realised that the
aircraft was too big for its routes, so the design was reduced in size to become the Super
VC10 Type 1151.
(Original Super VC10) Length 186ft, Span 146ft, Height 39ft 6in

BOAC's VC10 order originally totalled some forty-five aircraft. However, as time progressed,
this was reduced, and at one time nearly cancelled, until only twenty-nine aircraft were
procured. It was only through additional orders from the RAF for fourteen, and small
contracts from BUA, East African and Ghana Airways, that BAC were able to maintain
production at Weybridge, albeit at a very low rate, until the final delivery in 1970.

Throughout this period though, Vickers, and later BAC, were ever hopeful of expanding
the VC10 product range with a number of derivatives. Some of these included projects with
two or even three fuselages joined by stub wings married to Super VC10 outer wings, to
carry up to 450 passengers. Others were purely stretched variants. One very serious study
undertaken in depth was the DB265 project.

Vickers Superb (Super Super VC10) DB265

In 1965 BAC made proposals for a new redesigned and re-engined VC10 model, which carried a number of titles including the Superb, DB265 or Super Super VC10. This study saw a new double-deck fuselage joined to the Super VC10 wings and tail/fin unit with seating provided for up to 265, or a maximum of 286 at 34in pitch. Major changes adapted from the VC10 were increased thickness of the wing panels, ribs and spars, with minor modifications made to the flaps and slats. The main undercarriage was reinforced and the tail strengthened, while new nacelles housed the four Rolls-Royce RB178 engines of 27,500lb thrust.

BAC were proposing that Sud Aviation of France could become a subcontractor on the DB265, as on the VC10 with BAC, then happy to take a secondary role to Sud on the future Airbus, then under study. Sud's involvement on the project could have been up to 25 per cent. BOAC, who were quite interested in the programme, had originally been told that a decision would be taken by the government by October 1965, which would have enabled delivery by early 1968. The carrier was considering placing an order for around seven aircraft. However, as early government support was not forthcoming, this date soon stretched out to 1970.

Further studies were made to increase seating to 350, with lower deck seating increased from five to six abreast. A later development, the 265/80, also featured a new wing. Launch costs of the programme were estimated to be £40 million, a sum which BAC, already under financial problems due to the cancellation of the TSR2, could clearly not afford on their own. BAC wanted the government to give them a 100 per cent contribution, and to have the launch costs written off. However, a government report of the time saw estimated sales for this type of aircraft as being only thirty to forty by 1975, and thirty-five to fifty by 1980.

On 11 May 1966, it was announced by the Minister of Aviation that the government were not going to provide any launch funds for the DB265, which would have become the first jumbo airliner and, with its passing indigenous British long-range aircraft, design effectively ceased. BOAC of course went on to order the Boeing 747, and became wedded to Boeing thereafter. The only production on the DB265 project amounted to a small fuselage cross-section.

Span 146ft 8in, Length 204ft 9in, Height 42ft, Wing Area 2,948sq.ft

*Vickers VC10 DB265
An artist's impression of the
VC10 DB265 in BOAC
colours. The double-deck
design would have seated
up to 265 passengers and
would have been powered
by four Rolls-Royce
RB178 turbofan engines.
(BAE SYSTEMS – via
Brooklands Museum Trust)*

Chapter 4

A New Jet for BEA

The development of British European Airways' new jetliner for the sixties and seventies was one of the most important and intensely fought battles between British Aircraft manufacturers in the fifties. It was also one of the contributory factors for the restructuring of the British Industries that occurred over 1959/1960.

In 1952 BEA had tentatively set out a requirement for a four-engined airliner, that could carry around 120 passengers over a range of 500 miles at a speed of 550mph, to replace its 'Discovery' Viscount aircraft. Initially, the airline was very taken with the new VC7 jet programme and showed much interest, even though the airliner was conceived as a long-range transport for the RAF and, hopefully, BOAC. Other aircraft studied at the time included the Comet 3, Viscount 800 and a stretched Britannia with Proteus 3 engines. Both the Comet and Viscount were deemed too small, while the VC7 was considered, on technical grounds, as a suitable Viscount replacement. Sadly, the VC7 problems and later cancellation did not see BEA get their jet aircraft.

In what became a very short-sighted move and, despite the development of jetliners such as the Comet and Caravelle and its surprising interest in the VC7, BEA still felt that for its short-haul routes, turboprops were to be the powerplant for its new fleet for the sixties. In 1954 the company issued a specification for a larger turboprop successor to the Viscount, which had been successfully introduced into service a year earlier. The airline looked at new low and high-wing designs, with both circular and double-bubble fuselages, as well as Britannia developments powered by the Rolls-Royce RB109 and Bristol BE25. Vickers submitted designs included low- and high-wing four RB109 transports, with five-abreast seating for ninety-three passengers, and underfloor baggage holds. The low-wing design's wing span was 114ft and the overall length was 120ft. Vickers' other designs included stretched RB109 or jet variants of the Viscount (Type 870), followed by the Type 900, and finally the Type 951/953 low-wing RB109-powered Vanguard, of which BEA placed an order for twenty in 1956.

The airline was forced to re-adjust this decision hastily when it became evident that big turboprops were certainly not the future of mainline air travel, after its main European competitor, Air France, placed an order for a fleet of new jetliners. The French carrier's new Sud-Est SE-210 Caravelle jets could travel at over 450mph, and twelve aircraft were ordered in February 1956, nine months after the aircraft had made its maiden flight. Although the Vanguard was undoubtedly good, it was evident that while it was the right size of aircraft, it was now powered by the wrong choice of engines. What made matters worse was that Air France's Caravelles would be entering service even before BEA's much slower Vanguards would be delivered. With speed and jetliners becoming the new byword in travelling circles, it was inevitable that BEA would be forced to back down and, in July 1956, the very same month that the Vanguard contract was signed, a specification was issued by BEA for what was effectively the Vanguard's jet replacement.

The 1956 specification called for a new 100-seater jetliner to be powered by more than two engines, with the ability to carry a payload of up to 19,000lb out of 6,000ft runways over 1,000-mile sectors. Other important factors were that it should be able to travel at 600mph – faster than Air France's competing Caravelle – and be in service by 1964. This was quite a turnabout face for an airline who were insisting, just months before, that slower turboprops were the future for short-haul routes.

Interestingly, and despite issuing the above specification, BEA's chairman, Lord Douglas of Kirtleside, was still insisting that the turboprop Vanguard would, when it entered service, be the cornerstone of the airline's fleet, and that any new jets would only be required in small numbers. Yet, in 1957, just a few months after that statement, the carrier had to concede that jets were the future of short-haul transport and its new Vanguards would in effect be obsolete before even entering service. It has often been noted that BEA should have, when making

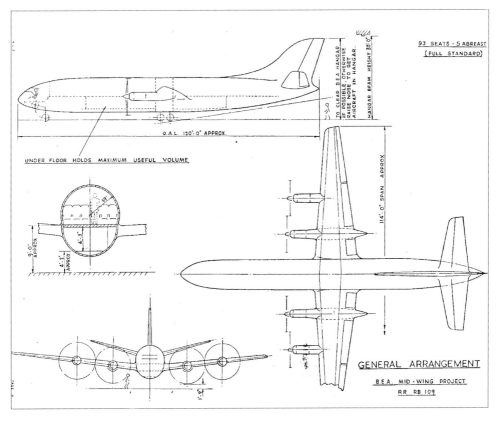

Vickers BEA Mid-Wing Project
A proposal for BEA by Vickers for a Viscount replacement aircraft, featuring a mid-wing layout and powered by Rolls-Royce RB109 turboprops, very similar in design to the chosen Vanguard. (BAE SYSTEMS – via Brooklands Museum Trust)

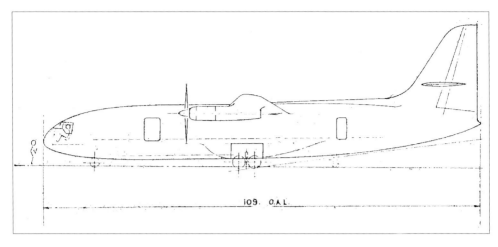

Vickers BEA High-Wing Project
An alternative Vickers high-wing layout for BEA's Viscount replacement, with the tailplane mounted midway on the fin. (BAE SYSTEMS – via Brooklands Museum Trust)

their decision to buy a large turboprop airliner, opted for a Rolls-Royce Tyne development of the similar sized Britannia in production for BOAC. This would have saved a considerable sum being spent on a similar product developed for their own use (and TCA's). Such a programme would have expanded the potential market of the Britannia, which was already becoming a lame duck with regards to major export orders and, could maybe have been used to sustain employment at Short Brothers & Harland in Belfast, which was always a government consideration at that time.

However, at the time there was no sense in combining both state airlines' fleet requirements, and so BOAC operated Britannia turboprops and BEA ordered its own large turboprop, the Vickers Vanguard. Neither aircraft sold in considerable numbers, yet used up a vast amount of capital and valuable manpower.

At last there was a hope that BEA's new jet could launch a new British attack on the airliner market, perhaps achieving success similar to the Viscount's just a few years earlier. Suds Caravelle was already attracting orders, with the major European carrier S.AS placing an order for six aircraft in June 1957. Time was of the essence to obtain orders from other European, Commonwealth and maybe even American carriers.

By now the airliner market was changing. New contracts from the state airlines were becoming fewer, and competition for each new contract was therefore fierce. BOAC had their own jetliner requirement for the sixties, to which a number of manufacturers had turned their attention. Indeed, de Havilland's earlier studies had tried unsuccessfully to produce an aircraft which met both specifications. It was therefore logical, with major domestic orders becoming ever scarcer, that nearly all the major British commercial aircraft manufacturers would turn their attention towards producing a new jet design. Designs were submitted from Armstrong Whitworth, A.V. Roe, de Havilland, Vickers, Bristol and Handley Page. Only Blackburn and Short Brothers & Harland of the big transport builders, appear not to have submitted projects. Those remaining manufacturers who did not bid were more military or smaller-aircraft orientated.

Vickers–Armstrong Studies

Initially, Vickers, sensing that BEA was beginning to change its mind with regards to a big turboprop airliner, began studying jet developments of the Viscount and Vanguard. A number of designs were investigated, which firstly included a 1956 study combining the Viscount shorter fuselage, with the Valiant wing and tail plus three Conway engines. By November 1956, studies were being carried out under the Vanjet and medium-range Transport monikers. These were for up to 100-seater jetliners utilising the Vanguard fuselage, to be powered by three Conway or Avon engines, two on the rear of the fuselage and the third buried within the tail with a new fin. The designs also featured new swept wings. The central engine design was unusual in that an S-shaped intake duct would feed the engine via an air intake which was located on the top of the fuselage.

Some studies carried dual designations including Vickers Vanjet VC10 Mk1 and 2, both tri-jets, the latter a three Rolls-Royce Conway-powered 100-seater, with an AUW of 160,000lb. Later VC10 schemes included the Mk3, a seventy-seater powered by four rear-engined Rolls-Royce jets (unspecified), with an AUW of 130,000lb and, in July 1957, a ninety-five-seater powered by four Rolls-Royce RA29 engines, with a cruising speed of 582mph.

When it became clear that BEA were going to stick with their order for the Vanguard, the Vanjet faded away as Vickers turned their attentions towards meeting the BOAC long-range jet contract, which also took on the VC10 legend.

(Vanjet Scheme 3) Length 98ft Span 93ft 5in, Wing Area 1,600sq.ft

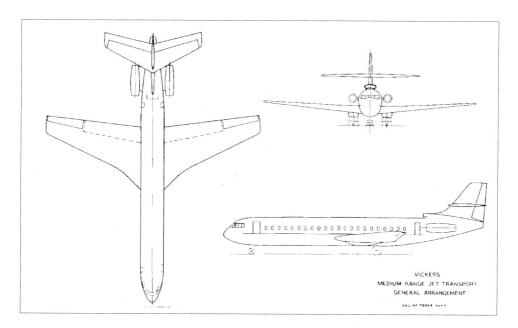

Vickers Medium-Range Jet Transport
One of a number of proposals carried out by Vickers under the Medium-Range Jet Transport study, which saw the Vanguard fuselage combined with a new wing and powered by three Rolls-Royce Conway or Avon engines, the third buried in the tail. (BAE SYSTEMS – via Brooklands Museum Trust)

Armstrong Whitworth 175

One of two Hawker Siddeley Group companies to propose a jet for BEA was Armstrong Whitworth, with the AW.175. A very elegant design looking a little like the Boeing 737, the 175's fuselage was 101ft long and 12ft in diameter, with an AUW of 108,327lb. Power was provided by four Bristol–Siddeley BE47C engines mounted in twin pods beneath swept wings of 35 degrees, with a maximum speed of 610mph. The tailplane was mounted midway on the fuselage. Hawker Siddeley decided only to submit one programme, and work on the 175 was incorporated into Avro's 740 submission.
Length 106ft 6in, Span 98ft 3in, Height 33ft 6in, Wing Area 1,750sq.ft

Avro 740

Avro was the first company actually to reveal its design for the BEA specification. The Avro 740 was originally proposed as either a three RB141- or four RB140-powered airliner seating seventy-eight passengers, with a cruising speed of 603mph. The tri-jet design was favoured and became Avro's proposal to BEA. The 740 was unique in featuring a butterfly tail-layout with the central engine mounted in a pod on top of the fuselage, with the other two engines mounted on the rear of the fuselage. Proposed powerplants were the Bristol Olympus 551 or Rolls-Royce RB141. The design incorporated a ventral airstair similar to that adopted by the BAC One-Eleven. First details of the swept wing project were revealed in July 1957, with development costs estimated to be in the region of £17 to 20 million.
Length 124ft, Span 98ft 11in, Height 27ft, Wing Area 1,750sq.ft

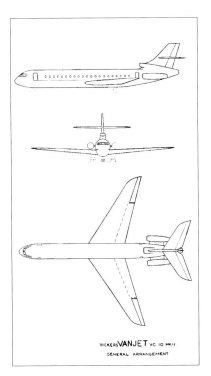

Vickers Vanjet
The Vanjet, or VC10 Mark II, powered by three Rolls-Royce Conway engines, could accommodate up to 100 passengers. (BAE SYSTEMS – via Brooklands Museum Trust)

Bristol 200

Development of the Bristol 200 began in 1956, with the study undergoing a number of layouts and engine configurations over the next couple of years. Initially, the design featured four BE47B (pure jet variant of Orion) engines and was proposed in either high- or low-wing layouts with provision for seventy-two passengers at five abreast seating. By January 1957, the new design could accommodate seventy passengers and was powered by either Bristol BE47 or Rolls-Royce (unspecified but probably RB135) engines of 7,000lb thrust, with an AUW of 110,000lb and a wing span of 91ft. Other studies included a high-wing airliner with a double-bubble fuselage and four engines, two on either side of the rear fuselage vertically on top of each other. Alternatively, low-wing designs with two or four engines mounted at the rear like the VC10, with a tailplane at mid-height on the fin were put forward. These studies were superseded in June 1957 by proposals with either three Olympus or four RB140 engines seating eighty-one passengers with a cruising speed of 610mph.

The final submission in February 1958 was for a tri-jet powered by three Olympus 553 engines of 13,000lb thrust mounted on the rear fuselage, the third centrally fed by an S-duct with a high tailplane mounted at the top of the fin. A maximum take-off weight of 120,000lb was proposed, with a range of 1,700 statute miles while carrying 100 passengers. An Mk2 variant also studied would have been stretched to seat up to 117 passengers and had a larger span. It was planned that the Bristol 200 would enter service in 1962 and, in order to maximise potential, export orders, especially to the all-important US market, had a proposed alternative powerplant in the J57, which was discussed with Pan–American Airways.
Length 121ft 6in, Span 91ft, Height 28ft 3in

De Havilland 119

The first proposal from de Havilland, the DH119, emerged at the end of 1956 and was an all-new design, although similar to the company's earlier DH118 proposal for BOAC. The 119 had a swept wing, mid-mounted tailplane and four Rolls-Royce RA29 Avon engines of 12,000lb thrust mounted behind the rear wing spars, with air intakes below the wings. With an all-up weight of 160,000lb, accommodation was provided for up to ninety-five passengers. For political reasons, the 119 was evolved into the joint BEA/BOAC airline requirement: the DH120.
Length 128ft 9in, Span 117ft 6in

De Havilland 120

Shortly after submitting the 119, de Havilland proposed a joint project in order to meet both the requirements of BOAC and BEA. Similar to the 119, the project featured the same wing/engine layout but was powered by either four Rolls-Royce RB140s (scaled-down Conway) or RA29 Avons, with an AUW of 190,000lb. Neither BEA or BOAC favoured the design, given that it was a compromise to meet both specifications and, in BEA's case was much larger than required. The project was quickly superseded in the project office by a dedicated project, once again for BEA.

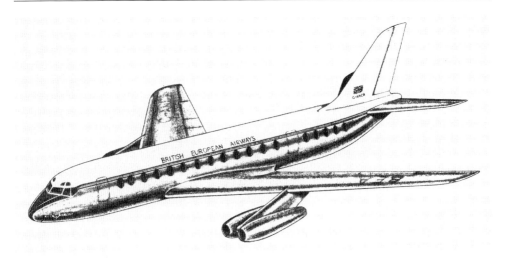

Armstrong Whitworth AW.175
An impression of Armstrong Whitworth's AW175 in BEA colours, whose four Bristol–Siddeley BE47C engines were mounted in pairs beneath the swept wings. (BAE SYSTEMS – via Ray Williams)

De Havilland 121

The 121 began life in May 1957 as a three- or four-engined jet, seating seventy-nine passengers, with a gross weight of 126,000lb. The tri-jet design was powered by three Rolls-Royce RA29 Avon engines, two of which were mounted on the side of the rear fuselage, with the third positioned centrally above the rear fuselage with a straight air intake. The tailplane was sited beneath the central engine. The four-engined study saw power provided by RB140s of 8,550lb thrust, which were mounted in pairs on either side of the rear fuselage.

By 1958 the 121, now a definitive tri-jet had adopted the now famous T-tail layout, with the second central engine adopting a similar layout to the Vanjet, being buried within the tail with an S-shaped intake duct. Power was initially to be provided by Rolls-Royce RB140s of 10,400lb thrust but, as the gross weight increased from 107,000lb to 122,500lb, these were replaced by the RB141 of 12,000lb thrust.
Length 126ft 8in, Span 107ft, Wing Area 1,920sq.ft

Handley Page (Reading) HP.R6

In 1955 short-term studies were undertaken at Handley Page, Reading, for a short-range high density transport aircraft to replace BEA's Viscounts. The highly aerodynamic design, with blown flaps and laminar flow wings, was originally put forward powered by Rolls-Royce RB109 Tyne engines, and later possibly with twin Conway engines. The design proposed more to meet the Vanguard specification, is also mentioned in early documentation for BEA's new transport but does not appear to have had too much effort expended on it and, as government records reveal, the submission was not taken very seriously.

Of the above designs, only three projects became serious contenders for the BEA order, those being the Avro 740, Bristol 200 and de Havilland 121. During 1957, the Conservative administration decided to use what would become one of the few new major commercial contracts as a carrot to encourage the British Industries to reorganise themselves into larger groupings. At this time there were still too many separate design teams (even though there was the loose grouping of the various companies of the Hawker Siddeley Group).

Initially, one of the most important conditions of the new aircraft was that it was to be privately financed. This was an interesting development and, whereas Avro, who with the backing of the vast Hawker Siddeley Group behind them, stated they were able to finance the development of the aircraft themselves, neither de Havilland or Bristol could afford to finance their offerings independently. It is interesting that even at this time it was considered that this new transport could be the last subsonic short-range jet transport to be designed in Britain. This was a number of years before the infamous Plowden Committee's recommendations.

As a consequence of the government's conditions for tendering for the order, a delay was incurred as the manufacturers began discussing prospective partnerships. The de Havilland company proposed a consortium under the old name of Airco (Aircraft Manufacturing Company) with Hunting, Fairey and rather interestingly, Bristol. It was also intended to include Saunders Roe (in which de Havilland was a shareholder) in a subcontract capacity, with Handley Page offering assistance.

Not surprisingly, Bristol did not want to play second fiddle to de Havilland (who were considered to be the 'royal family' of British airliner manufacturers) and decided to link up with the Hawker Siddeley Group in December 1957. A consequence of this proposed grouping was that the Avro 740 was dropped and the new Bristol–Hawker Siddeley combination on a 35 to 65 per cent split concentrated their efforts on the Bristol Model 200. It has been documented that in this grouping it was envisaged that Hawker Siddeley (Avro) would have been responsible for the airframe, while Bristol would have handled the systems.

It appears that there was a strong prejudice within BEA for using any product of the Bristol Aircraft company and that they were also not confident in Avro as a civil aircraft builder. On the other hand, de Havilland was the only British manufacturer with previous jet transport experience. It was also armed with all the valuable data from the Comet crashes, had major experience in structural fatigue and a good after-sales service. A further factor was that

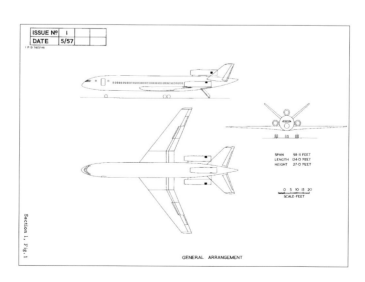

Avro 740
Avro's 740 tri-jet was an unusual design, featuring a butterfly tail, with the third engine mounted in a pod on top of the rear fuselage.
(BAE SYSTEMS)

de Havilland was used to working with Rolls-Royce, and Bristol (with their own engine company) were not, and of course the 121 was the natural follow-on to the Comet. As an interim measure, before delivery of the new jetliner, de Havilland was also offering the Comet 4B transport, and it was eventually ordered by BEA in August 1957.

BEA decided in 1958 that the 121 best met its requirements, even though Bristol continued to press their case for some time with the Model 200, which the government appeared to prefer, due to the stronger financial resources of the Bristol–Hawker Siddeley joint venture. In a last ditch attempt to gain a US order for the 200, Bristol took their project to the Americas and held talks with Pan–American. There was even talk of a Curtis Wright Zephyr US version of the Olympus engine. All this was to no avail, as BEA was resolute that the 121 was to be the selected aircraft.

On 1 August 1958, approval was given for BEA to place an order with de Havilland for twenty-four 121 aircraft with an option for an additional twelve aircraft. Having now decided on its new aircraft, BEA and de Havilland worked closely on the new project, tailoring it specifically for the airline's requirement. It could now accommodate up to 117 passengers and was powered by Rolls-Royce Medway engines. That it would certainly have been a world beater was clear, and it could have been developed further as there was much potential in the Medway engine for growth variants. Cruelly, this was not to be, as fate intervened in early 1959 when there was a sudden dip in traffic growth. Instead of seeing this as a temporary blip, BEA panicked, fearing it would now be operating a huge fleet of new aircraft but would be unable to fill all the seats.

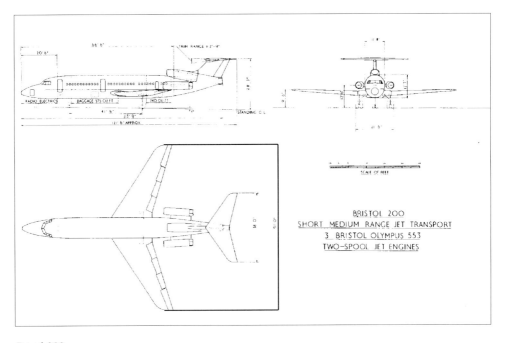

Bristol 200
The Bristol 200 was proposed in both three- and four-engined configurations. This, the final scheme, was powered by three Bristol Olympus 553 engines and, although favoured by the government, BEA ordered de Havilland's rival 121 Trident. (BAE SYSTEMS – via Bristol Aero Collection)

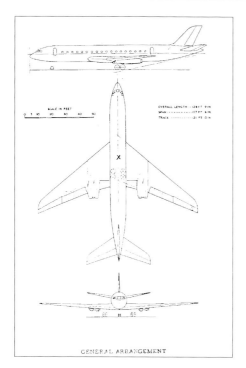
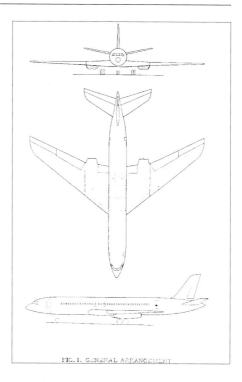

Above left: *De Havilland 120*
The de Havilland 120 was proposed as a compromise to combine both BEA and BOAC specifications for a new jet. Not surprisingly, neither airline favoured a joint project, which was quickly dropped. (BAE SYSTEMS – via de Havilland Heritage Museum)

Above right: *De Havilland 119*
De Havilland's first proposal to meet the BEA specification, the 119, was powered by four Rolls-Royce Avon engines. (BAE SYSTEMS – via de Havilland Heritage Museum)

With little resistance from the management at de Havilland, the 121 was subsequently cut down in size to accommodate only eighty passengers, and the Medway engines were replaced by the less powerful Rolls-Royce Spey. This was to cost the project immensely in the coming years, as both capacity and range were to become limited in comparison with the rival Boeing Model 727. Interestingly, de Havilland had invited representatives from Boeing to Hatfield to view the 121 line, in the hope of a joint production deal. However, a reciprocal trip to Boeing saw nothing of that company's future plans being revealed to de Havilland. In the event, BEA officially placed an order for twenty-four aircraft and twelve options of the scaled-down 121 Trident on 12 August 1959.

As has been well documented, Boeing produced an aircraft similar to the original 121 Specification. Whereas the Trident went on to achieve a production of some 117 aircraft, over 1,800 727s were manufactured, and led to future developments such as the 757. Over the years, many developments of the Trident were projected, even from the early days. They included the 1960 Mk2 variant as shown at that year's Farnborough Air Show, which was heavier with a stretched fuselage and a wing of a reduced sweep of 30 degrees, and more powerful Spey engines. However, all proposals suffered from the unavailability of a suitable engine.

One final interesting study emerged from Vickers and could possibly have regained some of the market lost by the decision to scale down the de Havilland 121.

Vickers VC11

The VC11 began life as the Type 1400, the design of which began in October 1959. Part of Vickers' policy at that time was to develop a family of VC10 derivative rear-engined transports, with the VC11 being proposed for short- to medium-range routes with an all-up weight of 170,00lb and a range of 1,500 nautical miles. Similar in design to a scaled-down VC10, the VC11 was also a low-wing design with boundary layer control and high lift devices, with a high T-tail and four jet engines mounted in pods two apiece on either side of the rear fuselage. The superiority of the design, it was claimed, lay in its small swept wings designed for the best possible cruising speed. The lower cruising drag which resulted allowed for smaller engines providing a lower thrust, and gave greater fuel efficiency. Power was to be provided by four engines mounted, as with the VC10, on the rear fuselage, with either the Rolls-Royce AR963-6 (a scaled-up RB163) or Rolls-Royce RB963-1 of 11,000lb thrust, while for the export market consideration was given to the Pratt & Whitney JT8D-1. Seating would have been provided for up to 138 passengers at 34in pitch in a six abreast layout within a cabin of 11ft 6in diameter, with passenger access gained from both a forward entrance and a ventral airstair. With BEA deciding the aircraft was too big, Trans-Canada Airlines (TCA), always a keen Vickers sales target and who had originally wished to purchase the cancelled

De Havilland 121 Trident
De Havilland 121 Trident prototype G-ARPA, seen taking-off from the company's Hatfield factory, was operated by BEA for ten years. (BAE SYSTEMS)

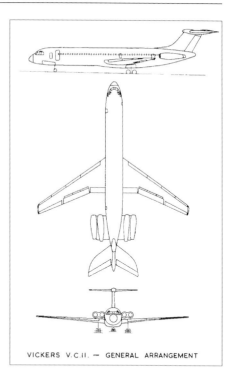

VICKERS V.C.II. — GENERAL ARRANGEMENT

Vickers VC11
Proposed as the smallest member of the Vickers family of
rear-engined jetliners, BEA found the VC11 too large, but
Trans–Canada Airlines placed a commitment for fourteen
aircraft. When Vickers became part of BAC, the VC11
was to be replaced by the One-Eleven. (BAE SYSTEMS
– via Brooklands Museum Trust)

VC7, found the aircraft ideal, and soon placed an option on fourteen aircraft. The first flight was originally planned for May 1963 although as the project developed, this date later slipped. The project was due to receive government backing to the tune of £9.75 million ,which was half the estimated launch costs of £19.5 million, with a quoted break even figure of seventy-two aircraft.

When Vickers became part of the British Aircraft Corporation, production was intended to be shared within the new group, with Bristol building the wing and tail, and Hunting, the fuselage. However, the formation of BAC had also brought with it Hunting's small 107 jet. The company's attentions naturally turned to what should be the correct course of action for its new jetliner programme. While the VC11 already had a potential customer, BAC could see that the market place was already crowded with the Trident, potential Trident 2, Boeing 727 and, to a lesser extent, the Caravalle. It therefore elected to pursue the small jet, which eventually became the One-Eleven. The VC11 was cancelled in spring 1961 and its government launch costs were transferred to the new jet. With hindsight, perhaps BAC should have stuck with the VC11, although the One-Eleven was of course built to the tune of 235 aircraft in the UK, with an additional nine Romanian-licence-built examples. The VC11 may also have prevented the debacle with the later Trident models.

Sadly, TCA, as in the case of the VC7, were unable to buy a Vickers transport. All future purchases, through what became Air Canada, were to go to American companies. BEA became wedded to the underpowered Trident, despite trying to order 727s a few years later and, due to the unavailability of a suitable engine, any major potential developments and valuable export orders were lost.

(October 1960) Length 136ft 2in, Span 106ft 3in, Height 32ft 6in, Wing Area 1,600sq.ft

Chapter 5

Supersonics

From the late 1940s onwards, it seemed that man's mission was to achieve even greater speed, and this was translated into supersonic military aircraft development, with the first major British design being the Miles M.52 (sadly cancelled in February 1946). The transition to a supersonic commercial transport was to take much longer.

Having led the way with commercial jet transports, it was natural that in order to capitalise on this initial success, Britain's design teams should turn their attention to Supersonic Transport aircraft. By the mid-fifties, the ground lost by the Comet accidents and VC7 cancellation could, it was hoped, be reclaimed with the production of hundreds of aircraft travelling faster than the speed of sound.

The study of supersonic airliners in Britain really began in 1954 at the Royal Aircraft Establishment (RAE) at Farnborough, when a working party was set up under Morien Morgan to investigate the possibility of a faster-than-sound transatlantic airliner. Its initial design was for an aircraft based around the Avro 730 supersonic bomber, with thin unswept wings and a long slender fuselage, only able to accommodate around fifteen passengers. The aircraft could have travelled at Mach 2 from London–New York but the all-up weight was estimated at above 300,000lb, with an excessive cost per passenger. It was evident that the development of such an aircraft was unjustifiable.

All this changed after the head of supersonic research at the RAE, Philip Hufton, went to America in 1955, and saw developments in supersonic aircraft, using the 'area rule' effect. This stated that if the shape of an aircraft's cross-sectional area was the same all along its length, the wave drag would be minimised. Encouraged by this, Hufton filed a report suggesting that a Supersonic Transport may now be feasible. A further line studied was an entirely new shape of aircraft which could be designed for supersonic flight – the delta wing. The upshot of all this was that the minds of those back at Farnborough, who just months earlier were saying that an SST could not be justified, now had their interest rekindled in a major way.

Among those now re-examining supersonic flight at the RAE was an aerodynamicist, Dr Dietrich Küchemann, who began to study delta designs. In order to further research, it was decided that the RAE alone could not look into all the problems that would need to be investigated, especially if Britain was to try and get ahead of the field as it had done with the Comet less than a decade earlier. It was decided that all the major parties in the industry, as well as airlines, government, ministries and the Air Registration Board, should be included.

Under the chairmanship of Mr (later Sir) Morien Morgan, deputy head of the RAE, the Supersonic Transport Aircraft Committee (STAC) was set up in October 1956. This

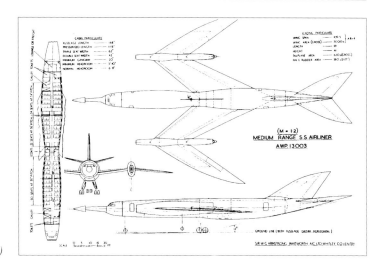

Armstrong Whitworth
AW.P13003
The M-wing planform
Armstrong Whitworth
AW.P13003 could carry
100 passengers over
medium ranges. (BAE
SYSTEMS – via
Brooklands Museum Trust)

committee had its first meeting on the 30 November 1956. Its two key points were to investigate the possible market for an SST and to define an operator's broad requirements so that areas of desirable research could be carried out. Among the representatives were all the major aircraft companies, namely: A.V. Roe, Armstrong Whitworth, Bristol Aircraft, de Havilland, Handley Page, Shorts and Vickers–Armstrong. These were joined in November 1957 by English Electric and Fairey. Also represented were the four main engine companies: Armstrong Siddeley Motors, Bristol Engines, de Havilland Engines and of course Rolls-Royce. Other representatives came from BOAC and BEA, as well as government departments: The Air Registration Board, The Aircraft Research Association, The National Physical Laboratory, The NGTE (National Gas Turbine Establishment), RAE, Ministry of Supply and Ministry of Transport and Civil Aviation. The committee foresaw the prestige that a successful SST would bring to Britain, as well as the possible military transport spin-off.

The committee looked at the problems of flying at speeds from Mach 1.2 to Mach 2.6, and the problems that were associated with materials, especially at a higher speed with detailed research carried out. In the event, two sizes of aircraft were proposed: a medium-range transport carrying 100 passengers over 1,500 miles at Mach 1.2 (800mph), and a Mach 1.8 (1,200mph) or faster long-range airliner carrying 150 passengers. Many different shapes of aircraft were to be investigated, including swept wings, variable wings, M-wings, slender wings and aircraft capable of vertical take-off. The committee also found that although a Mach 2.6 aircraft would probably be feasible, its development would take too long.

In the early stages, de Havilland concentrated on Mach 1.2 long-range designs with swept, M and delta wing planforms. The M-wing form was also investigated by Vickers, Bristol and Armstrong Whitworth. Shorts looked at both medium-range and long-range transports with swept and delta wings at Mach 1.5 and Mach 1.8, while Handley Page studies featured delta, cropped spearhead and swept wings at Mach 1.8. Avro looked at a medium-range straight wing Mach 1.8 transport.

The committee initially decreed that for the Mach 1.2 airliner, an M-wing or possibly swept wing would be preferable, while for the Mach 1.8, an integrated slender wing or long thin delta should be studied. At the time, total development costs of the Mach 1.2 design were put at £60 to 80 million, while those for the Mach 1.8 were around £95 million.

When the STAC's report was submitted in March 1959, the Ministry of Aviation acted quickly, with feasibility studies being commissioned for three aircraft types, from the Hawker Siddeley Group and Bristol Aircraft in September of that year. A major change was that the proposed speed had now increased to Mach 2.2. The Hawker Siddeley Group was chosen to study an integrated wing which was to be handled by its Advanced Projects Group, and resulted in a design with an all-up-weight of 320,000lb and a wing area of 6,000sq.ft.

Concurrent with this, Hawker Siddeley also undertook joint studies, with Handley Page, into Mach 2.2 airliners. Bristol Aircraft were to study a slender shape wing design with a distinct fuselage. Both companies were also asked to investigate a Mach 2.7 aircraft.

After reporting their feasibility studies in March 1960, it was announced in October that BAC (into which Bristol Aircraft had now been absorbed) had won the contract to further their design with a Ministry of Aviation contract of £350,000. The Bristol design was submitted in August 1961 as the transatlantic type 198, powered by six Olympus engines and accommodating 130 passengers, with an all-up weight of 380,000lb. It is interesting that in early government documents, questions had been raised about awarding the SST contract to Bristol, except in association with Hawker Siddeley, and under the latter company's leadership. Obviously these misgivings had later been dealt with.

However, a further design was later authorised from BAC for a smaller four-engined aircraft which became the Bristol 223. It could accommodate 100 passengers and had an all-up weight of 250,000lb. At around the same time, the French company, Sud Aviation, exhibited a model of their own SST at the 1961 Paris Air Show, the Super Caravelle, which bore an amazing resemblance to the 223. Great minds on both sides of the channel were obviously thinking along the same lines.

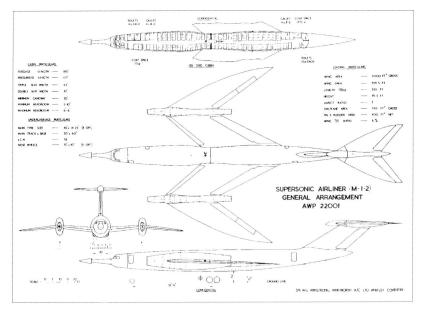

Armstrong Whitworth AW.P22001
The long-range M-wing Armstrong Whitworth AW.P22001 would have travelled at Mach 1.2.
(BAE SYSTEMS – via Brooklands Museum Trust)

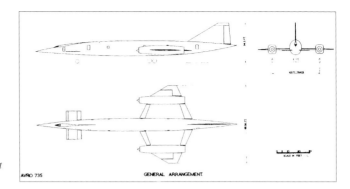

Avro 735
Developed from the Avro 730
long-range supersonic
Reconnaissance aircraft, the Avro
735 could carry 100 passengers at
Mach 1.8. (BAE SYSTEMS)

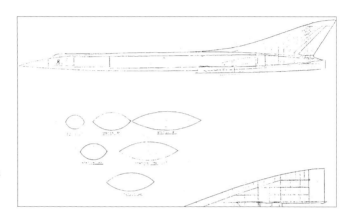

Avro 760
Side view of the Avo 760
integrated-wing supersonic airliner.
(BAE SYSTEMS – via Alan
Greenhalgh)

As is now well documented, in 1962 Britain and France decided to pool their individual studies, the Sud Super Caravelle and the BAC (Bristol) 223, into a new joint project which was to become Concorde. An agreement was signed between two governments in London on 29 November 1962, and registered in The Hague, with both countries having equal shares in the new programme. It became the first major collaborative aircraft venture. Despite many attempts by the British government to cancel it in its early days, the contract was binding, with no cancellation clause.

For such a major technological project, progress was swift, with the first metal being cut in 1965 and the first aircraft rolling out at the Sud Aviation factory in Toulouse on 11 December 1967. On 2 March 1969, this aircraft, F-WTSS, made its first historic flight from Toulouse, and a little over a month later on 9 April 1969, BAC's first aircraft, G-BSST, made its maiden flight from BAC's Filton factory. It is interesting that assembly lines were set up in both countries, as the project was so prestigious and so costly that it could not have been seen for one country to have taken all the glory. Thankfully, times have changed.

Sadly, although a technical 'tour de force', Concorde never attained the commercial expectations that had seemed so achievable when it was launched. As early as 1963, Pan Am had placed a conditional order for 6 aircraft which would have been delivered on a rotational basis with Air France and BOAC. As the flight development programme proceeded, the world into which the project had originally been conceived changed dramatically. Surprisingly, the abandonment of the US SST (Boeing 2707-200) in 1971 did much to harm the project's sales

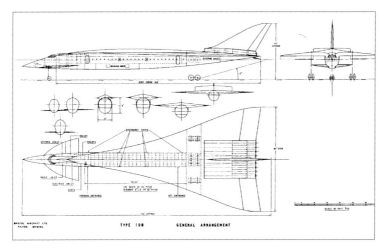

Bristol 198
The delta-winged
Bristol 198, powered
by six Bristol–Siddeley
Olympus engines.
(BAE SYSTEMS –
via Brooklands
Museum)

success. This may seem strange, as in most cases the withdrawal of a competitor boosts the success of the remaining projects, but overnight the Americans suddenly became more anti-noise pollution and, therefore, anti-Concorde. It would have been interesting to see if this would still have been the case if the Boeing 2707 had actually been realised. The fuel crisis, some two years later, was compounded with the anti-Concorde feeling, which caused spiralling inflation and world recession – the writing was on the wall for a noisy, small and fuel-thirsty new airliner. Only sixteen production aircraft were to be built, although this did provide thousands of jobs in Britain from the mid-sixties through to the end of the seventies. As early as 1967, total commitments to Concorde had totalled seventy-four aircraft from most of the world's major airlines. However, the problems in the seventies led to British Airways (BOAC) and Air France becoming the only customers, despite Letters of Intent from the Chinese carrier CAAC and Iraqi Airways. The last aircraft was delivered from the production lines in 1980. The supersonic journey had lasted from 1956 to 1980. The announcement that both British Airways and Air France were to end Concorde flights in 2003 could mark the last commercial supersonic flights for many years to come.

Armstrong Whitworth

Armstrong Whitworth carried out a number of design studies for Supersonic Transports. The AW.P13 from the company's Initial Projects Section was an M-wing planform study with engines mounted in nacelles at the wing kinks, with a sting-mounted nose cone located ahead of the cockpit to avoid drag penalty. Accommodation was provided for 106 passengers, with a maximum of six abreast at the fuselage's maximum width in the rear fuselage, while only single seats were on either side of the central gangway at its narrowest point. There was also provision at the rear of the fuselage for either a lounge or carriage of freight. Proposed as a medium-range transport travelling at Mach 1.2, the design had an all-up weight of 183,500lb. Length 181ft, Span 109ft 5in, Height 41ft, Wing Area 3,000sq.ft

The AW.P14, studied in conjunction with the AW.P13, featured a highly tapered swept wing with tailplane mounted on top of the fin, and an area-ruled fuselage with two rear-mounted

turbojets providing the power. Accommodation was provided for 100 passengers within the waisted fuselage, at a maximum of six abreast with an all-up weight of 202,400lb.
Length 184ft, Span 81ft

The AW.P22 of 1958 was very similar in design to the AW.P13, with an M-wing planform and waisted fuselage. It featured a T-tail arrangement and increased wing chord. Designed as a long-range transport with stage lengths of 3,450 miles, the lengthened fuselage could accommodate up to 126 passengers at a maximum of five abreast.
Length 210ft, Span 109ft 5in

Other studies undertaken by the company in 1957, with no AW.P numbers, included a VTOL supersonic delta-powered by 224 RB108 lift engines, with an AUW of 420,000lb, able to accommodate 136 passengers, with an additional four propulsion engines over a range of 3,000 miles. A further VTOL study seating ninety-six passengers was powered by 240 silenced RB108 engines plus propulsion engines.

Avro

The Avro 735, put forward in 1956, was based around the Avro 730 long-range supersonic reconnaissance aircraft. The 730 had been chosen to meet Operational Requirement 330/R156T, issued in 1954 for an aircraft capable of flying at Mach 2.5, with a minimum range of 5,000 nautical miles. The aircraft was well advanced when the Sandy's White Paper on Defence was published in 1957, which cancelled the project and ordered the test fuselage to be broken up. In its civil form, the medium-range Avro 735 could seat up to 100 passengers at five abreast in a fuselage of 11ft maximum width, and could travel up to 1,500 nautical miles at Mach 1.8. The design featured a light alloy structure all-moving noseplane, with trailing edge elevators and nose flaps all incorporating boundary layer control. The unswept wing carried eight Armstrong Siddeley P176 turbojet engines, mounted as four each

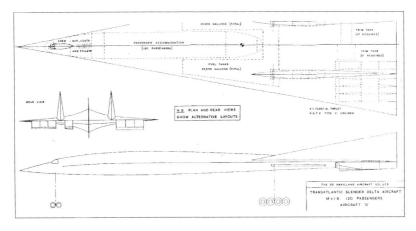

De Havilland Mach 1.8
A slender delta study from de Havilland, to travel at Mach 1.8 carrying 120 passengers. (BAE SYSTEMS – via RAF Museum Hendon)

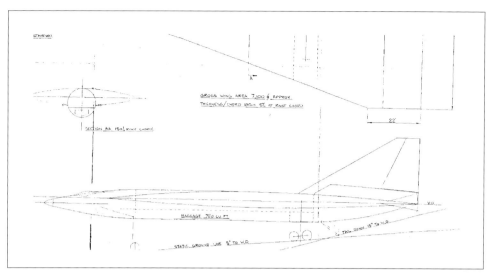

Fairey Project 91
Side view of the Fairey Project 91, a high-wing Supersonic Transport from December 1958, which would have accommodated 120 passengers. (Westland Helicopters – via BAE SYSTEMS)

in nacelles inboard of wing tips, each with variable-geometry air intakes and with each engine fitted with a variable convergent/divergent nozzle. Between the side of the fuselage and the engine nacelles, trailing edge flaps of boundary layer control were fitted, while fuel was carried within an integral wing tank. The undercarriage was a centrally-mounted unit with two subsidiary units, one from each engine nacelle. Designed for heights of between 40 and 50,000ft, the all-up weight was 264,225lb, with an estimated direct operating cost of £940 per hour.

Length 180ft, Span 68ft 56in, Height 34ft 5in, Wing Area 2,350sq.ft

The Avro 760 was an integrated wing project from 1958, powered by six jet engines. Accommodation was provided for 186 passengers, forty-two in a forward cabin at six abreast, and 144 in the split rear cabin, also at six abreast. Access to the cabin was provided by two airstairs in the centre of the aircraft.

Bristol

Bristol Aircraft proposed three major supersonic designs. The Bristol 198 began life in 1956 as an M-wing Mach 1.3 design, before evolving into a delta over wing engined Mach 1.8 transport. The definitive type 198 emerged as a Mach 2.2 delta airliner powered by six under wing Bristol–Siddeley Olympus 591 engines of 22,800lb thrust. The all-up weight was 385,000lb with seating for up to 122 passengers and a maximum range of 3600 miles with a ceiling of 60,000ft.

A number of other 198 projects were studied, including proposals in early 1960 by Dr A.A. Griffiths for VTOL and STOVL aircraft, seating up to 122 passengers over the London to New York route. The VTOL aircraft was assumed to fly off/on to a special ground fixture and, was therefore provided with no permanent undercarriage, the ground features having built in shock absorption with gridded surfaces to avoid ground suction effect. The all-up weight was 602,500lb with a landing weight of 347,400lb. The design facilitated the need for some seventy lift engines which required a large wing area of some 6,000sq.ft. Again, six engines would provide forward propulsion, and these were expected to be scaled-down Bristol–Siddeley Olympus.

(VTOL 198) Length 185ft, Span 94ft

The STOVL design, which was of a more fully-integrated wing body configuration had an all-up weight of 442,150lb and a landing weight of 261,000lb, with a take-off length of 4,500ft predicted. Up to thirty lift engines were mounted fifteen apiece on either side of the fuselage, and were sealed when not in use. The six propulsion engines, which were presumed to be Bristol Olympus, were carried in two nacelles beneath the wing. Take-off would have been characterised by a steep climb-out gradient, reducing jet-lift as speed built up.

(STOVL 198) Length 170ft, Span 78ft

Both the VTOL and STOVL designs employed lift assistance from propulsion engines obtained by deflecting the nozzles – with the greater part of the jet lift coming from lift engines. As a consequence of the lift engines, both of these designs were substantially heavier than the conventional 198 design.

Other studies included the April 1958 198B family of slender integrated SSTs with a gothic planform and a cabin fully submerged in the wing. Up to 120 passengers could be carried, and the wing had an area of some 8,000-8,500sq.ft. The 198S would have been

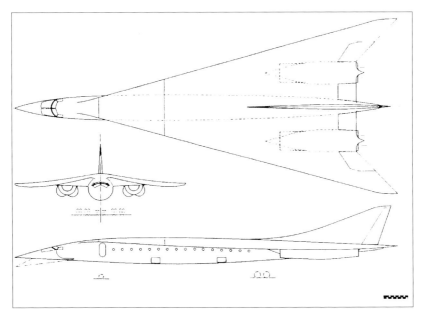

English Electric P30N
The P30N was one of a number of schemes from English Electric for supersonic airliners travelling at up to Mach 3. (BAE SYSTEMS)

constructed of steel and could achieve Mach 2.8. All the 198 studies were, however, considered too ambitious to be given government approval, and there was also concern with regards to the sonic boom created by such a heavy transport.
(198) Length 180ft, Span 78ft, Height 40ft 4in, Wing Area 5,270sq.ft

The Bristol 213 was a Mach 3 (1,900mph) transport study in 1959 which, because of the extreme velocities at such a speed, would have been made from steel and titanium to withstand the increased air friction heating. However, it was found that travelling at Mach 3 would only save an additional 10 per cent of time and, consequently, the project was shelved.

The final independent project to emerge was the Bristol 223 in 1961, a smaller four-engined design with a light alloy airframe which could travel at Mach 2.2 with transatlantic range, and had an all-up weight of 251,700lb. Of similar design to the 198, up to 100 passengers could be accommodated at 33in-pitch, with five-abreast seating in a fuselage of 10ft 10in maximum diameter. Power was provided by four Bristol–Siddeley Olympus 593 engines mounted beneath the ogival wing. The design was eventually amalgamated with the Sud Super Caravelle, with the end result becoming the BAC/Sud Concorde.
Length 176ft 6in, Span 70ft, Height 35ft, Wing Area 3,700sq.ft

De Havilland

De Havilland investigated a series of Supersonic Transports for the STAC and these included a Mach 1.8 slender delta powered by eight NGTE Type-C engines. A further study, the DH130, was of variable geometry with a cruise speed of Mach 1.15. This was powered by three Rolls-Royce RB178 Super Conway engines of 25,000lb, two positioned beneath the wings with the third in the fin. Up to 150 passengers could be accommodated in an economy layout, with a range of 2,350 nautical miles with maximum payload. The project was also proposed in a number of military guises and, after de Havilland was taken over by Hawker Siddeley, the project was transferred to Kingston. Here it re-emerged under the Advanced Projects Group as the HS1011 which, in its military guise, was tendered for the contract eventually met by the Nimrod.
Wing Area 2,700sq.ft

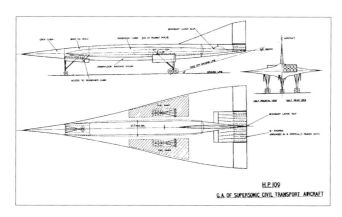

Handley Page 109
Handley Page 109 supersonic airliner. (Handley Page Association)

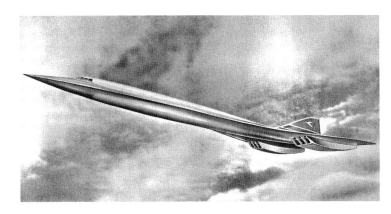

Hawker Siddeley HS1000 An artist's impression of the Hawker Siddeley HS1000 integrated wing design in BOAC colours. (BAE SYSTEMS)

English Electric P30

Under the P30 designation, English Electric's SST studies covered speeds up to Mach 3, powered by four or six engines, including variable geometry planforms. One study, which emerged in 1959, was of a high-wing design with six underwing-mounted Bristol–Siddeley Olympus 593 engines.

Fairey

Like all the companies represented on the STAC, Fairey undertook a number of design studies. These included Project 91, from December 1958, which was for a 120-seater airliner at six abreast, with passengers entering via a ventral airstair, similar to the BAC One-Eleven.
Length 157ft, Span 85ft, Wing Area 7,100sq.ft

Handley Page 109 and 110

Handley Page conducted both independent SST designs and a laminar flow Mach 2.2 project in 1960, collaborating with Hawker Siddeley Aviation. This was for a 150-seater airliner some 170ft-long with a wing area of 6,000sq.ft. Under the HP.109 moniker for a Mach 1.8 long-range transport, designs were studied of fully integrated, slender delta ogee, thin and thick wing types. One such study could accommodate 120 passengers at five-abreast seating with an all-up weight of 350,000lb.
(Thin wing study) Length 172ft 6in, Span 107ft 9in, Height 38ft 9in

The HP110 was a medium-range airliner proposed in either conventional or boundary layer suction variants, capable of travelling at up to Mach 1.3.

Hawker Siddeley

The Advanced Projects Group at Kingston investigated a number of SST designs. The project that emerged to meet the STAC feasibility study resulted in an integrated wing

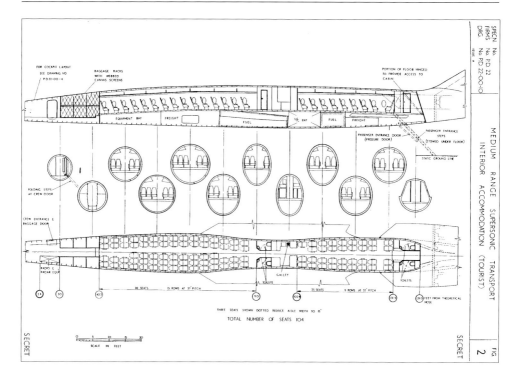

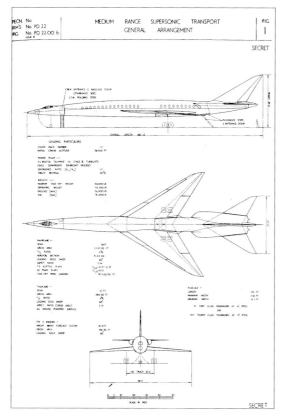

Above: *Short PD22 Interior*
Interior layout of the Short PD22
with 104 seats, showing the
waisted fuselage and passenger
entry via a ventral airstair.
(Courtesy of Bombardier Aerospace
– via RAF Museum Hendon)

Left: *Short PD22*
The medium-range Short PD22
featured a swept wing, and would
have travelled at Mach 1.3.
(Courtesy of Bombardier Aerospace
– via RAF Museum Hendon)

Opposite: *Short PD29*
The Mach 1.8 Short PD29
design featured a foreplane, adopt-
ed for trimming purposes.
(Courtesy of Bombardier Aerospace
– via RAF Museum Hendon)

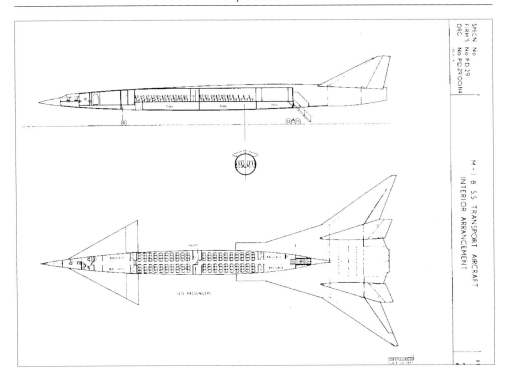

airliner under the APG designation HS1000, with an all-up weight of 320,000lb, and a wing area of 6,000sq.ft. Designed to carry 100 passengers at five abreast, the Mach 2.2 design was powered by six underwing engines. Further studies were undertaken of similar designs for Mach 2.7.

Length 179ft, Span 74ft 6in, Height 34ft

The company also undertook VTOL SST studies, but found that this type of aircraft was not suitable as a Supersonic Transport, given the extra power required and noise generated. The company's conclusion was that VTOL was not practical for a first generation SST.

Shorts

The PD22, from April 1957, was a swept wing medium-range design for BEA, capable of travelling at Mach 1.3 over stage lengths of 1,500 nautical miles. Designed to operate from 2,500yd fields, it had a gross weight of 216,000lb. Power was provided by four Bristol Olympus 531 Stage 2 engines and up to 104 passengers could be accommodated at four or five abreast. The fuselage with a maximum diameter of 11ft 8in was mostly of circular section, although waisted in the forward portion of the rear fuselage. Passenger access was via a ventral airstair.

Both high- and low-wing layouts were considered, with a tandem seating arrangement for the pilots under a 'teardrop' canopy. The engines were mounted on the rear of the fuselage with the tailplane mounted directly above. It was considered that the design could be used by BOAC for its short-length routes. Maximum take-off weight was 216,000lb and landing

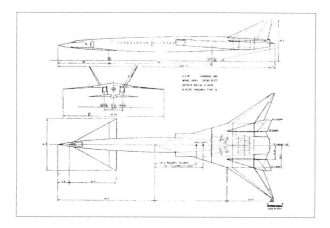

Short PD29
Short PD29 long-range Supersonic
Transport. (Copyright Bombardier
Aerospace)

weight, 165,000lb, with an initial cruise altitude of 38,000ft. The PD22 was to be mostly made from high strength aluminium alloy.
Length 180ft, Span 78ft, Height 39ft, Wing Area 2,220sq.ft

In April 1959, Shorts put forward the PD29, a long-range SST capable of travelling at Mach 1.8. Various designs were considered, with one of the most promising being rear-engined, featuring a foreplane adopted for trimming purposes, which showed large reductions in overall drag, due to lift over the conventional tailplane. Designed to carry up to 120 passengers at six abreast, and with a range of 4,600 nautical miles using a balanced field length of 9,000ft, the PD29 had an AUW of 380,000lb. Passenger entrance to the aircraft would have been via a ventral airstair, with power provided by eight engines of the NGTE Type B. One problem was that the fuel was carried in the pressurised fuselage beneath the passenger cabin, instead of being wholly within the wings. It was felt that the wing could be modified to extend forward in a future design, to produce stowage of fuel external to the pressure cabin. Shorts also undertook studies of a Mach 1.5 long-range delta, and the PD30, a Mach 1.8 long-range jet.
(PD29) Length 202ft, Span 97ft 75in, Height 38ft 5in, Wing Area 3,900sq.ft

Vickers

Project X, from October 1956, was a series of designs which were undertaken by both the Weybridge and Hursley Park design teams of Vickers. The Weybridge studies included M-wing designs to seat up to 100 passengers at five abreast over the London–New York route, with waisted wings and rear engines mounted around the fin/tailplane unit. The Hursley Park designs included high-wing layouts with podded engines.
(Weybridge M-wing Study) Length 160ft, Span 112ft, Wing Area 2,500sq.ft

Further studies included medium-range Mach 1.8 projects with straight wings, and the types 586 and 587, with variable geometry wings for medium-range routes, to accommodate 135 tourist passengers. Again, the engines were mounted at the rear in a unit to which the tailplane was also affixed.
Wing Span (wings extended) 115ft

After the selection of the joint BAC/Sud SST design, supersonic activity greatly diminished within British design teams, although one company, Handley Page, continued with studies.

Handley Page HP.128

The HP.128 was a short-range 'area-ruled' airliner, designed to cruise at Mach 1.15 without sonic bang at ground level. A model of the HP.128 was exhibited at the Farnborough Air Show of 1962. Originally a ninety-seater, the design grew to have 125 seats with seating at three, four and five abreast within the waisted fuselage. Designed to travel over stage lengths of 500 miles, the maximum all-up weight was 116,000lb. Power was to be provided by three scaled-up Rolls-Royce Spey engines, positioned within the fuselage tail side-by-side. Handley Page continued to study the project until the middle of 1964 but found it could not be competitive with aircraft such as the 727, with direct operating costs around 15 per cent higher. With the company short of funds, further development would have required partners, and so the project was sadly dropped.
Length 156ft, Span 67ft 6in, Wing Area 1,300sq.ft

Son of Concorde

Before Concorde entered service BAC and Sud were already looking at a follow-on variant, the series B, which was to become the standard model from production aircraft No.17.

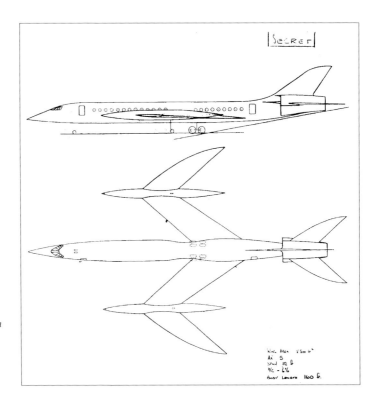

Vickers Project X
The M-wing Project X from
Vickers' Weybridge design
team.
(BAE SYSTEMS – via
Brooklands Museum Trust)

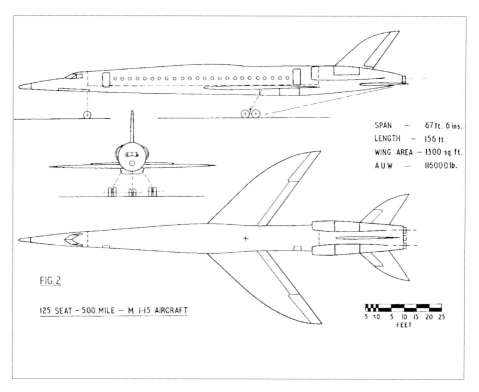

SPAN   —   67 ft. 6 ins.
LENGTH   —   156 ft.
WING AREA — 1300 sq. ft.
A.U.W   —   116000 lb.

FIG.2

125 SEAT – 500 MILE – M. 1·15 AIRCRAFT

5 10   5   10   15   20   25
FEET

Handley Page HP.128
Handley Page's HP128 was designed to cruise at Mach 1.15 without sonic boom at ground level. (Handley Page Association)

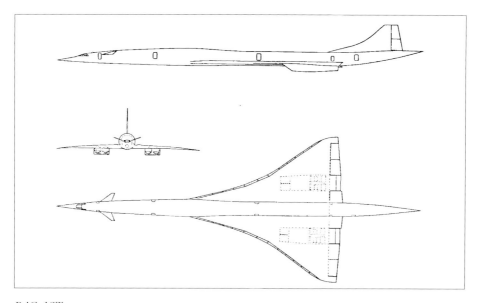

BAC AST
One of many mid-seventies follow-on designs from Concorde, this BAC Advanced Supersonic Transport featured a forward canard on the front fuselage. (BAE SYSTEMS)

BAE Supersonic Business Jet
An artist's impression of British Aerospace's proposal for a small supersonic business jet, seating up to twelve passengers, that was unveiled at Farnborough in 1986. (BAE SYSTEMS)

Changes on this model included a modified wing with extended wing tips, and full span droop leading edges, while the Olympus powerplant would have been improved with a new LP compressor. The curtailment of production at No.16 saw an end to this, although BAC continued to study advanced new supersonic designs. One such project from 1976 could accommodate up to 280 passengers, and had a range of 4,100 nautical miles and an all-up weight of around 750,000lb. Power would be provided by four Olympus BPR1.0 engines, and the design featured a small canard on the front fuselage.
Length 312ft, Span 122ft, Wing Area 6,633sq.ft

After BAC was incorporated into British Aerospace (BAe), further studies continued and, indeed, at the Paris Air Show of 1979, BAe showed a design of a Concorde follow-on project under a joint study with Aerospatiale and McDonnell Douglas for a 230-seater airliner with engines grouped in pairs, and canard foreplanes and leading edge slats. The powerplant was expected to be based on the core of the Olympus. The Advanced Supersonic Transport (AST) continued to be developed as a low priority at Filton, with studies of 300-seaters with separate engine pod installations mounted beneath an arrow delta wing.

However, in the smaller field of executive jets, British Aerospace did unveil, at the 1986 Farnborough Air Show, a design jointly undertaken between Filton and Hatfield for a small business jet. The design, with three engines, two mounted over the wing and the other in the tail, would have seated twelve passengers, and had a range of 3,800 miles.

While BAe maintained a very limited SST design activity through the nineties, various proposals for joint programmes with both European and American companies have surfaced at regular intervals. Whether there ever will be a son of Concorde remains to be seen, especially after the fatal crash of an Air France aircraft in 2000. However, with the new Airbus integrated company of BAE SYSTEMS and EADS, who knows what future studies may emerge. There is only one certainty in aerospace, and that is to expect the unexpected. One thing is for definite: should a new SST emerge it will certainly not be an all-British programme, and may even – if produced under Airbus – contain no UK airframe or design work at all.

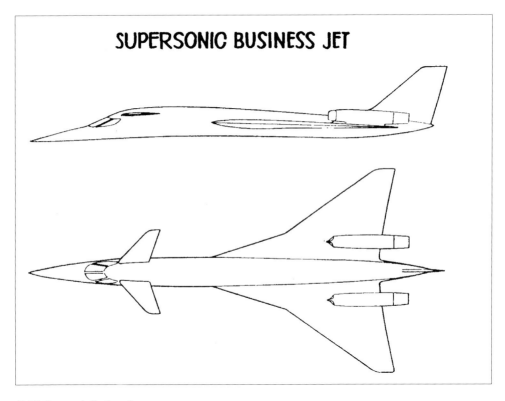

BAE Supersonic Business Jet
General arrangement of the British Aerospace Supersonic Business Jet, powered by three jet engines. (BAE SYSTEMS)

Chapter 6

VTOL Projects

By the mid-fifties, the technical lead that Britain had established in airliner development was already being eroded, and the anticipated success on the world market with the Comet had been lost. Therefore, it was vital for the British Aircraft Industry that investigations to be made as to where future markets, production and profits might lie.

Two new avenues presented themselves. The first was Supersonic Transports, and the second, Vertical take-off and landing transports. Through a British European Airways specification, it seemed there may be an opportunity for a new sponsored programme, with an all-important state airline requirement.

The BEAline Transport

British European Airways was heavily interested in the concept of VTOL transports during the fifties, having originally set up its Helicopter Experimental Unit back in 1947. The airline had operated services between Heathrow/Northolt–Birmingham, and Liverpool–Cardiff, which had led it to believe that only multi-engined helicopters would be able to operate successful passenger services. In late 1951, the airline issued an initial specification for a Vertical take-off and landing short-/medium-haul transport, for what became known as the 'BEAline Bus', and to which five British manufacturers proposed a number of schemes.

The August 1951 specification had ten major requirements. In its initial form it should be able to carry thirty passengers or a 7,000lb payload over 115 statute miles, and in its final form, thirty-five to forty-five passengers or a 10,000lb payload over 230 miles. Other requirements included fuel tankage to permit operation over 230 mile stages against a 46mph headwind, a commercial cruising speed of at least 138mph at 2,000ft, and the ability to operate from an area 400ft in diameter, with upstanding obstructions all round. A number of possible powerplant options were suggested, including the Centaurus, Hercules, Proteus, Ghost jets, Dart and Mamba.

Bristol 181

A 1953 tandem rotor project, powered by two Bristol Proteus engines of 3,940shp, with twin rotors of 72ft diameter. The 181 had an AUW of 48,000lb and could accommodate up to eighty passengers, with a design cruise speed of 226mph and a range of 300 miles.
Fuselage Length 100ft, Height 28ft 6in

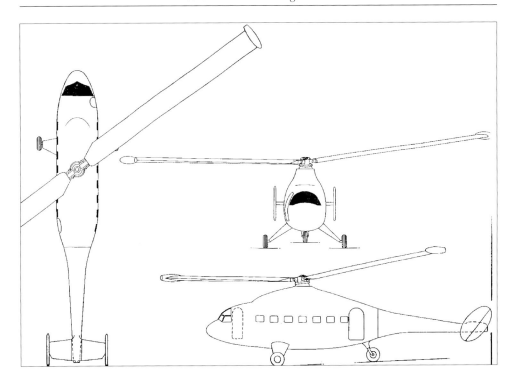

Above: *Percival P85*
Percival's original proposal to
meet the BEAline
specification was the P85.
(BAE SYSTEMS)

Left: *Percival P86*
An artist's impression of
the Percival P86 in flight,
in BEA colours. (BAE
SYSTEMS)

Fairey Rotodyne

Fairey undertook a number of design studies for VTOL transports, with a variety of powerplants and layouts. One study from 1947 had twin Leonides plus tip jet engines, and could seat fifteen passengers. By 1949 this had evolved into a twenty-seater with power provided by twin Armstrong Siddeley Mamba engines, with tip jet engines. Later studies involved both Mamba and Dart engines, again with tip jet engines. The definitive Rotodyne emerged in 1953, powered by Napier Eland N.E13 turboprop engines mounted underwing with an AUW of 33,000lb. In August 1953, the Ministry of Supply ordered a single prototype XE 521, which made its maiden flight from White Waltham on the 6 November 1957. In April 1958, it made the transition to and from autogyro mode.

(Prototype) Length 58ft 8in, Span 46ft 6in, Height 22ft 2in

(Civil Production Variant) Length 64ft 6in, Span 56ft 6in, Height 23ft 2in

Percival P86

Not originally renowned for helicopter manufacture, the Percival company had taken a great interest in this new form of transport and had been working on their P74 flying Oryx test bed since 1951. In response to the BEA specification, the company first proposed the P85 single rotor transport. This was replaced by the definitive proposal, the P86, a four-engined all-metal helicopter powered by Napier N Or. 101 turbo gas generators with a freely tilting twin-bladed rotor of 110ft diameter. The P86 was designed for simplicity and featured tip jet drive with power units buried within the fuselage. Seating capacity was arranged at four abreast for between forty and sixty passengers, together with all freight and mixed traffic, with up to two or three cars and twelve passengers being accommodated. By using a low pressure drive, it was hoped that the P86 would reduce the noise level. This was deemed to be very important, given that the aircraft was intended to be operated from within city centres. The stub wings of low aspect and uniform taper saw the outer 9ft fold down during hovering, to form the undercarriage structure. A maximum cruising speed of 132 knots was stated, with forty passengers being carried over a range of 200 nautical miles, and a maximum all-up weight of 29,200lb.

Fuselage Length 76ft 6in, Wing Span (wings spread) 39ft, Height 20ft

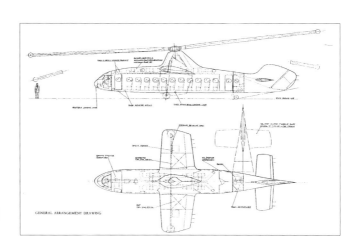

Percival P86
The four-engined Percival P86
could accommodate up to sixty
passengers, and featured a freely
tilting twin-bladed rotor of 110ft
diameter. (BAE SYSTEMS)

Saunders Roe P514
The Saunders Roe P514, also called the 'Rotorcoach', was powered by two Napier engines, and seated fifty
passengers. (GKN Aerospace)

Saunders Roe P514

Also known as the 'Rotorcoach', the P514 originated in 1952 and was a large tandem-engined transport with low stub wings and an all-up weight of 34,000lb. Power was to be provided by two Napier engines, which were fed by two ram orifices, one in the fin fillet and the other in the upper nose. The design also featured a ducted fan at the rear of the helicopter's centre fin, above which was a tailplane with twin rudders and endplates. Accommodation was provided for up to fifty passengers to travel up to 200 miles, and a large rear loading ramp was also provided.

Westland

Westland put forward two designs. The first, in 1951, was powered by an Armstrong Siddeley Double Mamba engine, and had seating for thirty passengers and a main rotor of 75ft. The following year a fifty-seater was proposed, utilising a common fuselage, but powered by either four Rolls-Royce Dart turboprop engines or three Napier Eland turboshafts, with a main rotor diameter of 85ft 5in.

The 1960 reorganisation of the British Aircraft Industry saw Westland emerge as the only UK company that continued to be active in the helicopter field, having incorporated the activities and factories of Saunders Roe, and the helicopter interests of Fairey and Bristol. Armed with these companies' product portfolios were three large vertical transports – the projected Bristol 194, flying Westland Westminster and Fairey Rotodyne. Naturally, only one of these could now be supported, so in 1960 the government selected the Rotodyne for

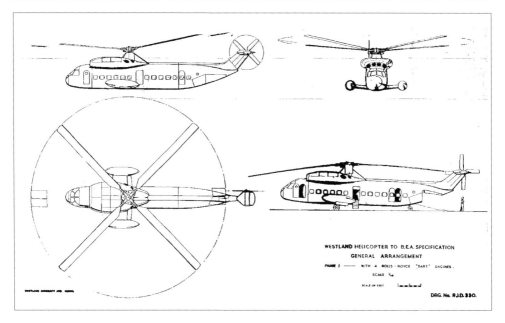

Westland BEAline
The four Rolls-Royce Dart-engined Westland proposal for BEA had a main rotor of over 85ft, while a similar design was powered by three Napier Elands. (Westland Helicopters)

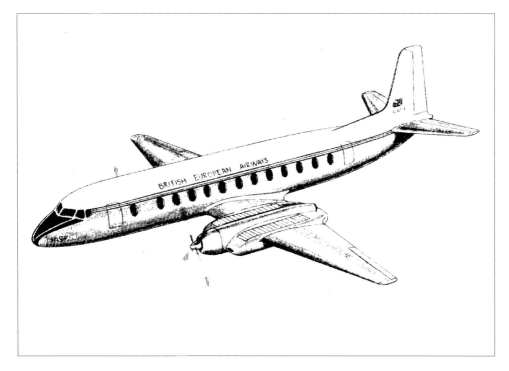

Armstrong Whitworth AW.176
An artist's impression of the Armstrong Whitworth AW.176, powered by two Napier Eland turboprops, with a further twenty ducted fan engines for vertical lift. (BAE SYSTEMS – via Ray Williams)

continuing development. However, the programme was subject to continued delays. The BEA order, proposed some nine years earlier, never materialised, even though the airline had indicated it might place a letter of intent for up to six of the developed variant in 1959. This was mainly due to the airline's requirements not being met, and the fact that noise was becoming a major issue. A provisional order was received from New York Airways for the larger Tyne-powered sixty-five-seater Rotodyne Type Z, with increased rotor diameter, wing span and an additional third fin. However, as RAF and BEA support for the project abated, especially given noise considerations, the letters of intent also disappeared. With no domestic support the project was finally cancelled on 26 February 1962.

BEA VTOL Transport

As well as embracing medium-sized passenger helicopters, BEA looked at other VTOL airliners seriously for a short time. To see what manufacturers could propose, a specification was issued in December 1957, calling for an aircraft carrying no less than forty passengers, which could travel over a 200 nautical-mile stage, cruising at no less than 300 knots. The aircraft should also be capable of future development to carry at least fifty passengers, and provide a standard of comfort needed for a two-hour journey. It should also be able to convert to all freight or passenger/freight configuration.

Armstrong Whitworth Studies

The AW.176 project saw an airliner of conventional appearance powered by two Napier Eland 4 turboprops, with seating for sixty-three passengers at five abreast in a fuselage of 10ft 10in diameter and an all-up weight of 66,500lb. To provide vertical lift, an additional twenty ducted fan NGTE engines were mounted in fairings, with five on each side of the turboprop engines. Length 86ft, Span 92ft, Height 29ft, Wing Area 935sq.ft

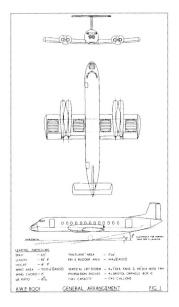

Armstrong Whitworth AWP 8
One of a number of studies from the Armstrong Whitworth Initial Projects Office, the AWP8 could accommodate fifty-two passengers, powered by four Bristol Orpheus engines with an additional four lift fans. (BAE SYSTEMS – via Ray Williams)

Opposite: Avro 749
The Avro 749, as proposed to BEA in February 1958. (BAE SYSTEMS)

Alongside the above study were those carried out by Armstrong Whitworth's Initial Projects Department. These included the AW.P8, a fifty-two-seater transport powered by four Bristol Orpheus BOr 12 engines, with an additional four mechanically-driven vertical lift-fans mounted in the wings to provide the main lift and, for pitch control, an additional single vertical lift-fan, located in the nose. The AW.P18 forty-seater development of the AW.176 featured a straight wing with eight scaled-up versions of the Rostat engine design of the NGTE proposed to provide lift, with six mounted vertically alongside the fuselage, and two horizontally under the fuselage. The AW.P20 of similar design featured redesigned tail surfaces and wing, with twelve ducted fan-lifting Rolls-Royce RB147 engines mounted alongside the fuselage, in two rows of three, with forward propulsion provided by an additional two pod-mounted Bristol Orpheus BOr 12 located at the aircraft's tail.
(AW.P20) Length 76ft, Span 70ft

Avro 749

Proposed in February 1958, the Avro 749 was powered by eight scaled up Rolls-Royce RB145 engines, mounted four each in two wing mounted nacelles, with accommodation for up to forty passengers at four abreast.
Fuselage Length 75ft, Span 77ft 2in, Wing Area 1,190sq.ft

Boulton Paul

Boulton Paul undertook a number of VTOL fan-lift airliner studies under Ministry of Supply contracts. Their first design, the P138, was a thirty-two-seater, powered by four Bristol Orpheus engines. This was followed in October 1957 by the P140, which featured a low swept wing and could accommodate up to eighty passengers. It was powered by eight Bristol Orpheus BOr 12 engines hung beneath the wing in nacelles, each containing two engines.

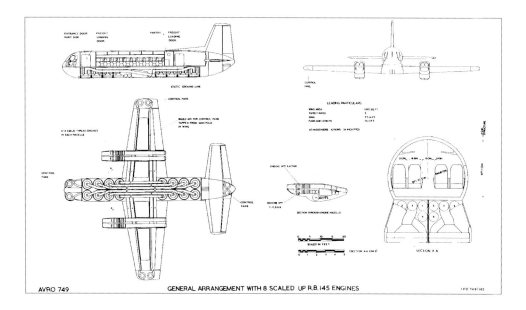

AVRO 749 — GENERAL ARRANGEMENT WITH 8 SCALED UP R.B.145 ENGINES

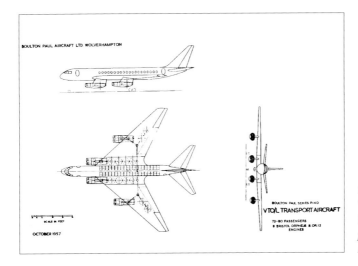

Boulton Paul P140
The low-swept wing Boulton Paul P140 accommodated eighty passengers. (Boulton Paul Association)

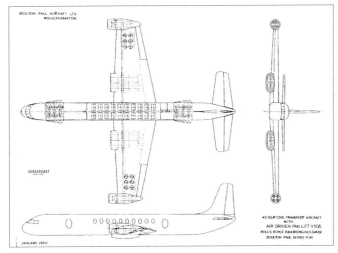

Boulton Paul P141
The air-driven fan-lift Boulton Paul P141. (Boulton Paul Association)

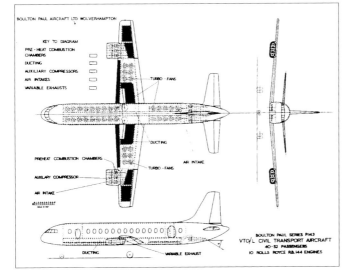

Boulton Paul P143
The Boulton Paul P143 was powered by ten Rolls-Royce RB144 engines. (Boulton Paul Association)

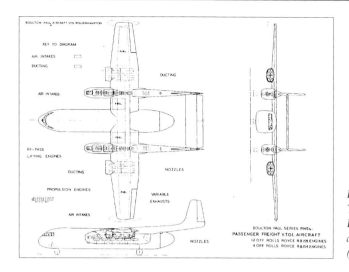

Boulton Paul P145
The high-wing pod and boom
Boulton Paul P145 was a
combined passenger/freighter design.
(Boulton Paul Association)

The P141 was a January 1960 project, and was an air-driven fan-lift VTOL airliner powered by Rolls-Royce RB108 engines, with seating for forty passengers. This was superseded by the P143, powered by ten Rolls-Royce RB144 engines, six mounted beneath the wing, with an additional four engines in the lower part of the rear fuselage. Accommodation was provided for up to fifty-two passengers.

P145

The P145 was a high-wing pod and boom passenger/freighter VTOL study to accommodate up to sixty passengers at six abreast from June 1959. Power was provided by four Rolls-Royce RB154 engines mounted beneath the wing, with an additional twelve Rolls-Royce RB153 by-pass lifting engines in a structure, from which extended the rear boom. Freight was loaded via a ramp through the opening rear door.
Length 70ft 5in, Span 100ft, Wing Area 1,250sq.ft

P146

The last VTOL study to come from Boulton Paul was the private venture P146 from November 1960. Accommodating up to ninety-six passengers at five abreast, the design featured low tandem swept wings and was powered by eighteen RB155 lift engines, four in each pod on the end of the main wings, and five in each pod on the forward canard wings. The aircraft was designed to cruise at 400 knots with a range of around 500 miles. Forward propulsion was provided by three rear-mounted modified RB163 engines.

Bristol Type 199

The Bristol Type 199 was a 1956 tilt wing convertiplane designed by Raoul Hafner, powered by four Rolls-Royce Tyne or Proteus engines of 4,000shp. The engines were mounted at the end of tilting wings, with a variable thrust line allowing for both forward flight and vertical

Model of the P.146 VTOL airliner project.

Boulton Paul P146
Model of the Boulton Paul P146, which shows the location of the eighteen RB155 lift engines. (Boulton Paul Association)

take-off. Up to fifty passengers could be carried at five abreast in a fuselage of 11ft diameter, with a range of 800 miles at a cruising speed of 400mph. The all-up weight was put at 60,000lb.

Fuselage Length 66ft, Wing Span 67ft 8in, Height 26ft, Rotor Diameter 48ft

English Electric P20 and P24

This designation encompassed a number of designs for a VTOL commercial transport with seating for up to 100 passengers, and with an AUW of 110,000lb. Four designs were studied: the P20A/1 featured a double-deck fuselage with a 60 degree delta wing, in which discreet engine and turbofans were mounted; the P20A/2, P20A/3 and P20A/4 all featured a conventional fuselage and tail, with a medium aspect ratio, unswept, untapered wing. Other changes between the three studies were in the wing area, number of lifting fans per engine and location of the propulsive fans. The P20A variants were all larger than BEA's requirement, but English Electric felt that low operating costs could be achieved and, that there would be sufficient traffic for the larger transport. Studies into VTOL aircraft were continued under the P24 designation between April and June 1958.

(P20A/1) Length 82ft 6in

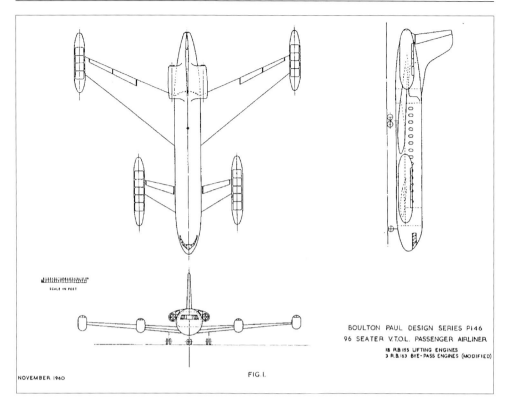

Boulton Paul P146
General arrangement of the Boulton Paul P146, the last VTOL transport study from the company. (Boulton Paul Association)

BEA issued an addendum in January 1958, stating that although the airline had no requirement in 1958 for a VTOL airliner, the specification had been issued to test the water to see what an airline's requirement for a VTOL airliner might be in the future. The carrier had also continued to monitor future helicopter developments, including the Hunting Percival P108, Fairey Rotodyne, Westland Westminster and the Bristol 194.

Bristol Type 194

This was a 1955 design for a compound tandem helicopter that evolved from a stretched Type 192, and was powered by four de Havilland Gnome engines of 1,175shp, in pairs, driving two six-bladed rotors. The design featured a rear rotor positioned at an acute angle, and a centrally located anhedral wing. Accommodation was provided for up to forty-eight passengers, with a cruising speed of 230mph and a range of 530 miles. The all-up weight was 33,800lb.
Fuselage Length 77ft, Wing Span 40ft, Height 24ft, Rotor Diameter 55ft

Sadly, despite strong interest, BEA never operated any of the large helicopters or VTOL transports proposed, although British Airways Helicopters ordered Boeing 234 Commercial Chinooks in the late seventies, with the first aircraft being delivered in December 1980.

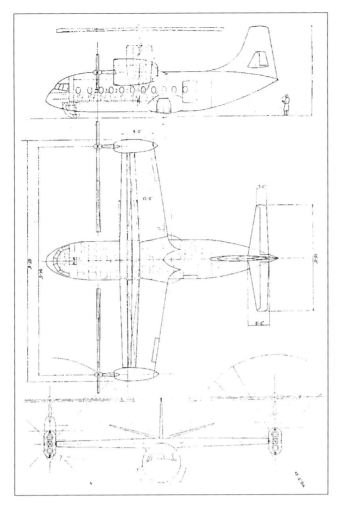

Left: *Bristol 199*
The tilt-wing Bristol 199
convertiplane, designed by Raoul
Hafner, had its four turboprop
engines mounted at the end of the
tilting wings. (BAE SYSTEMS)

Below: *English Electric P 24*
The English Electric P24 was
applied to a number of VTOL
studies developed from the earlier
P20 series. (BAE SYSTEMS)

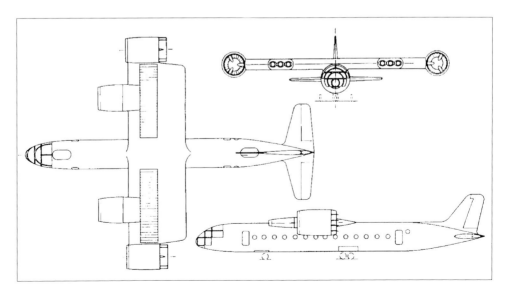

TARC VTOL/STOL Airliner

At the end of the sixties and early seventies, it seemed as if Britain might once again break new ground, with development of a VSTOL (Vertical Short Take-off and Landing) airliner, once more giving the country an advanced transport aircraft with major world market potential.

In 1966, the TARC (Transport Aircraft Requirements Committee) had presented its proposals for a VTOL airliner study, which were circulated to industry in March 1967. In 1969, the Ministry of Technology launched a regional transportation study with the setting-up of an inter-departmental body – the Joint Transport Research Committee (which included Mintech and the Ministry of Transport) to encompass many advanced transport forms. These included surface-based studies from the APT (Advanced Passenger Train), and tracked hovertrain as well as aircraft developments.

The TARC specification had called for a VTOL capable 100-seater airliner with a range of 450 miles with full payload, or 600 miles with a reduced payload, with submissions requested by September 1969. All three major British companies put forward proposals. BAC chose to study STOL aircraft, Westland tilt rotor proposals, while Hawker Siddeley (Hatfield) and Hawker Siddeley (Manchester), who still operated as separate design teams, put forward designs for Fan-lift and Controlled Circulation Rotor aircraft respectively.

BAC

BAC were of the conviction that noise would be a major consideration in future short-haul transportation and made studies of STOL aircraft that would be less complex than the VSTOL projects. BAC proposals were carried out under its 'Inter-Urban Air Transport Studies' and featured proposals for airliners with deflected slipstreams, conventional mechanical flap turbofans, and high bypass ratio aft-fans with lift engines. One study followed on from research carried out with Breguet on the 941, to meet the RAF Strategic Transport aircraft. This deflected slipstream design could seat 102 passengers in a 180in diameter fuselage with 2 + 2 + 2 seating and a wing span of 110ft. Although no definitive design ever emerged, work carried out was eventually incorporated into the QSTOL (quiet short take-off and landing) high-wing project of 1971, and later into RTOL (reduced take-off/landing) and RSTOL (reduced short take-off and landing) designs during the mid-seventies.

A further proposal to gain STOL understanding was to convert a 1-11 airframe with the fitting of RB162 or RB202 engines in wing pods. The intention had been to convert the prototype aircraft G-ASYD, fitted with RB162 engines, and able to seat up to sixty passengers at four abreast. Later designs for the 1-11 incorporated six RB202 high by-pass engines being fitted, three each into pods, which were attached to the wing just outboard of the trailing edge 'kink'. These were capable of being swivelled 45 degrees. Further changes to the basic design included increasing the Series 500 wing area, by employing larger chord flaps and increased span wing tips, while full span fully vented slats were also incorporated.

(1-11 STOL) Length 93ft 6in, Span 97ft 1in, Height 24ft 6in, Wing Area 1,125sq.ft

BAC STOL
An artist's impression of one of BAC's many studies into a short take-off and landing transport, which included deflected slipstreams, conventional mechanical flap turbofans and high bypass ratio aft fans with lift engines. (BAE SYSTEMS)

Hawker Siddeley

Hawker Siddeley at Hatfield had been studying VTOL airliners since the late fifties, and, in 1967, began major studies of commercial transports. The company was convinced that the future lay in VTOL for European civil aviation, for the late seventies and beyond and, over the proceeding years, spent millions of pounds on research and development with major wind tunnel testing of a number of projects. The philosophy was that airports with VTOL capability were inherently more flexible than STOL airports. During their investigation, Hawker Siddeley had looked at the full range of designs that could meet the requirements and. while Hatfield had concentrated on fan-lift, the Manchester design team had investigated a host of concepts which included compound helicopters and convertible rotor projects.

Early Manchester Studies

HS803

An October 1966 design for a VTOL transport with NGTE developed circulation-controlled rotors (CCR) of 60ft diameter. The HS803-02C variant of low-wing design could accommodate ninety passengers, with power being provided by four Rolls-Royce Spey 512 engines of 8,000lb, installed in pairs at the wing tips. The three-bladed rotors located at the wing tips immediately above the powerplants provided the vertical lift, and were

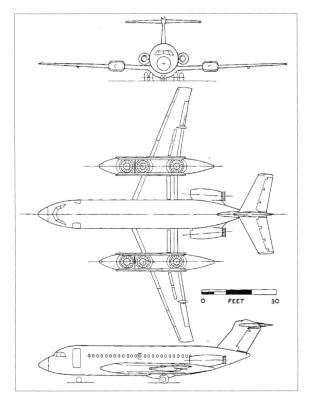

Right: *BAC One-Eleven STOL*
The BAC One-Eleven STOL design had
additional RB202 engines mounted in
pods, just outboard the wing-trailing edge
kink. (BAE SYSTEMS – via
Brooklands Museum Trust)

Below: *Hawker Siddeley HS803*
The Hawker Siddeley HS803 featured
NGTE-developed circulation-controlled
rotors. (BAE SYSTEMS)

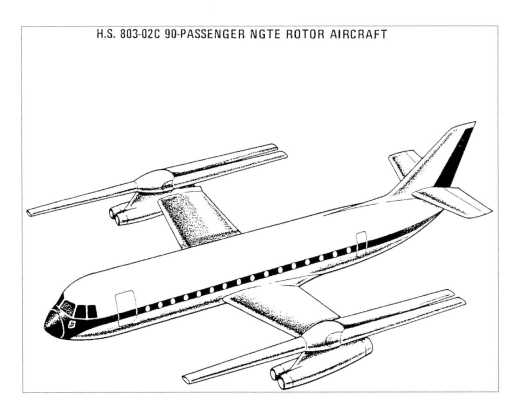

H.S. 803-02C 90-PASSENGER NGTE ROTOR AIRCRAFT

interconnected by cross shafting. The engine's cold efflux provided the circulation control ducted directly to the rotors. The design had an AUW of 105,936lb and could carry a payload of 18,000lb with a cruising speed of nearly 500mph.
Length 96ft, Wing Span 74ft, Height 26ft 9in

HS804

A further October 1966 design, the HS804, was a ninety-seater, and featured a high tilt wing layout powered by eight T64S5B engines of 5,350shp, mounted in pairs on the wing, driving four bladed propellers. To enable the necessary slipstream vectoring during transition, the wing had large chord double-slotted flaps, which were geared to the wing tilt mechanism, while for pitch control during vertical or low speed flight, a small mechanically-driven tail rotor was incorporated. The HS804-03C variant had an AUW of 105,900lb, could carry a payload of 18,000lb and had a cruising speed of 400mph.
Length 101ft 3in, Span 103ft

HS805

In January 1967, the design team at Manchester investigated three further transports under Type HS805. These were the HS805A deflected slipstream, the HS805B with mechanical flaps, and the blown flap HS805C. All these designs accommodated up to ninety passengers, with conventional high-wing layouts. The HS805A used a large chord double-slotted flap with the whole wing immersed in the slipstream of the four propellers, thereby achieving a large deflected slipstream. Power was provided by four under wing-mounted T64-GE-16 engines of 3,365shp, with the tailplane mounted midway on the fuselage. The design had an AUW of 82,220lb, could carry a payload of 18,000lb and had a cruise speed of 400 mph.
Length 92ft 3in, Span 86ft 9in, Height 27ft

H.S. 804-03C 90-PASSENGER TILT WING AIRLINER

Hawker Siddeley HS804
The tilt-wing Hawker Siddeley HS804
was powered by eight T64S5B engines
mounted in pairs on the high wing.
(BAE SYSTEMS)

H.S. 805A-09C 90-PASSENGER DEFLECTED SLIPSTREAM AIRCRAFT

Hawker Siddeley HS805
The Hawker Siddeley HS805 was a
number of studies of deflected slipstream
(illustrated), mechanical flap and blown
flap designs, seating up to ninety
passengers. (BAE SYSTEMS)

Hatfield Projects

HS133

A beautifully elegant airliner, the HS133 was a narrow delta fan-lift VTOL design with a low wing. A number of studies were made under this project number, including some with twin vertical tail surfaces mounted mid-span, and others with a more conventional fin/rudder, but no tailplane. The 133 design went to the limit of integration, both structurally and aerodynamically, and was estimated to achieve a cruise speed of 675mph. Vertical lift was provided by eighteen Rolls-Royce RB202 fan-lift engines of 7,500lb thrust, mounted in the wing root structure in two rows alongside the fuselage. In order to provide a smooth upper and lower wing surface during cruise flight, doors would close over the lift-fan air intakes and thrust vectoring louvres below which the lift-fans were positioned respectively. In addition, two propulsion engines of 18,500lb were mounted between the sides of the fuselage and the vertical tail surfaces. Seating was provided for up to 100 passengers in a design with an all-up weight of 100,000lb. This design carried the most technical risk, due to aerodynamic interference.

(HS133-B25C) Length 98ft, Span 60ft, Height 18ft 3in

HS139

The HS139 was a podded VTOL design with an all-up weight of 112,000lb, and featured a conventionally swept high-wing layout with two Rolls-Royce RB207-03 engines of 25,000lb thrust mounted in nacelles beneath for forward thrust. An additional battery of eighteen RB202 fan-lift engines of 7,250lb thrust were mounted in two pods at approximately mid-semi span, to provide vertical lift. Here, the lift system was applied to an otherwise conventional layout, with the lift and normal aerodynamic airflows largely separate, which would minimise interference. Adopting such a layout was seen in terms of extra weight and drag, and a reduced cruising speed. A number of designs were proposed, including T-tails, and mid-fin tailplanes,

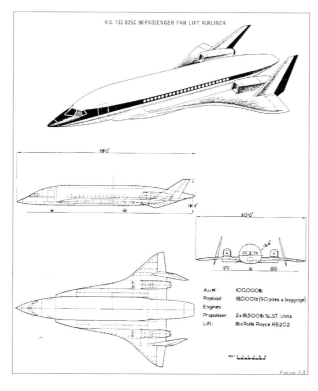

H.S. 133 B25C 90-PASSENGER FAN LIFT AIRLINER

95'0"

16'3"

40'0"

A.u.w.:	100,000 lb
Payload:	18,000 lb (90 pass. & baggage)
Engines:	
Propulsion:	2 x 18,500 lb SL.S.T. Units
Lift:	16 x Rolls Royce RB202

FEET

Figure 2.8

Left: *Hawker Siddeley HS133*
The narrow delta fan lift Hawker
Siddeley HS133, with twin vertical tail
surfaces. (BAE SYSTEMS)

Below: *Hawker Siddeley HS133*
Alternative photographic impression of
the HS133, featuring single fin and
underwing-mounted engines.
(BAE SYSTEMS)

as well as swept and straight wings. The HS139 B26 proposal featured seating for up to ninety passengers, had an all-up weight of 112,000lb and could cruise at 565mph.
(HS139 B21) Length 100ft, Span 81ft, Height 26ft 6in

When it became apparent that noise levels were becoming all important in a new environmentally-aware society, Hawker Siddeley decided to concentrate on two projects to present to the TARC – Manchester with the HS810 CCR design, and Hatfield with the fan-lift HS141.

HS810

The HS810 was a twin Circulation Control Rotor design, with rotors at each end of the wings, powered by paired RA 660-06 engines mounted in wing pods at the tips. Forward thrust was provided by three engines designated as RB211-20 of 17,100lb thrust, two mounted under wing and the third in the fin. The fuselage of 12ft 4in diameter had an internal width of 11ft 6in, and seated up to 102 passengers at six abreast, with an AUW of 142,000lb. The design initially looked promising. However, the use of rotors would have limited the aircraft's cruising speed to Mach .7, which, after the late seventies, was felt to be too slow for passengers. Rolls-Royce also felt that the RB202 lift-fan engine would be a quieter engine, which shifted opinion in Hawker Siddeley towards Hatfield's HS141.
Length 101ft 75in, Span 89ft 29in, Height 35ft 75in

HS141

The HS141 was Hatfield's last major VTOL airliner, and the Hawker Siddeley company's major submission to the TARC specification. Like its predecessors, the 141 underwent many design changes before emerging as a very elegant low-wing airliner, with modest sweep and a T-tail. The conventional low-wing design had clean aerodynamic lines and the simplest structure of all the VTOL designs with the partial integration of the fuselage and lift pods. It was also lighter and faster than earlier Hatfield studies. Two RB220 engines of 27,000lb thrust were mounted in nacelles beneath the wings for forward thrust, while 16 RB202's of 10,300lb thrust were mounted beneath sponsons on the side of the fuselage. First details of the project were released at the Hanover Air Show in 1970, with further information at that year's Farnborough Air Show. Accommodation was provided for up to 119 passengers at five abreast, although a normal load would have been 102 passengers. In earlier designs, the fuselage featured six-abreast seating, with a 12ft 4in diameter, and cargo holds sited on cabin floor level.

Later studies featured an 11ft 3in-fuselage diameter with underfloor freight holds, with stretched variants powered by up to twenty lift engines able to accommodate up to 150 passengers. It was envisaged that in full VTOL mode, a range of just under 400 miles would be possible, while a short take-off plus vertical landing would increase the range to 850 miles. Total development costs of the project were put at £200 million, including development of the lift-fan engine, with a possible in-service date of 1978/79.
Length 120ft 2in, Span 75ft, Height 29ft 10in, Wing Area 1,060sq.ft

General Arrangement

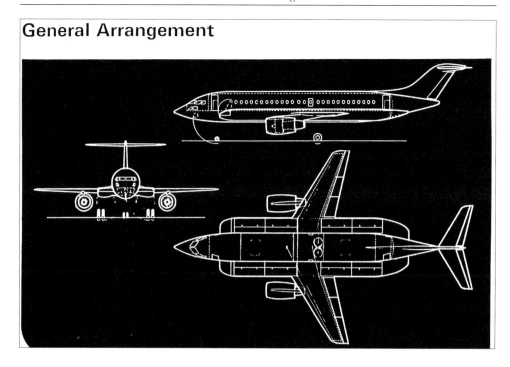

Hawker Siddeley HS141
General Arrangement of the Hawker Siddeley HS141. (BAE SYSTEMS)

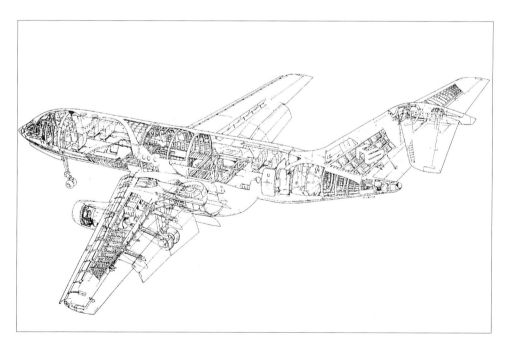

Hawker Siddeley HS141
Cutaway illustration of the Hawker Siddeley HS141. (BAE SYSTEMS)

Hawker Siddeley HS141
An artist's impression of the Hawker Siddeley HS141, showing the two underwing turbofan
engines and T-tail layout. (BAE SYSTEMS)

Hawker Siddeley HS141
Indicating the long fuselage-mounted sponsons, which housed the sixteen lift fan RB202 engines of the HS141.
(BAE SYSTEMS)

Westland WE01
The five-seater Westland WE01 executive research vehicle did progress as far as a convertible rotor rig set at
Weston-Super-Mare. (Westland Helicopters)

Westland Studies

Early Westland projects concentrated on tilt rotors and included the WE01, a 285mph executive research vehicle, for which a mock-up and some test rotors were built, including a convertible rotor rig set constructed at Weston-Super-Mare while wind tunnel tests were also carried out. The five-seater craft would have been powered by four Allison 250 turbines of 370shp, which would have been wing-mounted in pairs, with swivelling nacelles housing two four-bladed rotors of 19ft 6in diameter. A first flight was originally planned for 1971.
Length 32ft, Span 41ft

The larger WE02 high-wing tilt rotor was proposed in two variants – the seventy-seater WE02A, powered by four GET64-16 engines, and the heavier eighty-four-seater WE02B, powered by four GET64-S5B. Each system was driven by two pairs of coupled engines driving a large-diameter rotor. A first flight was planned for 1975. Information from both programmes was put into the Westland submission to the TARC.

Westland WG22 Convertiplane

Westland concluded that the only viable development for a VTOL transport, given the requirement for low noise levels, was a compound design with large-diameter lightly loaded

Westland WE02
The high-wing tilt rotor Westland WE02, information from which was incorporated into Westland's later VTOL submission, the WG22. (Westland Helicopters)

open rotors with a fixed high-wing layout using tilting wings. The new WG22 was to be a short-range VTOL transport of convertible rotor design. Studies were made of both six-abreast seating with a fuselage width of 12ft, and a single aisle or seven-abreast seating at 14ft 11in width, with twin aisles. The cantilever high-set wing with tapered outer panels would have, in order to achieve high lift, seen the entire wing's leading edge tilted by 30 degrees. The wing was also hinged at the rear spar, and could have been rotated to a maximum of 100 degrees at low speeds, with a high incidence stall aerofoil fitted. Power was to be provided by either four Rolls-Royce RB411-01s (shaft drive derivatives of the M57H) or the Avco Lycoming LTC-4V-4, both of which had a three-shaft layout, which would be carried two side-by-side in two wing-mounted nacelles. With 100 passengers, the WG22 had a range of 450 miles, while seventy-four passengers could be carried over a range of 800 miles, with a cruising speed of 460mph.
Fuselage Length 92ft, Span 101ft 1¼ in, Wing Area 1,387sq.ft

Hawker Siddeley, the keenest of all the companies on VTOL airliners, undertook studies that could have led to interim research being carried out, and these included a Trident conversion with RB202 engines mounted on each side of the front fuselage to gain RTOL experience. This was followed by the HS140 single fan-lift aircraft to gain general experience, and the HS145 executive fan-lift concept. The company also looked at building the 141 initially as a STOL aircraft, with 4, 6, 8 and 12 fan-lift engines, which could later lead to VSTOL capability.

The HS141 project continued to be updated by Hawker Siddeley on a private venture basis over the next few years, moving from VTOL to being more of a STOVL airliner. This involved exhaustive wind-tunnel testing on models costing several million pounds. However, noise concern was becoming greater and there was increasing environmental pressure against noisy transports such as Concorde. When this was coupled with spiralling inflation as the seventies progressed, the case for, and cost of, vertical take-off and landing airliners, meant that the projects were sent to the back burner, and were not revived when economic conditions improved.

Westland WG22
The 100-seater Westland WG22 convertiplane would have been powered by four Rolls-Royce RB411-01 or Avco Lycoming LTC-4V–4 engines. (Westland Helicopters)

Chapter 7

Feederliners

In the post-war era, one of the largest markets that presented itself was for a small feederliner aircraft, firstly to replace the de Havilland Dragon Rapide, and then, more importantly, the Douglas DC3 Dakota. The Rapide contract had first surfaced in 1949 as Specification 26/49. Many British manufacturers had turned their attentions to it, with designs from Blackburn (B84), de Havilland (Heron), Folland/Saunders Roe (Fo134/P132), FG Miles (Surrey 1), ML Aviation, Percival (P64/P65), Scottish Aviation, Shorts and Westland. No contract was ever awarded under this specification, although the de Havilland DH114 Heron was put into production and operated by BEA. However, as time progressed, passenger traffic increased to such an extent that the major market now became that to replace the ubiquitous DC3 Dakota. The prize for winning even a share of this enormous market was a tremendous inspiration to most of the airframe companies, whose designs constantly evolved and grew throughout the fifties and sixties, as seating capacity grew from fifteen-/thirty-to sixty /seventy-seaters as air transport correspondingly grew itself.

Avro and Manchester Studies

As one of the largest British design companies, A.V. Roe (Avro) at Manchester, undertook many feederliner studies from 1953 onwards. As with all the companies who undertook project studies, many of these were never investigated very deeply. However, the 771 and a number of 748 developments, did reach a more advanced stage.

Early studies carried out at Manchester were propeller-driven and included the twelve-seater twin Cheetah-engined Avro 700 from 1945, and Avro 715, a ten-seater four-engined prospective Dove replacement. These were followed by the Avro 723, powered by four Alvis Leonides from 1953 and the Avro 736 and 737, both powered by four Armstrong Siddeley P1.82 or Napier E223 engines. The Avro 747 high-wing passenger freight transport was also proposed, which was powered by two Rolls-Royce Dart engines. The larger Avro 754 of 1958 utilised the wing of the proposed Avro 745 NATO maritime patrol/reconnaissance aircraft. In a two-class configuration, this could accommodate up to eighty passengers, fifteen in first class at five abreast with a 39in-pitch, with sixty-five seats at 34in-pitch in the rear cabin. Freight was carried in underfloor compartments. The design of a low straight wing with tailplane mounted on the rear fuselage was not too dissimilar to an enlarged 748.

(Avro 715) Length 40ft 3in, Span 55ft, Height 15ft 11in

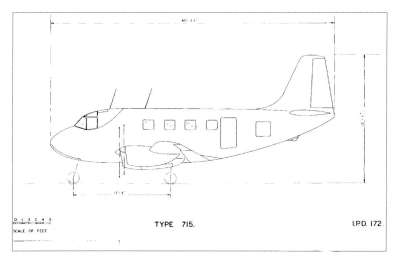

Avro 715
The prospective Dove replacement was the Avro 715. (BAE SYSTEMS)

However, Avro could see that the future for even feederliner aircraft lay with the jet engine and, consequently, their designs from the late fifties onwards were turbofan powered. One of the earliest of these was the Avro 750, put forward in 1958. This encompassed a number of twin- and four-engined designs. One of these featured a low wing and two rear-mounted engines with a T-tail arrangement. Many of the 750 design features were incorporated in the joint Bristol/Avro Jetliner. The Avro 751 of March 1958 was a low-wing rear-engined tri-jet, again with a T-tail, providing seating for up to fifty-six passengers at four abreast, with underfloor baggage holds.
(Avro 750) Length 97ft, Span 81ft 3in, Height 26ft 2in, Wing Area 1,200sq.ft

Avro 761

Put forward as a turbofan replacement for the Vickers Viscount in 1958, the 761 was a low-wing design with ¼ chord sweep of 32.5 degrees, with the tailplane mounted on top of the fin. Accommodation was provided for sixty-five passengers in a fuselage of 10ft 7½in diameter. The 761 had an all-up weight of 70,000lb and a range of 500 miles, at a cruising speed of 480 knots. Power was provided by two rear-mounted Rolls-Royce RB163 engines.
Length 92ft 5in, Span 87ft 75in, Height 24ft 5in, Wing Area 1,100sq.ft

Avro 771

The 771, which superseded the 761 in September 1960, was a slightly smaller design, again featuring the low wing and T-tail arrangement, and was aimed at the prospective jet Viscount replacement market. Matched against the BAC 107, both aircraft were rear-engined designs powered by two Bristol–Siddeley BS75s of 7,350lb thrust. Fuselage diameter remained at the 761's 10ft 7½in but ¼ chord sweep was now only 30 degrees. The small wing was cambered and twisted and featured leading edge slats and high lift Fowler flaps, giving good field

performance. Up to sixty passengers could be accommodated at five abreast, although a more typical layout was for fifty-four tourist-class seats or forty-six in two-class layout. Freight holds were provided underfloor to accommodate up to 310cu.ft of capacity. Maximum cruise speed was 560mph at 25,000ft, with a maximum payload of 12,000lb carried over stage lengths of 685 to 771 nautical miles. The design was hawked around for a short while but, as the company became more closely integrated within the new Hawker Siddeley Grouping, the new 748 turboprop began to occupy much of its effort, and the 771 was dropped.
Length 80ft 37in, Span 77ft 46in, Height 24ft 25in, Wing Area 800sq.ft

748 Jet Variants

The final designs to emerge from the Avro stable were based around the 748 turboprop. In an effort to obtain a new feederliner without the cost of developing a completely new aircraft, many configurations were tried out under the 748J designation.

The Avro 778 from 1960 was originally proposed as a rear-engined twinjet powered by the Rolls-Royce RB161 of 7,000lb thrust. Up to fifty passengers could be accommodated at four abreast with a range of 500 nautical miles, a design cruise speed of Mach 0.65 and a gross weight of 40,275lb. This proposal was superseded by a General Electric CF700 of 4,000lb thrust design. The new design used the same wing span as the earlier study but was slightly shorter, and could carry a payload of 9,200lb over 500 nautical miles, with a maximum all-up weight of 43,960lb. Much of the 748 design remained unchanged, although the wing span was reduced, and pods housed the undercarriage where the original engine nacelles were positioned. The rear fuselage was also redesigned and there was a new T-tail layout. A further 748 study, the Avro 781, also a twinjet, featured a reduced fuselage length. Subsequent 748 jet designs emerged under the Hawker Siddeley legend.
Avro 778 (Tri-Jet) Length 72ft 91in, Span 84ft, Height 21ft 17in, Wing Area 739sq.ft

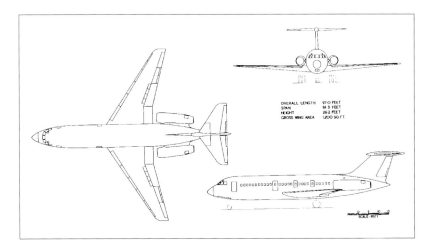

Avro 750
The Avro 750 designation was applied to a number of studies for small jet airliners, both twin- and four-engined, with many of the design features incorporated in the proposed Bristol/Avro Jetliner. (BAE SYSTEMS)

Hawker Siddeley (Manchester) HS806

The HS806 featured a lengthened 748 fuselage and was powered by two Rolls-Royce RB203 Trent engines, positioned on the rear fuselage. Like the 778, the undercarriage retracted into pods on the wing, mounted in the position of the original engine nacelles, while the tailplane was mounted on the fin.
Length 77ft 4in

Hawker Siddeley (Manchester) HS860

The HS860 was submitted to the Hawker Siddeley board as a comparison against Hatfield's HS136 proposal for a new feederliner project. The new model featured two rear-mounted Rolls-Royce RB203 engines of 9,970lb thrust, with wing mounted pods housing the main undercarriage. Other modifications were made to the wing and the fin unit, which was of greater angle and on which the tailplane was mounted. The range with a maximum payload of 14,800lb was put at over 600 nautical miles, with an all-up weight of 59,500lb. In the event, the Hawker Siddeley board decided to combine features of both the HS136 and HS860 into a completely new project, which emerged as the HS144.
Length 81ft 4in, Span 95ft, Height 26ft 35in, Wing Area 795sq.ft

Many of the studies later undertaken at Manchester were for design purposes and not intended as serious projects. These included the HS817 from 1970, a smaller variant of the HS144 powered by the Rolls-Royce M45H, and the HS823, a tri-jet ALF502 development of the HS146, to seat up to sixty-five passengers. Among the other designs was the forty-seater HS821 from 1971, with numerous powerplant options including the ALF502, ATF3, T53 and T55, and advanced turboprops including the HS831 from 1975, and high-wing HS835 from 1976. One design studied seriously for a number of years was the HS832.

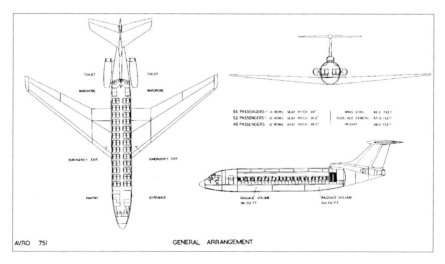

Avro 751
Avro 751 twinjet which could accommodate up to fifty-six passengers. (BAE SYSTEMS)

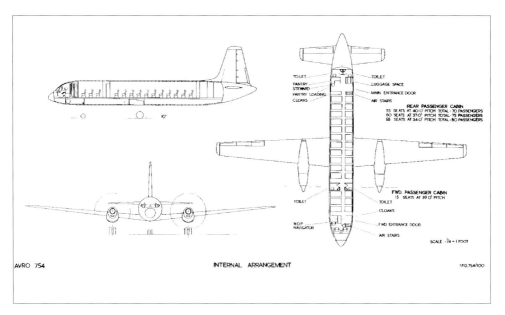

Avro 754
One of the last large turboprop designs was the eighty-seater Avro 754. (BAE SYSTEMS)

Hawker Siddeley (Manchester) HS 832 – 748 Series 5

Leading on from the HS827 twin ALF502 jet 748 development was the HS832, originally designated HS748/502 (to indicate the use of the original powerplant, the Avco Lycoming ALF 502), which featured turbofan engines mounted over the wing on the same structure that carried the Dart engines. When later studies included variants powered by the Rolls-Royce M45 of 7,136lb thrust, the designation was adjusted to the HS748 series 5. This design featured a fuselage stretched by some 7ft 6in, enabling accommodation for up to sixty-four passengers, a dihedral in order to keep the tailplane clear of the jet exhaust and the addition of adaptive braking and lift dumpers. Hawker Siddeley did go as far as to consider fitting two overwing-mounted ALF 502s on a new 748 airframe, to be used for flight testing and demonstration, and which may have also led to retrofitting of Dart-powered models with the ALF502 engines. By late 1976/77, the British industry was being reorganised once again, and the new British Aerospace Corporation began to look seriously at new civil aircraft projects. Seeing the need for a small feederliner, the company weighed up the derivative jet 748 against Hatfield's all-new 146 design, which had been kept ticking over for a couple of years. Seeing more potential in the latter, jet 748 developments were dropped.

Since becoming part of British Aerospace, Manchester Division continued with new designs, including the 100-seater HS839 in 1979, and the HS840 and HS848 projects designed for the Fuel Efficient Aircraft Technology (FEAT) specification. The late eighties saw new designs for high-speed commuter aircraft emerge and, following the taking over of the 146 project from Hatfield, came the original larger replacement the RJX (BAe 857), a 90- to 120-seater twinjet powered by BR715 engines. It was originally hoped that this model would be produced in co-operation with Taiwan.

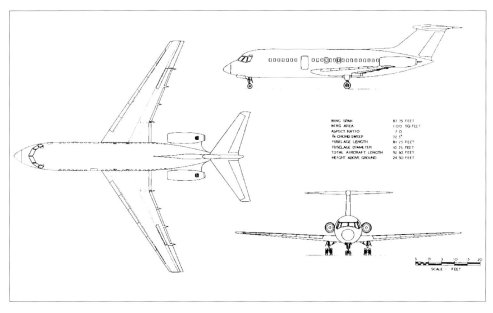

Avro 761
The Vickers Viscount replacement Avro 761 was powered by two rear-mounted Rolls-Royce RB163 engines.
(BAE SYSTEMS)

Blackburn

The Blackburn company had been absent from the commercial market since the failure of the Beverley/Universal to attract commercial orders, and the decision not to order any Rapide replacement aircraft. These earlier studies had included the four Gipsy Major X-powered B-77 and B-84.

Blackburn B-105

A new larger feederliner, the B-105 Baronet, was proposed in 1953. It was to be a low-wing transport to be powered by four Bombardier engines, which was basically a scaled-up B-84 to seat up to eighteen passengers. With an all-up weight of 12,000lb, a payload of 3,500lb could have been carried over a range of 100 miles, with a cruising speed of 170mph at 5,000ft.
Length 47ft 6in, Span 75ft 11in, Height 18ft 8in

Blackburn B-106

The larger B-106, also of low-wing design, was powered by four Turbomeca Marcadau turboprops of 475hp, which would have been produced under licence by Blackburn. Accommodation was provided for up to twenty-six passengers at three abreast, with a maximum take-off weight of 22,500lb. It was envisaged that a payload of 8,000lb would be able to be carried over stages of 100 miles at a cruising speed of 240mph.
Length 57ft 6in, Span 87ft 3in, Height 20ft, Wing Area 750sq.ft

Avro 771
An impression of the Avro 771, a smaller version of the 761 proposed to replace the Viscount in September 1960. (BAE SYSTEMS)

Blackburn B-110

In 1958 the company turned its attention towards a definitive DC3 replacement aircraft, and the B-110 was the end result. The low-wing design saw the tailplane mounted midway on the fin with two rear-mounted turbofan engines (although turboprop designs had also been studied), and it could accommodate up to twenty-eight passengers at four abreast. It was a very much smaller aircraft than other DC3 replacement designs and, in fact, looked like an enlarged business jet, and was similar in many ways to the DH126. Designed to operate from small airfields including grass airstrips, it would have been powered by two turbofans of 3,200lb thrust, with a take-off weight of 19,600lb. The B-110 was an advanced design, yet failed to cater for the increase in passenger numbers then being experienced.
Length 56ft 2in, Span 62ft, Height 19ft 6in, Wing Area 538sq.ft

De Havilland and Hatfield Projects

The de Havilland company at Hatfield was, alongside Vickers, the premier commercial design and production team in Britain. Naturally, the company which had developed its own niche product, the Dove, turned its attentions towards a DC3 replacement market. That the factory continued these studies after its amalgamation into Hawker Siddeley Aviation, and then British Aerospace, showed the seriousness attached to such a potential market. However, it was not until 1981 that the fruits of their labour actually took to the skies with the first flight of the 146.

De Havilland 123

Initial studies by de Havilland for a small feederliner came under the moniker of the DH123 from Hatfield's sister factory, the old Airspeed works at Christchurch. In 1959, the company revealed a W.A. Tamblin design for a high-wing twin turboprop design, with a wing very similar to that of a scaled-down Ambassador. The new design, unveiled at the 1959 Farnborough Air Show, could accommodate up to forty passengers at four abreast, had a maximum take-off weight of 22,100lb, and was powered by two Gnome engines of 1,150shp. However, with the major reorganisation that occurred in 1960, and de Havilland's absorption into the Hawker Siddeley Group, the 123 was now finding that it was competing with a sister company's project, namely the Avro 748, that had already been launched and had obtained orders. The 123 was dropped and de Havilland instead turned its attention towards a jet feederliner.

Length 60ft 6in, Span 81ft 3in, Height 20ft 3in, Wing Area 550sq.ft

De Havilland 124

Very little information about this project has survived, except that it was a low-wing aircraft that could accommodate forty to forty-eight passengers at four abreast, with two rear-mounted Rolls-Royce RB145 engines of 5,700lb thrust. Freight was to be carried in forward fuselage holds. The 124 project was quickly superseded by the 126.

Length 60ft, Span 81ft, Wing Area 550sq.ft

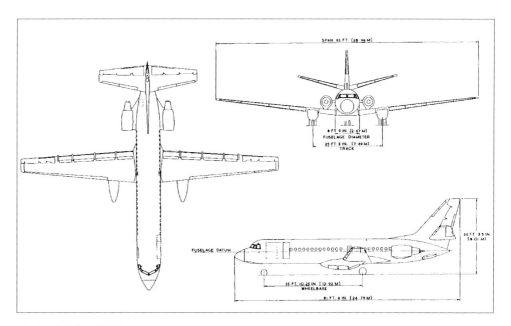

Hawker Siddeley HS860
One of many proposed jet developments of the Avro 748 was the Hawker Siddeley HS860, which was compared against Hatfield's HS136 to fulfil Hawker Siddeley's new feederliner project.
(BAE SYSTEMS)

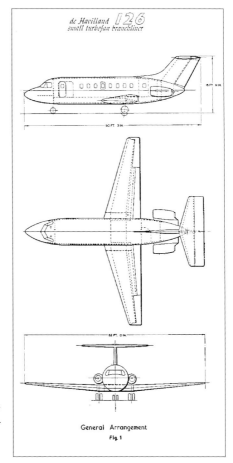

De Havilland 126
Looking like a larger 125, the de Havilland 126 was put
forward in 1960, and would have been powered by either
Rolls-Royce RB172 or General Electric CF700 engines.
(BAE SYSTEMS – via de Havilland Heritage Museum)

De Havilland 126

The last of the feederliner projects to bear the de Havilland legend, the 126 was a low-wing rear-engined jetliner put forward in 1960, and resembled an enlarged 125. Original power was to be provided by two de Havilland PS92 or PS92Bs. However, when de Havilland Engines were acquired by Bristol–Siddeley, the 92 was abandoned, leading to the Rolls-Royce RB172 and General Electric CF700 being put forward as replacements. The 126 design continued to evolve, growing from its initial thirty seats with a maximum take-off weight of 22,500lb, to a 29,250lb maximum take-off weight, and accommodating thirty-two passengers in 1964. The major problem for all small jetliner manufacturers at the time was the availability or non-availability of suitable engines, and for any new aircraft to be able to provide operating costs better than older available aircraft they were due to replace.

Another issue at the time was re-engining older aircraft with newer fuel-efficient engines, such as the Napier Eland turboprop. Nevertheless, considerable interest in the project was shown, especially from Australian operators, including Ansett, who were impressed with the aircraft's proposed short stage lengths and short field performance.

Length 62ft 8in, Span 67ft, Height 19ft, Wing Area 600sq.ft

Hawker Siddeley HS131

Now under the Hawker Siddeley banner, the HS131 was Hatfield's shortlived replacement for the 126, and this time utilised components from its turboprop stablemate, the Hawker Siddeley (Avro) 748. In order to reduce costs, the 131 used the 748's flightdeck and front fuselage, in addition to many systems and interior furnishings. These were married to a new wing, tail unit and landing gear. As with the 126, accommodation was provided for up to thirty-two passengers with a maximum take-off weight of 30,000lb. The search for suitable engines proved to be the problem once more, as studies were made using the Rolls- Royce RB172, Bristol–Siddeley BS304 and, again, the General Electric CF700.
Length 62ft 8in, Span 67ft, Height 20ft 3in, Wing Area 640sq.ft

Hawker Siddeley HS136

In 1964, Hatfield produced the 136, a completely new aircraft of low-wing configuration that was originally a rear-engined design, powered by RB172 engines. This was continually evolving so that by 1967, a new engine, the Rolls-Royce RB203 Trent (one of the company's new three-shaft engines), was under development, and the design was revised to feature underwing engines of 9,730lb-thrust. The project now resembled a shrunken Boeing 737. Many reasons were put forward for this radical development, including eliminating the deep stall problem that the One-Eleven had suffered. However, with the engines so close to the ground, there was now always the problem of ingestion of debris. This was even more important for such a small feederliner compared to the 737, as by its nature the 136 was expected to be operated from unprepared airstrips. The 136 project continued to be studied until the end of 1968, by which time it had grown considerably from its initial beginnings as a forty-seater at four abreast, into a ninety-three-seater at six abreast in its series 200 guise. A first flight was proposed for 1969/70, with deliveries due to commence from the middle of 1971. The majority of manufacture was expected to be split between the Hatfield and Portsmouth factories. The aircraft had now expanded from its original small feederliner brief, and would have been marketed against the smaller One-Eleven variants and the F28. In this final form, the project was compared against the competing Hawker Siddeley Manchester HS860, to see which project should be the company's new feederliner project.
(Series 200) Length 82ft 8in, Span 90ft 6in

Hawker Siddeley HS144

With engine ingestion found to be a major obstacle to the 136, and the 860 being a derivative aircraft, the Hatfield and Woodford design teams joined forces to provide a definitive new feederliner transport. The HS144 that emerged in 1969 was an elegant rear-engined low-wing aircraft powered by two Rolls-Royce RB203 Trent engines of 10,640lb thrust, featuring a T-tail and a seating capacity of up to eighty passengers at five abreast, with a maximum take-off weight of 64,100lb. The position of the engines over the wing's trailing edge was to improve the centre of gravity while also providing, aft of the engines, a passenger entrance door. The engine intakes, which were over the trailing edge of the wing, would now be protected from ingestion. Two variants were to be offered, the series 100 for up to sixty-two passengers, and the series 200, seating up to eighty passengers. The 144 was a thoroughly workmanlike aircraft and, although talks were held with SNIAS of France for a joint venture, it was felt to be well within the capabilities of the Hawker Siddeley Group to finance the project on a purely nationalistic approach. But fate was to intervene, firstly with the decision by Fairchild of the US to abandon their own small feederjet development of the Fokker 28, the F228, which was to be powered by Rolls-Royce's new Trent engine, which caused the engine company to slow down work on the engine. The second development was far more serious: the cost overruns on the development of the RB211 were to cause the bankruptcy of Rolls-Royce in the early part of 1971, and put paid to many commercial studies of the time, the Trent engine being one of them.

(Series 200) Length 96ft 3in, Span 83ft 4in, Height 26ft 3in, Wing Area 767sq.ft

Hawker Siddeley had lost its powerplant, and the 144 was once again a project that remained on the drawing board. However, Hatfield's next study, the 146, which began in April 1971, was at last to give the factory a new product and, although it achieved an elongated gestation through cancellation in 1974, just a year after it was officially launched, the aircraft's design continued to be refined. When British Aerospace officially came into being in 1978, the

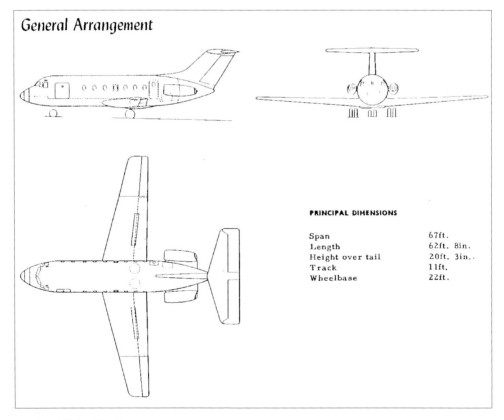

General Arrangement

PRINCIPAL DIMENSIONS

Span	67ft.
Length	62ft. 8in.
Height over tail	20ft. 3in..
Track	11ft.
Wheelbase	22ft.

Hawker Siddeley HS131
The Hawker Siddeley HS131 utilised components from the HS748, including the flightdeck and front fuselage.
(BAE SYSTEMS – via de Havilland Heritage Museum)

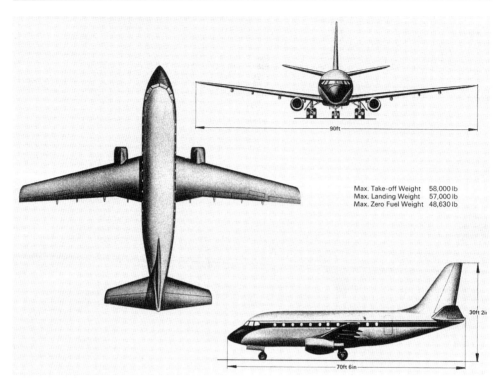

Max. Take-off Weight   58,000 lb
Max. Landing Weight   57,000 lb
Max. Zero Fuel Weight   48,630 lb

Hawker Siddeley HS136
The Hawker Siddeley Hatfield HS136, looking like a baby Boeing 737. (BAE SYSTEMS – via de Havilland Heritage Museum)

design was relaunched – for a time under the FeederJet Aircraft (FJA) designation – and made its first flight around three years later. In 1992, the 146 was superseded by the Avro RJ production, which continued until 2002. Its successor, the third generation re-engined RJX, made its first flight in 2001, but BAE SYSTEMS declined to spend further monies on its development and, after three aircraft had flown, including two prototypes, flight testing and production was abandoned. In total, 394 146 aircraft of all series were produced. Both the latter 146 derivatives' production was undertaken at the former Avro factory at Woodford.

English Electric

Although English Electric were never to build a post-war commercial transport, the company's design team engaged in a number of interesting studies of transport aircraft, among which were a number of feederliners.

English Electric P7

In the late 1940s, English Electric studied a couple of unnumbered transport projects, one of which in 1948 was an eight-seater Dragon Rapide replacement of low-wing design, powered

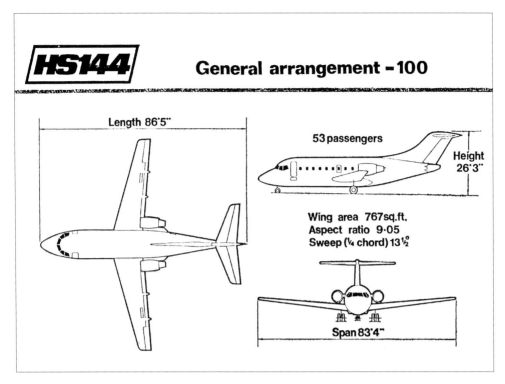

Hawker Siddeley HS144
The elegant T-tailed HS144 came from the joint Hatfield and Manchester design teams. However, fate intervened when work on its Trent engine slowed, and then stopped when Rolls-Royce collapsed. (BAE SYSTEMS – via de Havilland Heritage Museum)

by two engines driving one propeller mounted in the nose of the aircraft. In June 1953, the company undertook a major study of a DC3 replacement aircraft, under the project number P7. This low-wing fixed undercarriage monoplane was powered by a single Armstrong Siddeley Double Mamba engine, again mounted on the nose of the aircraft. In a report undertaken in May 1953 to investigate a Dakota replacement, English Electric found this formula to be the only one that could better the DC3 in comfort, safety and economy. It was also found that the design could accommodate boundary layer control and could be utilised for a variety of roles, including freighter and air ambulance, besides its feederliner role of carrying up to forty passengers. The design had an all-up weight of 30,000lb, a maximum cruising speed of 240 knots and a still air range of 1,450 nautical miles. While it continued to be discussed for a number of years, it was never to appear as a hard product.
Length 67ft 5in, Span 95ft, Height 15ft 5in

English Electric P29

By November 1958, English Electric's thoughts had turned towards a Viscount replacement, and the P29 was proposed. The high-wing T-tailed design had four underwing Rolls-Royce RB145 jet engines mounted in pods. With seating at four abreast, up to fifty-two passengers

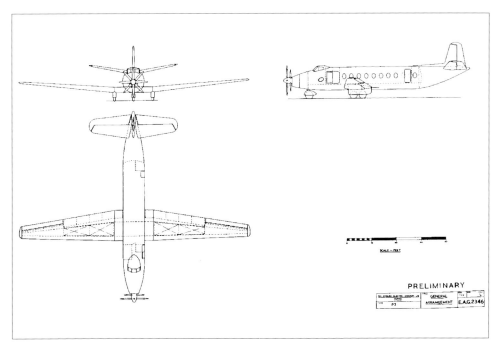

English Electric P7
A prospective DC3 replacement was the English Electric P7, powered by a single Armstrong Siddeley Double Mamba engine. (BAE SYSTEMS)

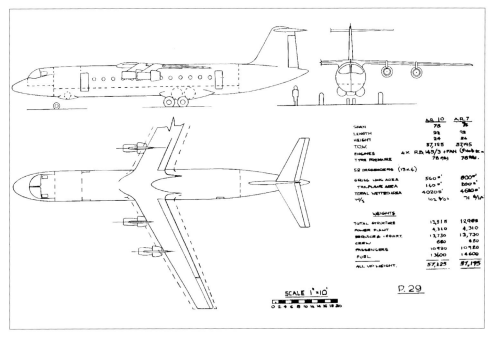

English Electric P29
The high-wing English Electric P29 was proposed in 1958 as a Viscount replacement. (BAE SYSTEMS)

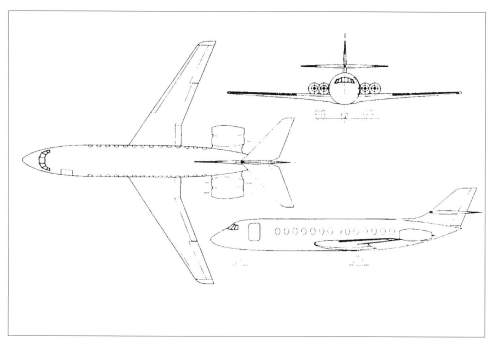

English Electric P32
The English Electric P32 was proposed in either twin- or four-engined variants. (BAE SYSTEMS)

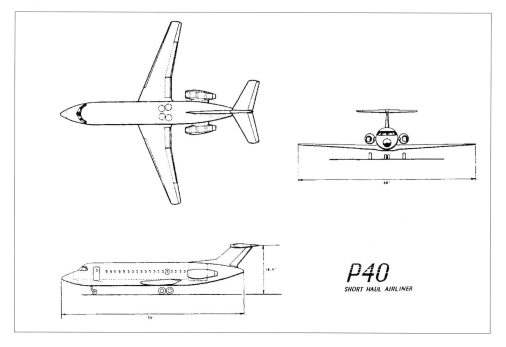

English Electric P40
The short-haul English Electric P40 twinjet from 1962. (BAE SYSTEMS)

could be accommodated. Two studies emerged, both with the same length and span, but with differing wing areas. The AR10 had a gross wing area of 560sq.ft, while the larger AR7's was 800sq.ft. The AR10 had an AUW of 57,125lb, and the AR7, 57,195lb.
Length 92ft, Span 75ft, Height 24ft

English Electric P32

In 1959 the P32 replaced the P29 project. This was for a low swept wing aircraft with a mid-fin mounted tailplane, to be powered by rear-mounted engines, either two Rolls-Royce RB163s of 10,100lb, or four 5,000lb Bristol–Siddeley BS75s. A seating capacity of up to fifty-six passengers was proposed, leading the design to fall into the same category as other proposed British small jets. When Hunting, Bristol and Vickers, along with English Electric, merged to become British Aircraft Corporation in 1960, the 107 was chosen to be the new company's feederliner project.

English Electric P40

One final short-haul feederliner design study to emerge from Warton was the P40 of 1962. This followed the same principle as the P32 in being rear-engined. The major differences were the placing of the tailplane on top of the fin and being powered by two Bristol–Siddeley BS75 engines of 6,500lb thrust. The wing was of 20-degrees sweep and the design's maximum take-off weight was 37,000lb. Propeller variants were also considered.
Length 76ft 5in, Span 68ft, Height 19ft, Wing Area 576½sq.ft

English Electric P40
An artist's impression of the English Electric P40, carrying the new British Aircraft Corporation title.
(BAE SYSTEMS)

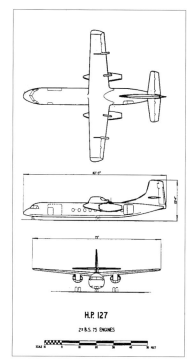

Handley Page HP.127
Utilising many Herald components was Handley Page's HP.127,
which could accommodate seventy passengers. Power was provided by
Bristol–Siddeley BS75s, and later, Rolls-Royce Spey Junior engines.
(Handley Page Association)

Gloster Studies

After the Sandy's White paper of 1957 and the subsequent cancellation of many of Britain's future military projects, all the aircraft companies were forced to re-examine their future design and production plans, and attention was turned towards commercial transports. Gloster, which was never a transport aircraft builder and, having lost the F153D, appeared to have no future, so had to investigate new projects with the utmost urgency. From 1958, the company undertook numerous commercial studies, including feederliners with capacities from thirty to eighty seats, some with area-ruled fuselages. However, these proposals remained purely design studies, and never reached a serious design stage. One further detailed investigation was made into the company's abortive attempt to take over the Aviation Traders Accountant project. In the end, some of the information obtained from this research was used by their sister company, Avro, in their competing 748 project.

Handley Page

Handley Page had always considered itself to be a builder of large aeroplanes, but the re-organisation of the British Industries in 1960 had left the company without any major new commercial transport. This was ever more apparent after the decision not to order the HP.111C (Treble One) transport for the RAF, which could have possibly led to an airliner derivative. After the company had taken over Miles Aircraft in 1948, it inherited the basis for a project which became the HP.R7 Herald, and it was from this aircraft, which was selling slowly, that future derivatives were studied, so that the company could remain in the commercial arena.

Handley Page HP.127 'Jet Herald'

The HP.127 was studied at Cricklewood during 1962, and revealed at the Farnborough Air Show later that year. Utilising many of the Herald's components in order to keep costs down, the HP.127 featured a stretched fuselage to accommodate up to seventy passengers with a take-off weight of 53,000lb. Power was provided by two Rolls-Royce RB183/1 Spey Junior engines (originally BS75s) of 8,850lb thrust, mounted under the wing with the jet pipe nozzles positioned aft of the passenger accommodation. Other major changes included an increased fin area, cropped tailplane and shorter wings. Provision was made to carry up to seventy passengers at 30in-pitch over 580 miles at 455mph, or forty-four passengers at 34in-pitch over 1,280 miles. Various layouts were proposed, including a combi with twenty-eight passengers and a 14½ft hold, while in all-freighter mode the usable volume was 2,177cu.ft. An alternative design aimed at the military market featured rear-opening doors, making the aircraft suitable for carrying large missiles or vehicle dropping. It was planned that the HP.127 could enter service by 1965.
Length 86ft 8in, Span 80ft, Height 23ft 4in, Wing Area 785sq.ft

Handley Page HP. 129 'Mini Jet Herald'

Concurrent with the HP.127 was the HP.129, a mini-jet Herald to seat up to thirty passengers. The design saw a reduction in the length of the fuselage and wing, with the standard Herald nose portion, tapered rear fuselage, outer wing and tips retained. A new wing centre section was incorporated, and the new centre fuselage incorporated pods to house the main undercarriage. Another change was the relocation of the front crew door to the starboard side. The tailplane and fin were also redesigned to smaller areas. Engine choices, as well as the Spey Junior, included the Rolls-Royce RB172, Bristol–Siddeley Orpheus and General Electric CF700, and a turboprop version was also studied.
Length 58ft 3in, Span 57ft 4in, Height 20ft 2in

Handley Page were unable to provide funds to build either or both of these projects, and faced stiff competition on the HP.127 from the new F28 (already launched) and smaller variants of the One-Eleven and DC9. At that time, the small size of the HP.129 had not yet been proven in the market. Indeed, the VFW-Fokker 614, which was aimed at the same market, failed, with only a handful being built. The company faced the same problems as the other manufacturers targeting the small jet market at the time, namely the lack of a suitable engine.

Hunting Percival Projects

The Percival Aircraft Co. had undertaken studies for small feederliners for many years, including designs for the Brabazon 5A (Percival P41 and P42) and the Rapide replacement, P64, and P65. The company later began to look at larger feederliners, and new projects were submitted for applications for Certificates of Airworthiness on 23 September 1955. These were for six studies: the P87, P92, P95, P101, P106 and P107.

Percival P87

The Percival P87 was a high-wing design with twin pusher Napier Oryx turboprop engines mounted on the wings, with 10ft 6in diameter propellers. The tailplane was mounted low on the fin and the wing design had double-slotted flaps. Up to thirty passengers could be carried in the pressurised fuselage at four abreast with a small freight hold below the cabin floor. The design featured a removable pressure bulkhead which incorporated a passenger entrance door, while, for military applications, there was a rear-loading door and ramp that would enable carriage of a vehicle. The design had an empty weight of 12,500lb, and a gross weight of 26,000lb.
Length 62ft, Span 90ft, Height 22ft 6in, Wing Area 900sq.ft

The Percival P92 was a twin Rolls-Royce Dart pressurised aircraft, with a maximum weight of 32,500lb, while the Percival P95 was a pressurised twin Napier Gazelle-powered aircraft, with a maximum weight of 26,000lb, to seat up to twenty-four passengers. The unpressurised Percival P101 was powered by four Alvis Leonides, with a maximum weight of 26,000lb, while the Percival P106 was studied in both high- and low-wing configurations, had an AUW of 20,000lb and was powered by four Blackburn Turbomeca Marcadau.

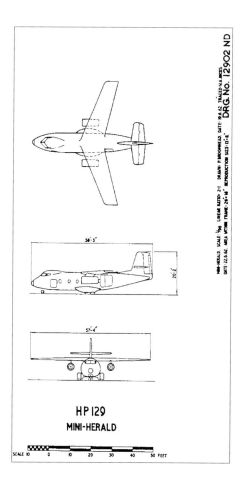

Handley Page HP.129
The thirty-seater Handley Page HP.129 'Mini Herald' was proposed with many different powerplants, including the CF700, Orpheus and RB172. (Handley Page Association)

Percival 107

After looking seriously at the P87, major company effort was directed towards the Percival P107, later given the designation Hunting 107, as a replacement for the Viscount. Many different studies were made under the 107 Type number. One of the early intentions had been to embody the Comet 4 nose section complete with windscreen structure. Other studies included designs with moderate wing sweep and engines incorporated into the tailplane, extending from the rear fuselage with a maximum take-off weight of 33,000lb, with a cruising speed of 410 knots and a range, with thirty passengers, of 300 nautical miles (dimensions listed below). A further study saw a low wing of 20-degrees sweep and tailplane mounted midway on the fin, accommodating up to forty-eight passengers at four abreast, over a range of 1,000 miles. A wooden mock-up of this project was built, and development costs were put at £5 million in July 1958. The company even registered the proposed prototype aircraft as G-APOH. Originally powered by two Bristol Orpheus engines, in September 1958 these were replaced by Bristol BS61 and then BS75 engines, at which time the aircraft's capacity increased to fifty-six passengers.

Length 66ft 9in, Span 77ft 6in, Height 23ft 3in, Wing Area 775sq.ft

With the integration of the Hunting company into the new British Aircraft Corporation (BAC), the Hunting 107 was chosen, along with the Vickers VC11, to see which programme should spearhead the new company's commercial project range alongside the VC10. Original plans were for the 107 to be a joint venture with Bristol Aircraft, with that company building the fuselage and having final assembly at Filton, while Hunting would manufacture the wing and tail. In the event, although Bristol did become involved in its successor aircraft, the One-Eleven, the 107 was taken under the Vickers/Hunting umbrella, being re-designated the BAC 107.

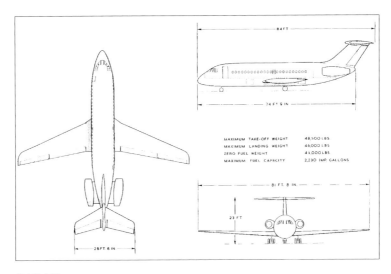

BAC 107
Originating under Percival Aircraft as the P107, the design evolved under the British Aircraft Corporation to become the BAC107, a fifty-nine-seater twinjet.
(BAE SYSTEMS)

BAC 107

The 107 design continually evolved, both under Hunting, and then, when joined with Vickers, through BAC. Throughout this time it remained rear-mounted, jet powered by two Bristol–Siddeley BS75 engines, although later designs featured a T-tail instead of the original cruciform layout. With seating to be provided for up to fifty-nine passengers at five abreast, and with a maximum take-off weight of 48,500lb, it would be pitted against the new Hawker Siddeley Group's proposed Avro 771. The design saw a wing of 20-degrees sweepback with a cruising speed of 500mph. For a short time, the two British companies were offering the market's joint short-/medium-haul projects – BAC, the 107/VC11, and Hawker Siddeley, the Avro 771/de Havilland 121 Trident, with some considerable effort expended on the sales front for these joint projects, especially in the Australian market. At a BAC board meeting in March 1961, the 107 was given the go-ahead, together with what was at the time a larger derivative, the 111 (to be powered by Rolls-Royce Spey engines), while the VC11, competing for the same funds, was dropped. It was even considered that the RAF might be interested in taking up to fifty 107s as a Varsity and Valetta replacement.

However while contracts were soon obtained for the 111 (now called the BAC One-Eleven), the 107 failed to attract any orders and, although it remained on offer throughout 1961, the decision by Bristol–Siddeley to cease development of the BS75 engine, saw the project quietly dropped. By this time, the 107 was nearly identical to the 111, except that 37in had been removed from the fuselage – the equivalent to two seat rows, in order to balance the reduced weight of the BS75 engine plus a reduced fuel capacity and thinner metal skin gauges.

Length 84ft, Span 81ft 8in, Height 23ft, Wing Area 825sq.ft

Jetstream 51/71
Revealed at the 1993 Paris Air Show was the Jetstream 51/71 family of advanced twin turboprops. A lack of partners, and Jetstream Aircraft's incorporation into Aero International (Regional), killed off the project. (BAE SYSTEMS)

Scottish Aviation and Prestwick Studies

Scottish Aviation had been studying a number of small transport aircraft since 1944 including a twenty- to thirty-seater and low-wing Rapide replacement. Later studies centred on developments of the Pioneer and Twin Pioneer. The forty-seater Turbo Pioneer General Purpose Aircraft from 1956 was powered by two Rolls-Royce Dart 506 engines. The Super Twin Pioneer from 1958 featured a stretched Twin Pioneer fuselage to seat up to twenty-two passengers, and was powered by two de Havilland Gnome P1200 engines, with a retractable undercarriage. It was estimated that a 4,000lb-passenger load could be carried at 208 knots over a 200 nautical mile stage length. Work on this project was stopped in 1959, owing to financial difficulties.

After Scottish Aviation became part of British Aerospace, Prestwick concentrated on building the Jetstream series of small transports. The Paris Air Show of 1993 saw the company reveal details of the Jetstream 51/71, a fifty-two- to seventy-eight-seater high- speed transport featuring new technology wings, cockpit, 4,000hp engines and a T-tail which, it was hoped, would enter service in 1997. Engines under consideration included the GMA2100. The Jetstream 71 had a maximum take-off weight of 60,000lb, a maximum cruising speed of 350 knots and a range, with seventy-two passengers, of 950 nautical miles. The Jetstream 51's maximum take-off weight was 50,000lb, and it could carry fifty passengers over 990 nautical miles, with a maximum cruising speed of 360 knots. British Aerospace made it clear that any new transport aircraft would have to be undertaken as a collaborative venture. However, the commuter market was becoming even more crowded, with potential new competitors from Spain and Indonesia. In 1996, BAe (Avro and Jetstream divisions) joined with ATR, forming the short-lived Aero International Regional group AI(R), which included the competing and highly successful ATR42/72 range, and the J51/71 was quietly dropped.

(J71) Length 101ft 7in (J51 80ft 4in), Span 95ft 1in, Height 23ft 9in

Shorts Studies

Short Brothers had always been considered builders of large aircraft, especially with their luxurious flying boats and bombers. However, after the company's move to Belfast, the market for military aircraft vastly decreased, and it was also the end of large flying boat's era. The company was forced to turn its attention to commercial transports, firstly with Comet production (later cancelled) and then with Britannia manufacture for both the RAF and airlines. Concurrent with these were their own transport studies, many of which were directed towards the small airliner market. The company had already submitted designs to meet the Rapide replacement Specification 26/49 with low-wing ten- and fifteen-seaters (undesignated). Later studies included the twin Gazelle or GE T58-powered PD26 and PD27, followed by the short-range PD60.

By the early sixties, the company was studying a small DC3 replacement aircraft, the PD65, which underwent many design changes. Both turboprop and turbofan variants were investigated, with high- and low-wing layouts, and numerous engine positions. Eventually, by July 1965, a definitive low-wing design had emerged with engines mounted in long nacelles above the wing. Seating was provided for up to thirty passengers at four abreast, with

an AUW of 32,500lb, maximum cruising speed of 457mph and a range of 1,000 miles. Even
for such a small project, Shorts knew it would need partners.

At one time it was plausible that a joint design would emerge between Shorts, VFW and
Fokker, similar to their F28 agreement. At the 1965 Paris Air Show, the companies looked
at combining work on their respective projects. VFW-Fokker had already been working on
the VFW614 and, it was hoped that Shorts could become involved in this project,
incorporating PD65 features, with a share of up to 30–35 per cent. It would probably involve
wing and tail manufacture. However, in a strange move, the British government at the time
elected that any partner in a small jet study should be Hawker Siddeley, who were at that time
working on their own HS136 project. The PD65 thereby failed to be realised and the
HS/VFW-Fokker tie-up never materialised.
Length 67ft 2in, Span 69ft 9in, Wing Area 685sq.ft

After concentrating on stretched variants of the Skyvan, namely the 330 and 360, in 1985
Shorts presented the 450, a further stretch of the 360 which, it was hoped, would be built
with the new Tucano partner, the Brazilian company Embraer. The 450 design unveiled at
the Paris Air Show could accommodate up to forty-nine passengers, with an AUW of
32,250lb, and featured a fuselage stretched by 9ft 4in, with a revised main gear arrangement
and elongated sponsons. Other changes included a new wing centre section, heightened tail,
and new engines of 1550shp powering six-bladed propellers of 9ft 9in diameter. With a
maximum payload, a range of 460 miles could be travelled. It was hoped the project would
be in service by 1987. With intense competition being envisaged in the forty-seater market,
especially from the ATR42, and because of the decision by Embraer not to collaborate on
the project, the 450 was dropped at the end of 1985.
Length 84ft 2in, Span 79ft 1in, Height 26ft 7in, Wing Area 539sq.ft

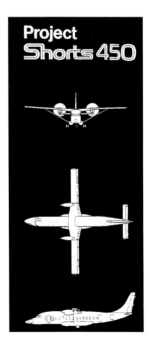

Short 450
The Short 450 was a stretched forty-nine-seater development of the 360, from
1985. (Courtesy of Bombardier Aerospace)

Short FJX
An artist's impression of the Short FJX twinjet. (Courtesy of Bombardier Aerospace)

At the Paris Air Show, 1987, Shorts, together with new partner de Havilland Canada, unveiled the NRA90 after an initial memorandum of understanding had been signed between the two companies at the Farnborough Air Show in 1986. This accord looked into new twenty-five-seater designs offering a comfortable 'widebody' fuselage, a cruising speed of 300 knots and seat mile costs 25 per cent better than current or projected thirty-seater aircraft. The NRA90 encompassed two designs, both featuring a fuselage with a 95in diameter (2.41m), 6ft headroom and a three-abreast layout. The first design, the NRA90A, was a conventional high-wing turboprop design of 1,600ehp, with a maximum cruise speed of 315 knots (583kph) and a high-speed cruise range of 705 nautical miles, and a maximum take-off weight of 23,350lb.

The NRA90B was a low-wing pusher design powered by two rear fuselage-mounted turbine engines of 1,600ehp, driving contra-rotating propellers. The model B was slightly faster with a maximum cruise speed of 340 knots (630kph), but with a comparable range and a maximum take-off weight of 22,250lb. The development costs of the NRA90 were put at between $250 to 300 million, and it was this high cost and the feeling that there was an insufficient market in which to recoup these costs, that killed the project.

(NRA90A) Length 60ft 8in, Span 64ft 9¼in, Height 20ft 10½in, Wing Area 350sq.ft
(NRA90B) Length 68ft 1in, Span 54ft 7½in, Height 24ft 5in, Wing Area 324.4sq.ft

In March 1988, Shorts announced their final airliner project to date. The FJX was a low-wing feederliner seating between forty-four and forty-eight passengers at four abreast in a fuselage of 113in diameter, with two underwing-mounted turbofan engines, a maximum take-off weight of 41,300lb and a range of 800 nautical miles. Possible powerplants included the CFE738 and PW300/X. At the Farnborough Air Show of 1988, Shorts exhibited a mock-up of the fuselage, and discussions were held with a number of interested airlines, including British Airways and the Airlines of Britain Group, some of whom were requesting an early stretched variant. Development costs of the project were put at £500 million, for which Shorts were prepared to contribute around 30 per cent. The company was, therefore, looking for potential partners to share development. Discussions were held with a number of companies including MBB, which included incorporating the design to become the smallest member of the proposed MRC75 range of airliners. The decision by HM Government to sell Shorts led to the FJX becoming a major factor in any new partner's plans for the company. However, in 1989, when the Canadian Transportation group Bombardier reached an agreement to purchase the complete company, the FJX was dropped. Shorts became a major partner in the Canadair Regional Jet, ironically the FJX's major competitor, building large fuselage assemblies and other components.

Length 79ft 9in, Span 74ft 2in, Height 25ft 9in

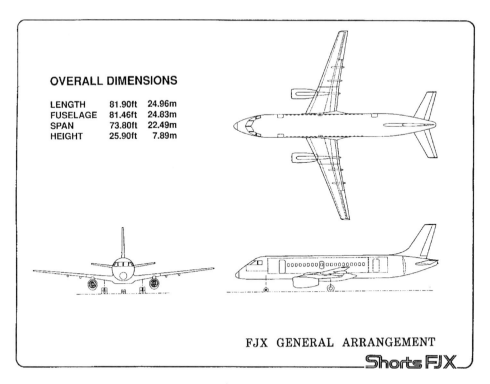

OVERALL DIMENSIONS

LENGTH	81.90ft	24.96m
FUSELAGE	81.46ft	24.83m
SPAN	73.80ft	22.49m
HEIGHT	25.90ft	7.89m

FJX GENERAL ARRANGEMENT

Shorts FJX

Short FJX
Development of the FJX was cancelled when Shorts was taken over by Bombardier in 1989. (Courtesy of Bombardier Aerospace)

Chapter 8

Airbus Studies

On 26 September 1961, the Transport Aircraft Requirements Committee (TARC) authorised Dr M.J. Lighthill (Director of the RAE) to chair a working party on short-range medium-cost air transport (more commonly known as the Lighthill Committee). The committee included representatives from the aircraft manufacturers, Ministry of Aviation, SBAC (Society of British Aircraft Constructors), ARB (Air Registration Board), the state airlines BEA and BOAC, together with the BIATA (British Independent Air Transport Association) and was to be guided by the RAE at Farnborough. Its brief was to study as wide a range of aircraft in all manner of configurations from jet flap and boundary layer ingestion to tandem-wings and canards. Studies were to be made of both new and derivative projects which included the Trident, VC10, Belfast and also the Canadair CL-44. In terms of costs, it was natural that developments of existing airframes be explored alongside entirely new designs. Concurrent with this committee was BEA's issuing of an outline requirement for an 'ultra short-haul, low-cost airliner'.

The working party met on six occasions between 10 January 1962 and 9 January 1964, to examine the long-term possibilities for reducing the operating costs of short-range transport aircraft, and this included new aircraft ideas. Three main panels were set up: Operations – which looked at the costs and revenues of an Aerobus type aircraft; Technical – which looked at short-range aircraft designs but not specifically all-wing; and the All-Wing Panel – which looked, as its title suggests, at the technical possibilities of all-wing designs.

All-Wing Studies

The All-Wing panel decided to commission three different designs from Whitworth–Gloster, Bristol and Handley Page. The latter two companies would submit all-wing transports. Bristol's was a compound delta and Handley Page's was a compound sweep. Whitworth–Gloster would produce a conventional design with an almost unswept wing and two rear-mounted jet engines. All the transports would be 100-seaters which could operate for two consecutive (non-refuelling) 250-mile stages, with normal reserves. Studies were also undertaken purely for comparative cost estimates, on similar transports with capacities of up to 250 passengers.

Handley Page HP.126 Aerobus

Many studies were made under the HP.126 designation of varying sizes. The basic design featured a compound swept wing with a 35-degree sweep constant chord centre section

housing the passengers, and a more highly swept outer wing for stability with wing tips. A forward stub fuselage would house the flight deck plus two passenger doors. Two further entry doors were provided in the wing-leading edge, which also held passengers' baggage. The cabin could house up to 102 passengers across the inner half of the span, and consisted of a shell made up of intersecting circular cylinders which ran parallel to the leading edge. Power was originally to be provided by four NGTE Type 'F' engines mounted at the rear of the centre section, with intakes on the wing upper surface. Later proposals were to use four by-pass turbojets with a total thrust of 29,000lb, with a maximum all-up weight of 78,000lb and a cruising speed of Mach 0.7. Handley Page later undertook studies of the 154-seater HP.134 Ogee Aerobus, with an integrated thick wing single central fin and rudder, powered by three turbojet engines.
Length 72ft 5in, Span 78ft, Wing Area 2,180sq.ft

Bristol

Bristol's submission was a delta-wing design of 62 degree leading edge sweepback, with a 34 degree tip extension, and slightly swept forward trailing edge. Accommodation was provided for 104 passengers, housed in a cabin which covered the inner third of the span, with a wing thickness of 19–21 per cent. Like the HP.126, the flight deck was located in a forward stub fuselage, with power being provided by four NGTE 'F' powerplants of 7,000lb thrust, which were to be strut mounted in pairs from the wing leading edge at mid-semi-span. A cruising speed of Mach 0.765 at 20,000ft was proposed, with an all-up weight of 81,420lb.
Length 74ft 75in, Span 74ft, Wing Area 2,022sq.ft

In July 1963 each panel produced its report. The conclusion reached was that a market would exist for a 100- to 150-seater short-stage aircraft in the seventies, which would probably be jet powered, but that all-wing designs held no clear advantage over conventional designs. The report added that it was hoped that further work would continue on such designs.

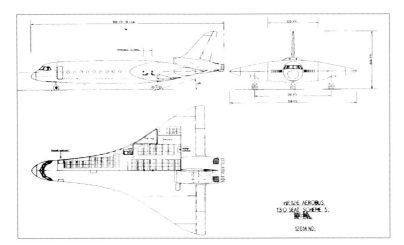

Handley Page HP.126
One of a number of schemes proposed by Handley Page under the HP.126 designation
for an all-wing airliner. (Handley Page Association)

BEA's Airbus

BEA's specification for its proposed airbus (ultra short-haul low-cost airliner) was issued in 1964, and was for a 150- to 200-seater able to operate high density routes such as London–Amsterdam, Paris and Manchester, and was seen as a replacement for its Vanguard fleet. With the likelihood of this being one of the last major subsonic domestic orders for many years to come, it was natural that the major airframe companies would turn their attentions towards meeting such a potentially large order. With its Trident just entering service, Hawker Siddeley looked at seeing how best its new jet could be adapted to meet this new specification. Various derivatives were proposed, from simple tri-jet stretches to 120-seater twin designs. However, there were also some more ambitious proposals put forward.

'Double-bubble' Trident

The 'double-bubble' Trident saw the aircraft's original upper fuselage lobe combine with a new lower fuselage. The upper fuselage provided seating at six abreast, while the new lower fuselage had five-abreast seating, with a well provided for the passenger aisle. In total, up to 200 passengers could have been accommodated. The passenger cabin in the new lower deck would have been provided forward of the wing, with the lower deck aft of the wing being used for freight. The total height of the new fuselage would have been 15ft 11in. Powerplants proposed included Rolls-Royce Conway and Aft-fan Rolls-Royce Speys.

Hawker Siddeley HS132 'Bident'

The HS132 was first proposed in 1964 as a twin-engined Trident development, designed specifically for low cost operation on high density routes. Power would have been provided by two Rolls-Royce RB178-14H engines of 28,100lb thrust with an all-up weight of 144,500lb.

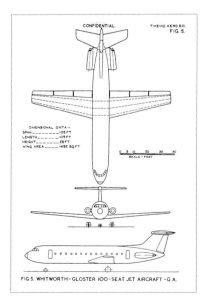

Whitworth–Gloster Jet
The conventional Whitworth–Gloster 100-seater jetliner, which was used as a comparison against the Handley Page and Bristol all-wing airliners. (BAE SYSTEMS – via Handley Page Association)

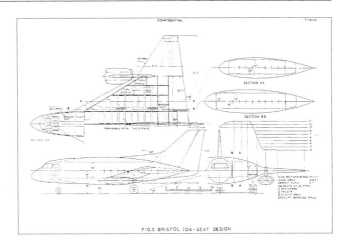

Bristol All-Wing 104-Seater
The delta-winged Bristol all-wing
design could accommodate 104
passengers. (BAE SYSTEMS –
via Handley Page Association)

Major parts of the 121 Trident were retained, in fact more than 60 per cent of the 132 utilised the same components. The major changes were a fuselage stretched by 24ft, and a redesigned rear fuselage to accommodate the twin engine installation, and to provide the necessary tail-down ground angle with the longer fuselage. The new stretch provided accommodation for up to 164 passengers in economy-class. The Trident IE wing was utilised with a 3ft increase in span, and the replacement of double-slotted flaps by large chord-tabbed Fowler types. The horizontal tail of the Trident was retained, together with a substantial part of the fin and rudder. The major difference was in the lower part of the fin which was redesigned due to the centre engine's removal. Final development costs of the project were put at around £30 million.

Later studies included the HS132B/C with 180-192 seats, and the HS132D with 219 seats. The major problem with the HS132 was that with aft engines the majority of any stretch had to be forward of the wing, which caused severe nodding loads. On the later variants, a deepened forward fuselage was considered to provide greater rigidity. Hawker Siddeley did talk to the French aerospace industry about collaboration on the project but BEA was of the impression that the aircraft was too small for their needs, so Hawker Siddeley turned their attention to a larger underwing engine Trident development.

Length 137ft 6in, Span 98ft, Height 29ft, Wing Area 1,458sq.ft

Hawker Siddeley HS134

Following on from the HS132, Hatfield put forward the HS134 Airbus. The first designs from 1966 saw the Trident's T-tail unit being utilised, combined with a stretched fuselage to seat up to 183 passengers, coupled with a new wing of 25-degrees sweepback, beneath which were mounted two Rolls-Royce RB178 engines in pods. By the time of the final configuration in 1967, the new design featured a swept fin, tailplane mounted on the rear empennage, and two underwing-mounted Rolls-Royce RB207 engines of 28,000lb thrust. In this new design, up to 210 passengers could be accommodated. The project, now very similar in design to Boeing's later model, 757, looked like a winner, but Hawker Siddeley did not have the resources to fund the project themselves, and again needed to find a European partner to share the costs and risks of the project.

Length 143ft 6in, Span 116ft 3in, Height 41ft 2in

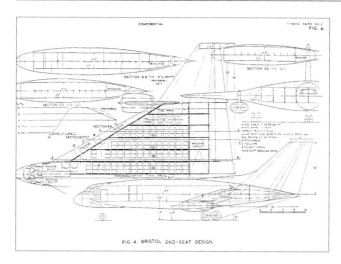

Bristol All-Wing 260-Seater
The larger 260-seater Bristol all-wing study. (BAE SYSTEMS – via Handley Page Association)

Other studies looked at by Hawker Siddeley included double-deck designs with seating for 226 passengers, and single-deck designs with 183 seats, powered by the RB178. Other Trident variants considered were powered by Conway engines or had a new wing and engines to seat up to 190. They also designed new studies with integrated fuselages and one with a raised flight deck design similar to the later 747, to accommodate 236 passengers.

Shorts Studies

Although no longer a major commercial airliner player, Shorts did engage in a number of studies towards Airbus type aircraft. With their own Belfast freighter project, it was logical that the company would investigate a derivative for BEA. One such study was for the airline to fly three adapted Belfast turboprops on the London–Glasgow route, which would have cost around £9 million. The Belfast airframe could accommodate up to 280 passengers on two decks – a mock-up of the airframe had been exhibited at the Farnborough Air Show. Other Shorts studies included a possible development of the CL44 put forward from Canadair in 1965. The proposed CL44J, which Canadair hoped to produce with Shorts, would feature a 13ft stretch to accommodate up to 196 passengers, six abreast at 34in pitch, and would have been powered by Rolls-Royce Tyne engines. The aircraft would have been available by 1967/68. Proposals were made for up to half of the airframe being built in Britain.

A further design, the PD75, also came from the Belfast design office in 1965. This was a double-deck low-wing airliner seating up to 200 passengers, powered by four turbofans mounted in vertical pairs above the wing, with the tailplane mounted on the rear fuselage.

British Aircraft Corporation

BAC's early thoughts about a BEA jet centred predominantly on developments of the VC10 long-range jet. Early studies included double-deck variants to seat 196 or 285 passengers, powered by the Rolls-Royce RB178. Later, their attention turned to a short-term interim project. This new study, to be powered by RB178 engines, featured a fuselage lengthened by 11ft 8in to seat up to 213 at 32in, and a reduction in span of some 15ft, with a cruising speed of 600mph. To secure an Airbus order from Air France, BAC proposed the study as a joint venture with French company Sud (already a subcontractor on the VC10), with that company also taking a possible 25 per cent stake in the proposed DB265 VC10. BAC would then take a secondary role to Sud on any proposed new Airbus project. It was planned that first deliveries of this variant of the VC10 could be by early 1969, with BAC hoping for a possible order of ten aircraft from BEA.

It was during this period that the British government became intent on pursuing collaborations with Europe. In 1965, the government released a report into the industry and its future which became known as the Plowden Report ('Report of the Committee of Inquiry into the Aircraft Industry' appointed by the Minister of Aviation under the chairmanship of Lord Plowden 1964-65). Among many proposals in this report was the advocation that all future airliner projects were to be undertaken as collaborative ventures with Europe, bar some small aircraft. Many of the report's conclusions were negative, and provided a field day for competitors who could seize on the fact that Britain appeared to be abdicating from airliner design and manufacture. It saw no predestined place for an aircraft industry in Britain and the need to purchase from the United States the most complex of weapon systems.

The tone of this report meant that any future airliner projects, especially one of the Airbus size, would have to be undertaken as a European, rather than, as had previously happened, a national, project for the state carriers. The report also stated that manufacturers should pay 50 per cent of any launch costs of new projects. One good point to come out of the report was that any future projects should not be tailor made for one carrier – à la VC10 and Trident, and that there should be a sustained drive towards the export market.

As a consequence of this, BEA's new fleet requirement led to contacts being made with representatives firstly from France, and then from Germany, to see if a new project could evolve for the three state airlines – BEA, Air France and Lufthansa. In November 1965, the British and French governments issued an Anglo-French Outline specification for an airbus type to seat around 200 passengers with a range of 810 nautical miles. Hawker Siddeley, although maintaining independent studies with the Trident derivatives, now also turned its attentions towards a new grouping with French companies Breguet and Nord, which evolved into the HBN series of projects. BAC discussed the possibility of joining its Concorde

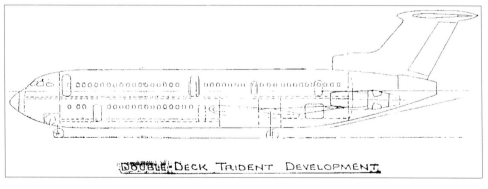

Double-deck Trident
Combing the Trident's original upper fuselage with a new lower fuselage provided the proposed Double-deck Trident with accommodation for up to 200 passengers. (BAE SYSTEMS)

partners, Sud, on the Galion project and, in January 1966, Germany was brought in to discussions at a governmental level. Proposals that were to emanate from these studies encompassed a wide variety of engine proposals, from four Spey or JT8 to three Conway or JT3, and twin RB178 or BS123s.

Hawker Siddeley/Breguet/Nord – HBN Studies

The Hawker/Breguet/Nord team put forward five proposals to meet the Airbus requirement, the main design being the HBN100. This was a conventional design submitted in April 1966, with a low wing of 30-degrees sweepback and leading and trailing edge lift devices, with an AUW of 207,360lb. The widebody circular fuselage would have provided seating for 261 at nine abreast, with freight holds mounted conventionally under the cabin floor. Propulsion would be provided by two Pratt & Whitney JT9D-1 or later Rolls-Royce RB178 engines of 44,000lb, mounted in underwing pods. A cruising speed of 600mph was envisaged, with a design range with full passenger load and reserves put at 1,200 nautical miles. Development costs of the project were put at £80 million and, with further engine growth, would have allowed for a larger 300-seater aircraft by 1975.
Length 146ft 8in, Span 129ft, Height 49ft 10in, Wing Area 2,200sq.ft

The other major study carried out against the HBN100 was the HBN101, a bulbous-looking horizontal double-bubble fuselage design, with a high wing and two underwing engines, with freight carried in underfloor holds. This configuration would have presented major structural problems as, against the more conventional HBN100 design and development, costs would consequently have been higher.

The remaining designs all featured double-decks, with the HBN102 a mid-wing study with underwing engines and a freight hold in the lower decks centre section. The HBN103 was again a mid-wing design with underwing engines, with the freight hold located on the lower deck aft of centre section, while the low-wing HBN104 had rear-mounted engines with the freight hold on the lower deck forward of the wing.

Hawker Siddeley HS132 The twinjet Trident development HS132 would have been powered by two Rolls-Royce 178 engines. (BAE SYSTEMS)

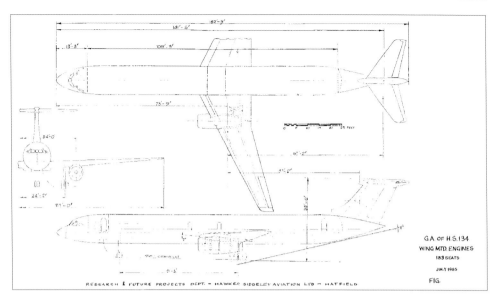

Hawker Siddeley HS134
Early 1965 drawing of the HS134, still utilising the Trident's t-tail unit. Later designs incorporated a swept fin,
and looked remarkably like the Boeing 757. (BAE SYSTEMS)

European Airbus

The Hawker Siddeley team chose the HBN100 for its submission, while Sud, with Dassault, put forward the Galion. The eventual Airbus design was larger but followed the HBN100 very closely. In a strange move, the Breguet and Nord teams which were involved with Hawker Siddeley, were replaced by the French government, who nominated Sud Aviation to be the chosen French partner. The first three-way discussions between Hawker Siddeley, Sud Aviation and the German Arge Airbus grouping (who had also been studying the double-deck VFW505 250- to 300-seater design) took place in September 1966, with a formal approach to the three governments being made on 15 October 1966. The new combined group's project now became known as the A300 Airbus.

In this initial form it had been decided that Sud Aviation would hold design leadership on the airframe, and Rolls-Royce, on the engine supplying the RB207. Shareholdings in the airframe were to be Sud and Hawker Siddeley with 37½ per cent each, and Germany, through the newly set up Deutsche Airbus GmbH, with the balance. It is interesting that an early German proposal for Airbus production saw Britain providing the engines through Rolls-Royce, France providing the aircraft's equipment and Germany building the airframe. Thankfully, such a proposal was not taken too seriously.

British European Airways had seen a requirement for an interim aircraft to precede the 300-seater Airbus, to help with capacity problems and replace the carrier's Vanguards, Comets and Viscounts. The carrier, usually so pro-British, requested permission to order a huge fleet of Boeing 737 and 727 jets, but were told by the Minister of Aviation that any new order would have to be placed for a British aircraft, and so began the battle between BAC and Hawker Siddeley to meet this potentially massive contract.

HBN100
The HBN100 was proposed as a future Airbus by Hawker Siddeley, with Breguet and Nord of France. (BAE SYSTEMS)

A300
The A300, in its original form, showing the flags of the three original partner countries, including the United Kingdom. (BAE SYSTEMS)

BAC Two-Eleven
The BAC Two-Eleven, in the colour scheme of Autair, who placed a provisional contract for two aircraft just days before the project was cancelled. (BAE SYSTEMS – via Brooklands Museum Trust)

BAC Two-Eleven

BAC, left out of the Airbus programme, began studies of short-haul versions of the VC10. These then lead into a new six-abreast fuselage stretch of the One-Eleven, the 'Super One-Eleven' powered by Rolls-Royce Conway engines, and then into a new design, the BAC Two-Eleven. This project, very much like a scaled-up One-Eleven, was again rear-engined and featured a T-tail.

The design continued to evolve throughout 1966/67, growing from Spey to Conway power before the definitive Two-Eleven emerged – an advanced short-/medium-haul airliner with very low seat mile costs, exceptionally good take-off performance, low airport noise levels and low fuel consumption. Power was now to be provided by two Rolls-Royce RB211-08 by-pass engines of 36,000lb thrust. Accommodation was to be provided for up to 219 passengers in a high density six-abreast fuselage, with an internal diameter of 142in. The more common layout would have been for 203 tourist seats, or 176 passengers in a mixed-class configuration, with 22 first-class and 154 tourist seats. Commonality with the One-Eleven was maintained with the fin and tailplane being directly scaled-up from the One-Eleven, as was the wing from the One-Eleven 500. With a full payload, the aircraft's range was 1,380 nautical miles, with a maximum take-off weight of 189,000lb. It was envisaged that the aircraft would make its first flight in late 1970, and could be in service with BEA by 1972. Development costs were put at £60 million, with additional costs for the RB211 engine.

BEA was so enthusiastic about the aircraft that they stated that had it been available earlier, then they would have chosen it over the Boeing 727, as it was seen as being quieter, had cheaper operating costs, better airfield performance and was at the start of its development life. Plans were also afoot for stretched variants of 225 and 250 seats. In early 1967, the airline asked permission to buy up to thirty aircraft, with an additional ten options. Meanwhile, co-operation deals were discussed with a number of European companies, including Shorts (rear fuselage and other components) and Sud (whose contribution in building the wing could have been for up to 30 to 35 per cent of the aircraft) while final assembly would have been carried out at BAC's Hurn facility. The government delayed – the Plowden report had not

BAC THREE-ELEVEN

General Arrangement

Overall length	183 ft 7 in.	55.95 m
Wing Span	147 ft 0 in.	44.80 m
Overall Height	43 ft 4 in.	13.20 m

BRITISH AIRCRAFT CORPORATION
the most powerful aerospace company in Europe

BAC Three-Eleven
General arrangement of the BAC Three-Eleven. (BAE SYSTEMS – via Brooklands Museum Trust)

advocated any more all-British projects, and they were also very keen to be seen to be European. In early December 1967, two further British carriers showed their faith in the aircraft, with Laker Airways and Autair ordering three and two aircraft respectively. Other airlines were also showing interest, including British Eagle and US carriers, Aloha and Mohawk. However, on 15 December, the president of the Board of Trade announced that the government had decided not to support the project, citing the high development costs and uncertainty of the size of the market – BAC saw a market for between 250 and 300 aircraft. Interestingly, the later 757, which expected almost the same market, has now reached a production of over 1,000.

Length 165ft, Span 125ft 9in, Height 35ft, Wing Area 1,860sq.ft

BEA, now told that it could not have the aircraft it wanted, reverted back to its initial choice of the Boeing 727. The government was adamant however, that BEA could not order American, and so it came to be that on 13 March 1968, an order was placed for twenty-six of the stop-gap Hawker Siddeley Trident 3s. The project, a stretched Trident 2 with an additional booster engine, was never a commercial success, and only obtained one further contract from China for two aircraft.

BAC Three-Eleven

Now without the Two-Eleven, BAC realised that the company would need a new project in order to remain in the mainline commercial transport market. Even before the Two-Eleven had died, the company had begun working on designs of wide body jetliners at Weybridge, and these came to the fore in 1968. In the summer of that year, the company revealed what it was hoped would be its new transport aircraft, the BAC Three-Eleven, which was destined to become the most important airliner ever proposed in Britain. Designed to seat up to 270 at nine abreast, or a maximum of 300 passengers, this was a direct competitor to the European Airbus A300, which the UK government was still at the time backing. Initial government response to an all-British project was lukewarm. BAC continued to invest in the aircraft, until

BAC Three-Eleven
The engineering mock-up of the
BAC Three-Eleven under
construction at BAC's Weybridge
factory. (BAE SYSTEMS – via
Brooklands Museum Trust)

BAC Three-Eleven BEA were strongly behind the Three-Eleven, and placed a provisional contract at the 1970 Farnborough Air Show. (BAE SYSTEMS – via Brooklands Museum Trust)

a definitive project emerged. The Three-Eleven, like its earlier sister aircraft, looked like a fatter and much larger One-Eleven. This time, however, the aircraft was completely new and powered by two rear-mounted RB211-61 engines. The low wing, of 25-degree sweep, featured the latest high lift concepts that were being designed at Farnborough, and looked to be a major potential seller. The design had a maximum take-off weight of 303,000lb, with a maximum cruising speed of 489 mph.

The Three-Eleven was then taken over by events. A government decision on production of the A300 was needed by 1 July 1968. However, this was dependent on there being orders for some seventy-five aircraft from the three sponsoring state carriers. When this was not forthcoming it was agreed that the aircraft, which had now grown to seating some 300 passengers, was just too big, and a decision was made to scale it down.

The new design, the A300B, now no longer needed the big RB207 engine, and could use either the General Electric CF6-50 or Pratt & Whitney JT9D-15 engines, or indeed, Rolls-Royce's own RB211. In March 1969, and still with no orders, the British government decided that it could not continue financing the project, and withdrew. The French and German governments elected to continue with the programme, and signed an agreement on the 29 May 1969. Hawker Siddeley, elected to continue with the programme and signed an agreement, with Sud and Deutsche Airbus in June 1969, to design and manufacture the wings.

It was now that the Three-Eleven began to get attention from the British government who, against their own report into the industries, began to support an indigenous British transport aircraft. BAC had been receiving encouraging noises from a number of carriers who had visited the mock-up built at Weybridge, and commitments were placed by Laker, Court Line, Tarom and Bavaria. However, the company stated that they would need orders for fifty aircraft before they could proceed to production for an aircraft whose development costs were estimated to be at least £150 million. BAC were prepared to fund half of this themselves, with the balance being met by the government, and risk-sharing partners who included Shorts and Scottish Aviation. Talks were also held with Romanian, Yugoslavian and Polish companies, Boeing, and the Japanese, Italian and Dutch industries. Plans were drawn up for assembly of the aircraft at BAC's One-Eleven assembly site at Hurn, near Bournemouth. But just as the Labour administration appeared ready to give the project its support, the June 1970 general election and surprise Conservative win meant there was a whole new delay for the project, as the new government began to look at all its spending plans. In the meantime, components began to be cut on the project, the engineering mock-up was under construction and, at that year's Farnborough Air Show, BEA made a commitment to twenty aircraft. All that was remaining was a Treasury go-ahead.

Sadly, when the financial troubles of Rolls-Royce began to hit the equation, government money began to be required to keep the company afloat. In the late sixties, Rolls-Royce had been fighting to get its new RB211 on board one of the new American widebody jets. In its bid to achieve this, it offered a fixed price contract to supply engines to the Lockheed L1011 programme. This was all well and good and the deal was applauded as a major British export success, providing employment and making a large contribution to the balance of payments for the seventies and beyond. But all did not go well with the development of the RB211 engine, and when it had to be redesigned with added weight, the cost overruns could not be met, and so Rolls-Royce began to sink into the financial mire. In 1970 the situation became so bad that the government was forced to provide funds. For the Conservative party, whose election motto had been about no more lame ducks and less government control, Rolls-Royce proved to be the complete opposite, when money began to be pumped into the company at an alarming rate, just to keep it and all its major defence contracts afloat.

The main result of this occurred on 3 December 1970, when the government announced that, due to Rolls-Royce using up all available funds, they could not provide finance to cover the 50 per cent of total development costs of the Three-Eleven. At the same time, a Hawker Siddeley proposal to rejoin the Airbus and launch the B7 variant – which would have given the company design leadership – was also thwarted. So it was with that one decision, and due in most part to another company's financial mistakes, that Britain lost its last chance to design and build a new indigenous mainline transport.

On 4 February 1971, Rolls-Royce was declared bankrupt, and the non-interventionist government ended up having to nationalise the company in order for it, and its lucrative military and RB211 contracts, to continue. As was to occur on many occasions, both before and after this, the airframe sector of the British Industries was sacrificed at the expense of Rolls-Royce.

Length 183ft 7in, Span 147ft, Height 43ft 4in, Wing Area 2,713sq.ft

BAC Three-Eleven
Freddie (Now Sir Freddie) Laker was always a supporter of the British Aircraft Industry. With Laker Airways, he placed commitments on the Three-Eleven as well as the earlier Two-Eleven, and through British United Airways he launched the One-Eleven. (BAE SYSTEMS – via Brooklands Museum Trust)

Chapter 9

Car Ferries and Flying Boats

It can be seen that most of the projects put forward by British manufacturers until the sixties were to meet the requirements of the state carriers. However, a small number of other potential markets also opened up for the independent airlines, and these included the replacement for the Bristol Freighter Car Ferries.

Car Ferries

A historic date in British air travel was 13 July 1948, with the inauguration of Car Ferry services by the legendary Silver City Airways when the third prototype Bristol Freighter G-AGVC carried two cars and passengers between Lympne in England, and Le Touquet in France. Initially operated as a charter service, and then under association with BEA, the services proved so popular that they were later expanded to many European destinations. Services had begun using the Bristol 170 Mk21, which could carry two cars and twelve passengers. In 1953 these were supplemented by the 170 Mk32, which could accommodate three cars and twenty-three passengers. Meanwhile, a new airline, Air Charter, later Channel Air Bridge, had also been set up by Freddie (later Sir Freddie) Laker, to operate similar services radiating from Southend Airport. The age of the Car Ferry had arrived.

As the years progressed, both carriers would turn their attentions to what aircraft would eventually replace the ubiquitous and reliable 170, whose usage would be limited by the finite life and metal fatigue relating to the number of landings. At that time, there were no suitable aircraft available to handle such a requirement for a second generation ferry vehicle. Silver City Airways, for example, wanted a larger freight hold to accommodate up to ten cars or, in all-passenger configuration, up to 100 passengers. Channel Air Bridge's specification, issued later in 1959, called for a low-first-cost unsophisticated aircraft, with a 70ft-hold to accommodate five British cars and twenty-five passengers, a payload of 8 tons and with space for a toilet and galley. Both carriers agreed that any Freighter replacement must be faster and quieter.

Coincidentally, with this, the Air Ministry had issued a specification in 1955 for a medium-range freighter under OR323, which would be capable of carrying a load of 25,000lb, but which would also appeal to commercial operators. This led to a number of proposals submitted to meet this requirement, also being proposed as having Car Ferry capability.

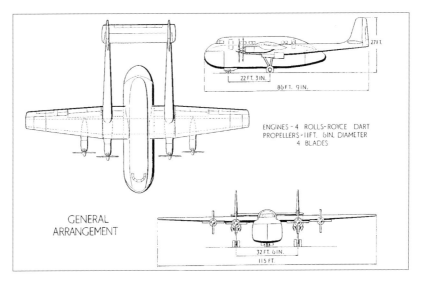

Armstrong Whitworth AW.670
Developed from the Armstrong Whitworth Argosy, the AW.670 could accommodate six cars,
with front and rear loading via clamshell doors. (BAE SYSTEMS)

Armstrong Whitworth AW.670/671

The AW.670/671 was a development of the high-wing twin-boom AW.650 Argosy. Powered by four Rolls-Royce Dart 526 engines, the 670 'Air Ferry's' major difference was an extended upper deck beyond the flight deck which could seat up to thirty passengers in two cabins, twenty ahead of the wing centre section and ten aft. The wider lower deck had a cross-section of 15ft, was 42ft long between doors, and 7ft high, and could accommodate six cars at two abreast, being accessed by front and rear clamshell doors, allowing direct drive on/drive off operation. The wing was slightly altered compared to the Argosy, with slightly shorter flaps and minor centre section modifications to cater for the wider fuselage. Designed specifically for short/medium routes, a capacity payload could be carried over stage lengths of 200 nautical miles. A further development of the 670 was the 126-seater AW.671 Airbus, whose lower deck was furnished for tourist-passenger operation, and could accommodate an additional ninety-six passengers, with light hand luggage, at eight-abreast seating in triple and paired units, with twin aisles. Both the 670 and 671 had a maximum take-off weight of 82,000lb, and a cruising speed of 239 knots. Silver City Airways was among a number of carriers who showed serious interest in the project in 1960.
(AW.670) Length 86ft 9in (AW.671) 86ft 75in, Span 115ft, Height 27ft, Wing Area 1,458sq.ft

Alongside the regular project were a number of studies by the Initial Projects Section of the Technical Department. One of these was a Car Ferry design, which may have been the AW.P23. This 1958 study was a high straight-wing design powered by two Rolls-Royce Dart engines, which could accommodate four cars and twenty-one passengers, or in all-passenger configuration, a maximum of seventy-two seats, with an AUW of 39,360lb.
Length 75ft, Span 92ft, Height 26ft, Wing Area 1,027sq.ft

Aviation Traders Low Wing Freighter ATL-95

Proposed in January 1956, the ATL95 was a dual-role development of the Accountant, to be either a military transport under the OR323 proposals, or a civil passenger/freighter with moderate pressurisation. Powered by two Rolls-Royce Dart RDa8 engines, or alternatively two Armstrong Siddeley Mamba P160 engines, with propellers of 12ft diameter, the design utilised the entire Accountant outer-wing, including fuel tanks and leading edges. The tail surfaces were increased in size while the undercarriage followed the Accountant design. Further savings were predicted by using as many hydraulic and electrical components from the sister aircraft as possible. Featuring two decks, the upper deck was moderately pressurised and circular in section, with an internal diameter of 9ft 4in, and a passenger cabin of 40ft 6in. This could accommodate forty passengers at four abreast. The lower compartment of rectangular section had an internal floor width of 9ft, and a clear height of 7ft 9in. At 46ft-long, this could accommodate three large cars loaded through a large rear ramp, or forty-five passengers in double and triple seating, with a forward freight hold of 760cu.ft. The maximum take-off weight was 52,000lb, and a payload of 9,190lb could be carried 1,500 nautical miles.

Fuselage Length 90ft 10in

Avro 772

The Avro 772 was proposed in January 1960 as a Car Ferry/passenger airliner. Three schemes were studied. Version A had seating for ninety passengers at eight abreast, with a single central aisle in a rectangular fuselage or six cars. Version B could accommodate six cars and twenty-five passengers, or ninety passengers at seven abreast, with two aisles, again within a rectangular fuselage. The final variant, Version C, was a pressurised design of semi-circular cross-section, which could carry six cars and twenty-five passengers, or ninety passengers, again at seven abreast with twin aisles. When in car-carrying mode, the twenty-five passengers were accommodated in a rear cabin with rear-facing seats, baggage area and toilet. Version C had the widest internal floor width, which was some 15ft 5in wide. All three designs were of high wing with a raised flight deck, and tailplane mounted on the rear fuselage, with front loading doors.

Fuselage Length (A) 82ft, (B) 86ft, (C) 87ft75in, Span 125ft 2in, Wing Area 1,200sq.ft

Armstrong Whitworth AW.670
An artist's impression of the
AW670, showing its high-wing and
twin-boom design.
(BAE SYSTEMS)

Blackburn Universal

Silver City Airways showed some early interest in the Universal, a civil derivative of the Beverley, which had an increased range. This could accommodate up to forty-two passengers at four abreast in the tail boom, with five motorcycles and six cars accommodated in the hold. Cars would have been loaded alternately on a two-tier arrangement with an electrically-driven screwjack lift raising the vehicles to the rail level, from where they would have been pushed and then locked into position. In all-passenger configuration, up to 160 passengers could be accommodated. A maximum gross weight of 127,000lb was proposed, with a maximum speed of 244mph. A payload of 45,700lb would have been carried over a range of 760 miles at 172 mph.

(Universal) Length 99ft 1in, Span 162ft, Height 33ft, Wing Area 2,916sq.ft

Bristol 179

Designed in September 1951, the 179 was a high-wing monoplane with twin booms for both civil and military operations, powered by two Hercules 272 engines. The aircraft featured a new wing design with the latest in flap technology permitting a higher weight take-off, retractable undercarriage and greater capacity for carrying fuel over the B170 Freighter. The hold of 41ft 3in was nearly 10ft longer than that of the 170 and, at a width of 8ft 10in, could accommodate sixty-eight passengers at five abreast. The aircraft's cruising speed was 190mph

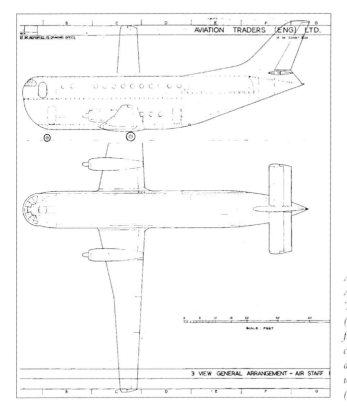

Aviation Traders (Engineering) ATL 95
The Aviation Traders (Engineering) ATL95 was derived from the earlier Accountant. It could carry three cars on its lower deck and forty passengers on the upper deck. (Aviation Traders (Engineering) Ltd)

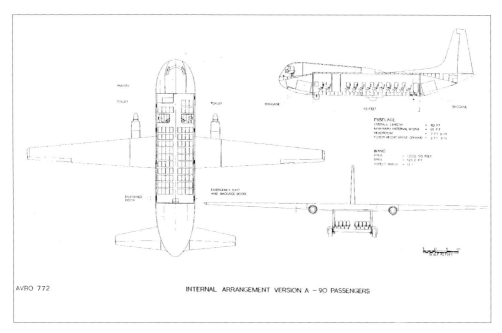

Avro 772
The Avro 772 was studied in three variants. Version A featured a rectangular fuselage, with provision for six cars or ninety passengers. (BAE SYSTEMS)

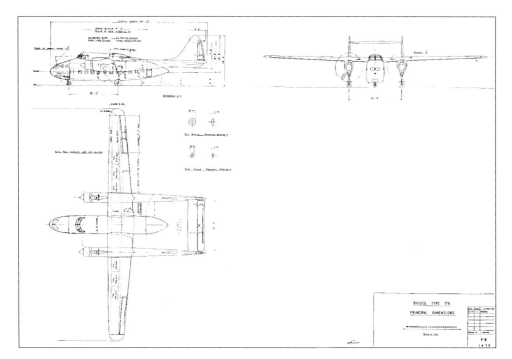

Bristol 179
Designed to replace the Bristol 170 freighter, the Type 179 was proposed in both commercial and military applications. (BAE SYSTEMS)

with a maximum range of 2,500 miles and a take-off and landing weight of 48,000lb. Many roles were envisaged for the aircraft, including Car Ferry accommodating two cars and twenty passengers, passenger-only aircraft, freighter, troop transport, paratrooper and air ambulance.
Length 84ft 3in, Span 120ft, Height 26ft 6in

Bristol 179A

Following on from the 179 in 1953, Bristol put forward the 179A, a completely new design featuring a high wing, single fin and retractable undercarriage, again powered by two Hercules engines, with a take-off weight of 48,800lb, a range of 2,140 miles, and a cruising speed of 190mph. To retain the low speed characteristics of the 170, the 179A was fitted with double-slotted flaps and reversible propellers. Freight was to be loaded via a rear-loading door beneath the upswept rear fuselage. This was made to open outwards to provide an aperture as large as the cross-sectional area of the hold, to allow for the dropping of military stores. Again suitable for a variety of roles, the 179A could accommodate two cars and ten passengers, or a maximum of sixty passengers at five abreast, in a hold with a maximum width of 9ft.
Length 83ft 6in, Span 125ft, Height 32ft

Bristol 216

Proposed in 1959, the 216 designed for Silver City Airways was to have been undertaken as a joint venture with Breguet of France. The high-wing design was very similar to the earlier Bristol 179A, but with a raised flight deck à la Carvair. Power was to be provided by two Rolls-Royce Dart engines, and the maximum take-off weight was 64,000lb, with provision for six cars and their passengers. It would have a cruising speed of less than 300mph. After the formation of BAC, the 216 was dropped.
Span 140ft

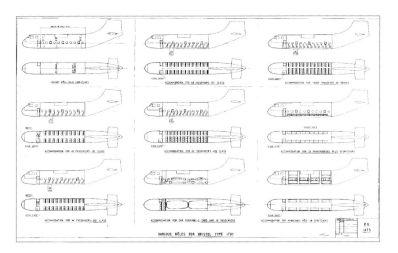

Bristol 179A
The Bristol 179A was a new high-wing design, with various roles, including
Car Ferry, all-passenger and military transport. (BAE SYSTEMS)

Handley Page HP.R8
An artist's impression of the Handley Page (Reading), HP.R8, showing the clamshell front doors with space for six cars at two abreast. (Imperial War Museum London: Negative No. HP.322)

De Havilland

De Havilland undertook a design study for a Silver City Car Ferry in 1960. It featured a high wing and was powered by two turboprops. The cockpit was located above the freight hold with provision for passengers in the rear fuselage. The tailplane was mounted midway on the fin. The project was never a serious study and was not allocated a de Havilland project number.

Handley Page (Reading) HP.R8

One of the most in-depth Car Ferry studies was carried out at the old Miles factory at Woodley under the aegis of the HP.R8 project. Put forward in 1959, the HP.R8 used much of the Herald structure, with the basic mainplane retained with a new parallel chord centre-section plus strength modifications, and an enlarged tail unit. The nose undercarriage was now non-retractable, and power was provided by Rolls-Royce Dart RDa7 engines. A flattened oval section fuselage was proposed, with clamshell doors at the front. The new car deck was 15ft wide and 45ft 6in long, with provision being made for six cars, with thirty passengers carried in the rear fuselage. The flight deck was located above the freight hold.

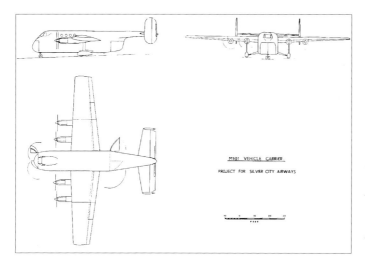

Miles M.101
Proposed to Silver City
Airways in 1953, the M.101
(later called 102) was powered
by four Rolls-Royce Dart
engines. (Miles Aircraft – via
Grahame Gates)

A maximum weight of 53,800lb was estimated, with a cruising speed of 210mph with a range of 500 miles. In all-passenger configuration, the HP.R8 could accommodate up to 100 passengers at eight abreast, with an observation lounge at the front of the fuselage with bar area. Models of the project were exhibited at the Farnborough Air Show in 1960, with a unit price of £250,000 being quoted. At the time Silver City Airways were taking quite a considerable interest in the project.

Length 82ft 2in, Span 120ft, Wing Area 1,176sq.ft

Miles M.101/M.102

Initially called the 101, this was later adjusted to the 102 after the connotations of the R101 Airship. The M.102 was proposed to Silver City Airways in August 1953, and could carry six cars and their respective passengers, who were accommodated in a cabin some 19ft long and 12ft wide, which was located behind the flight deck and above the freight hold. A maximum all-up weight of 55,000lb was quoted, with power provided by four Rolls-Royce Dart 605 engines of 1,400shp providing a maximum speed of 220mph, or cruising speed of 200mph. The design of mid-wing featured twin fins and clamshell doors at both the front and rear of the aircraft. The fixed undercarriage was supported by struts extending from the inner engine cowlings.

Length 89ft 6in, Span 110ft, Height 24ft, Wing Area 1,760sq.ft

Shorts PD16

The PD16 was a high-wing unpressurised monoplane with twin fins carried from the wings on booms, a single tailplane, and fuselage suspended from the wings by four fixing points. Designed primarily as an economical freighter, variants were considered to accommodate up to eighty passengers, or thirty-two passengers together with six vehicles. A number of different configurations were made, including Pi tail, beaver tail, tadpole tail and twin boom, with a part cabin mock-up built. Like most of the other Car Ferry designs, the flight deck was positioned above the forward main hold with large clamshell doors at both the front and

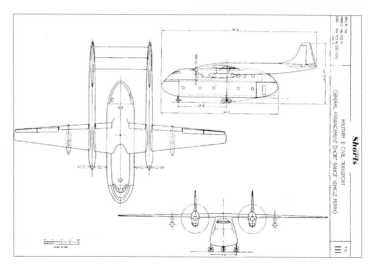

*Short PD16
General arrangement of the
short-range vehicle ferry
variant of the Short
PD16, showing the
extended upper deck.
(Courtesy of Bombardier
Aerospace – via RAF
Museum Hendon)*

back for loading/unloading freight, and with a maximum internal diameter at floor level of 14ft 6in. Power was to be provided by two Bristol Proteus engines, which were to be later replaced by Bristol BE25, Napier Eland 4 or Rolls-Royce Tyne. In the Car Ferry version, the upper deck was extended beyond the flight deck, and featured an enlarged fuselage which could seat thirty-two passengers at four abreast, with toilet. The dedicated passenger variant featured a semi-circular fuselage with seating for eighty passengers at six abreast, with toilets and galley, and underfloor freight holds, and had an all-up weight of 69,000lb.

(Car Ferry Variant) Length 90ft, Span 122ft 72in, Height 34ft

(All-passenger variant) Length 87ft 2in, Span 122ft 72in, Height 29ft

Vickers Car Ferry

Put forward to meet OR323 in 1956, the Vickers Type 799 was a high-wing design powered by either two Tyne or four Dart turboprops with a raised cockpit. Up to thirty-six passengers would be housed in a side cabin at two abreast, alongside accommodation for eight cars.

Length 106ft, Span 140ft, Height 34ft

The replacement for the Bristol 170 Freighter threw up the financial costs of developing an aircraft which would very specifically meet the requirements, in the first instance, of only two carriers – Silver City Airways and Channel Air Bridge. The specification originally drawn up by Silver City attracted quotations from a number of aircraft manufacturers, but they were requiring orders for at least twenty aircraft to keep costs down – which was a higher number than the market could afford at that time. Channel Air Bridge opted for a proposal from sister company Aviation Traders (Engineering) Ltd, to convert DC4s into car/passenger carrying aircraft – with the ability to provide a hold of some 69ft, accommodating twenty-four passengers, and which was faster than the 170. The resulting Aviation Traders (Engineering) ATL98 Carvair was ordered by CAB to the tune of ten aircraft, with a further eleven built for other carriers. In 1960, Channel Air Bridge became part of the new British United Airways Group, with Silver City Airways also becoming part of the group in 1962. When the

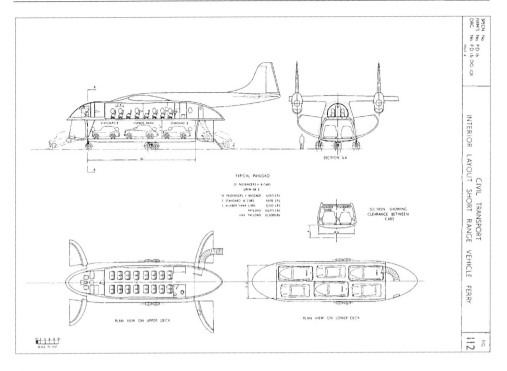

Short PD16
The interior layout of the PD16 shows provision for six cars on the lower deck, and thirty-two passengers on the
upper deck. (Courtesy of Bombardier Aerospace – via RAF Museum Hendon)

two operations were merged, in July of that year, to form British United Air Ferries, the new
Carvair fleet gradually replaced that of the 170.

In 1966, Aviation Traders investigated studies of Carvair derivatives of both the Douglas
DC6 and DC7. The development of the latter was given the name Carvair 7. Both featured
extended upper decks (a study which had first been carried out when the original ATL98
Carvair was studied) and were powered by Rolls-Royce Dart RDa10 Mk542 engines driving
Dowty reversing propellers. With an extended upper deck, accommodation would be
provided for twenty passengers with toilet and galley, with six cars being carried in the freight
hold, or five cars and an additional thirty-forty passengers in a rear compartment, again with
galley and toilet. Sadly, the company could not justify the cost of these developments.

Flying Boats

At the war's cessation, air transport was no longer the preserve of the rich, who would
be flown in slow transports in the utmost luxury cruise liner style. Speed was now becoming
essential. However, the lure of flying passengers in the lap of luxury was still a powerful
design force, and a number of companies still aspired to make new flying liners for the fifties
and beyond. The history of the Saunders Roe Princess, of which three aircraft were built
but only one flown, is well documented, but there were a number of other projects
put forward.

Blackburn B-49 Clydesman

The last passenger flying boat design study by Blackburn, the B-49, came outside the recommendations of the Brabazon Committee, but around the same time as the Saunders Roe Princess. Envisaged as a high-wing all-metal monoplane with single fin and rudder, power was to be from six Rolls-Royce Clyde 1s with six bladed Rotol contra-rotating propellers of 14ft diameter. An early variant had retractable wing floats, and was also designed as a cargo carrier with two fuselage top hatches fore and aft of the wing centre section. Accommodation was provided for 160 passengers over a range of 2,500 miles at a mean cruising speed of 269mph, and a gross weight of 310,000lb. A maximum speed of 307mph was quoted at an absolute ceiling of 20,000ft. Another design saw seating for eighty-five passengers on the lower deck, with the upper deck for freight and crew rooms.
Length 148'ft, Span 202ft, Wing Area 5,000sq.ft

Saben-Hart

Saben-Hart were a London-based firm of consultants who operated an Aircraft division at Bournemouth. The company studied the trends that were occurring in freighters, and firstly looked at the transport of oil across the world's trouble-spots, but, when this was rejected on economic grounds, attention turned towards the transport of bulk items. The company did not have the staff to undertake detailed design of the projects or manufacture, but the studies certainly aroused interest.

Two projects were put forward in 1957. The Freighter study was a monster of an aircraft of high-wing design, with a span of 476ft, and loading doors forward and under the rudder. Power was to be provided by turboprops of 25,000–27,000shp, probably Pratt & Whitney, with a payload of 1,000,000lb. The airliner study featured a skate type hull and was powered by large turbojets mounted within the swept wing of 325ft span. It was envisaged that up to 1,800 passengers would be accommodated within a fuselage with no windows.

The project failed to progress as at least £20 million was required to fund construction of a prototype, production of which would have had to be undertaken by an established manufacturer willing to undertake such a mammoth project. Despite this, some interest in the project was shown by at least one shipping company, and by the Dutch airline KLM.

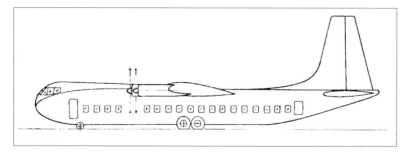

Vickers Car Ferry
The Vickers Type 799 Car Ferry was proposed in either twin Tyne- or four Dart-powered variants. (BAE SYSTEMS – via Brooklands Museum Trust)

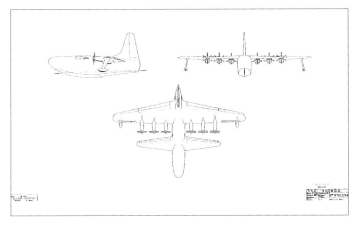

Blackburn B-49B
The Blackburn B-49
Clydesman was the
company's last passenger
flying boat. The B-49B, as
shown, was an alternative
proposal showing an unusual
design layout. (BAE
SYSTEMS)

Saunders Roe

One of the most famous names in British flying boat history, Saunders Roe had been engaged in many studies since 1945. The majority of these were developments of the Princess, including landplane, stretched and jet variants. However, two other serious designs did emerge from Cowes.

P135 Duchess

Designed by Henry Knowler, first details of the Duchess were revealed in Aeroplane magazine in May 1950. Saunders Roe had investigated a number of previous proposals, including the P123, powered by either Centaurus pistons or Proteus turbines, and the P131, the design of which was supplanted by the definitive P135. The premise of the design was to achieve the maximum economy in operation over stages of between 1,300 and 2,000 miles. The all-metal medium-range Duchess was to be capable of cruising at 500mph, with a flight crew of four plus two cabin crew servicing seventy-four passengers, with 66lbs of baggage per passenger and 3,500lb freight inside a pressurised cabin, although a maximum level speed of 550mph was envisaged. Power was by six de Havilland Ghost engines, with three in each wing root between the spars. In order to achieve the high critical Mach number required, the thicker root section was swept back more severely than the outer portion, while stabilising floats retracted to the extreme tip of the wing, their profile drag offset by their beneficial effect on aspect ratio of wing. Using SBAC standard methods for assessing direct operating costs, it would have been the most economical medium-range airliner in the world at that time. The all-up-weight was put at 130,000lb. One carrier particularly interested in a jet-flying boat was Tasman Empire Airways – who held serious talks with the company in 1950.
Length 124ft 6in, Span 135ft 6in

P192

A gargantuan of an aircraft, the P192, was proposed after a consultant for the shipping line P&O wanted to investigate an enormous 1,000-seater airliner with accommodation similar to that

Saunders Roe P192
This impression of the
massive Saunders Roe P192
shows off the twenty-four
Rolls-Royce Conway engines
mounted in the wing. (GKN
Aerospace Services)

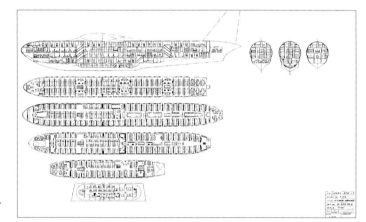

Saunders Roe P192
With accommodation on five
decks, the Saunders Roe
P192 could carry up to
1,000 passengers and freight.
(GKN Aerospace Services)

provided inside a luxury liner. Easily the largest aircraft ever seriously designed in Britain, the P192 was enormous in every aspect: it was twice as long as the Boeing 757, and had a wing span nearly half that again of the Boeing 747. The fuselage was of constant diameter, being some 33ft across, and the design also featured two large 'v' tails. Power was to be provided by twenty-four Rolls-Royce Conway engines of 18,500lb thrust, which were positioned within huge delta wings mounted above the fuselage – wings which were in fact large enough to accommodate engineers who could have stood up inside them to carry out maintenance work. The accommodation was laid out over five decks to enable passengers to eat and sleep on board, with lounges and bars. It included some fifty-three toilets and, like a ship, a pursers office.

The flight deck, or control deck, was of immense proportions, more akin to a luxury liner. Designed for the then all-important Australian route, it was envisaged that, like the great liners, passengers would take-off from Southampton Water and then stop in Fanara, Karachi, Calcutta (for a halfway stop), Singapore, and Darwin, before arriving in Sydney some forty-eight hours later. The legs between Karachi and Calcutta, and Singapore and Darwin, were designed for sleep periods, while at the other stops, refuelling would have taken place while meals were served. The all-up weight of this massive design was 1,500,000lb.

Length 318ft, Span 313ft, Height 88ft

Shorts Projects

Short S.A7/S.46

This was a small high-wing flying boat powered by two Cougar engines. The cockpit was raised slightly higher than the passenger cabin, which could accommodate up to fifteen passengers at three abreast, with small buffet, toilet and rear baggage compartment.
Length 58ft 2in, Span 82ft, Height 22ft 10in, Wing Area 666sq.ft

Short S.A8/S.47

The S.A8/S.47 design, developed from the Shetland, was a four Napier Nomad compound engined high-wing double-bubble fuselage design, providing accommodation on two pressurised decks for up to fifty-two day passengers, and which could cruise at 20–25,000ft. The unswept wing featured a light tapered box-spar construction. The upper deck featured a large flight deck, providing for the pilots, radio operator, navigator and engineer, together with four crew rest chairs and a staircase to the lower freight hold. Accommodation was provided on the upper deck for eighteen passengers, with toilets and bar together with dining compartments, a galley and forward freight hold. The lower deck provided for thirty-four passengers at four-abreast seating, together with a library and freight holds at front and rear. The Shetland hull's 12ft6in-beam was retained. A landplane variant was also proposed for BOAC's LRE Specification.
Length 118ft 6in, Span 160ft, Wing Area 2,262sq.ft

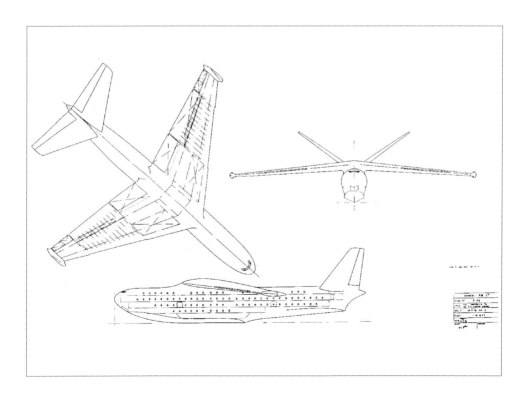

Opposite: *Saunders Roe P192*
The Saunders Roe P192 flying
boat, showing off the V-tail layout.
(GKN Aerospace Services)

Right: *Saunders Roe Duchess*
The elegant Saunders Roe Duchess
was designed by Henry Knowler for
the medium-range routes.
(GKN Aerospace Services)

Below: *Saunders Roe Princess*
Only one Saunders Roe Princess
G-ALUN ever flew. The other two
aircraft built were cocooned at
Calshot, before all three were
scrapped. (GKN Aerospace Services)

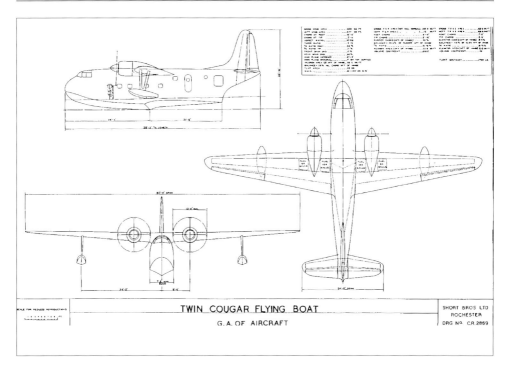

Short S.A7
Short S.A7/S.46 fifteen-seater Twin Cougar flying boat. (Courtesy of Bombardier Aerospace)

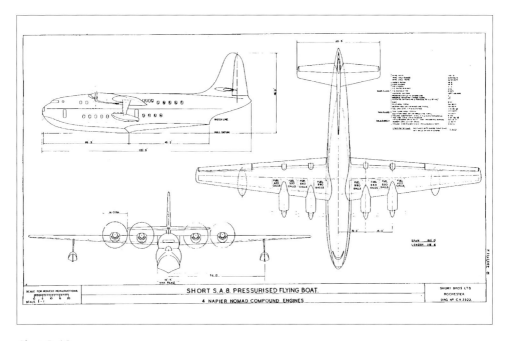

Short S.A8
The four Napier Nomad-powered Short S.A8/S.47 pressurised flying boat. (Courtesy of Bombardier Aerospace)

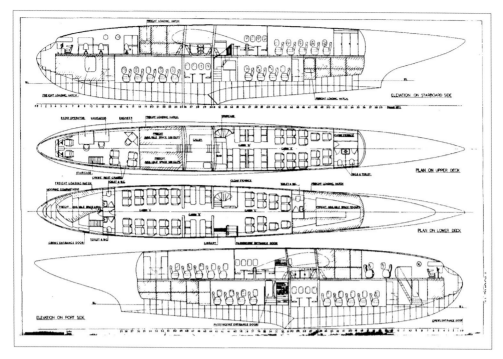

Short S.A8
Interior layout of the twin-decked Short S.A8/S.47. (Courtesy of Bombardier Aerospace)

Other Shorts Studies

Long Stage Empire Flying Boat

The long stage flying boat from 1946 provided provision for up to 106 passengers in day/night configuration, over two decks. The upper deck contained ten cabins together with dressing rooms and toilets, and two promenades and a galley were situated in the centre of the aircraft below the high wing. The cockpit was also located on the upper deck, with additional captain's cabin and crew's dressing room. In addition to the two pilots, provision was made for an engineer, navigator and WT operator. Two staircases led down to the lower deck, where daytime seating was provided in cabins, together with toilets, dressing rooms and cocktail bar. The freight holds at the front and rear provided 575cu.ft and 794cu.ft of storage space respectively. The high-wing design was powered by eight engines unspecified (probably Perseus), and was probably a development of the S.30 Long-Range Empire boat.
Hull Length 152ft, Span 232ft

Hercules Twin-Engined Flying Boat

This twin-engined Hercules flying boat was one of the last designs proposed from Rochester, and provided accommodation for up to twenty passengers at three abreast, in a design similar to the S.A7, again with a raised flight deck.

Chapter 10

The Seventies and Beyond
Collaboration Looms

1970 was to prove a difficult year for the British Aircraft Industry – two companies of vital importance made untimely exits from the world stage. The collapse of both Beagle (in the private aircraft sector) and then Handley Page (once one of the most powerful names in British aviation) within the space of six months, were the precursors to the final nail in the coffin that occurred at the end of the year. The financial woes of Rolls-Royce – possibly the most famous British company in the world – were ultimately to lead to the cancellation of the BAC Three-Eleven, and a refusal to rejoin the Airbus programme as a full partner. The early part of the following year then began with the bankruptcy of Rolls-Royce. It was no wonder that the British commercial aircraft industry was forced to re-examine itself with regards to both its current and, more importantly, future position. It was also becoming evident that in all but the smallest of transports, international collaboration was becoming the order of the day. This was nothing new – besides Concorde and the original Airbus studies, Britain's aircraft manufacturers had been involved in talks on many earlier joint projects. BAC had discussions on the original CL-1011 (Tristar) and the proposed Japanese YS33 jet transport, Hawker Siddeley held talks on a joint feederliner with VFW-Fokker, as did Shorts, who were already risking sharing partners with Fokker on the F28 Fellowship. However, at the same time as these collaborative studies were being undertaken, indigenous British projects were still continuing to be designed. As the seventies progressed, the climate changed dramatically. Rising inflation and increasing development costs made collaborative projects become the norm. Those projects, then on British drawing boards, were to remain purely design studies.

The joint decision by the new Conservative administration on 3 December 1970 not to back the Three-Eleven, and not to rejoin the Airbus A300B programme as a full partner (with design leadership on the proposed A300B7 for Hawker Siddeley), meant that with one cut of the knife, Britain was to be excluded from potentially the most important aircraft market of the next decade – the new subsonic short-/medium-range widebody transport.

How different it had all seemed just a year and a half earlier, when the world's major airlines were visiting BAC Weybridge to view the Three-Eleven mock-up, and Hawker Siddeley were still the major partner with Sud on the A300B programme. While it is true that Hawker Siddeley continued to be involved as a major subcontractor on the A300B (a foresight by the company using its own money that was to prove invaluable ten years later when Britain rejoined the group), the company was no longer a full partner. This meant that they had no direct say in the project, nor did the British equipment sector receive the potential major contracts that it might otherwise have expected to. With just one decision, taken in order to save Rolls-Royce, the blue-eyed boy of Whitehall, and to maintain the increasingly expensive Concorde programme, Britain's ability to design and build major transport aircraft was sacrificed.

The options open to the industry as 1971 advanced were few, with the hopes and new projects of the previous year now evaporated. The two major airframe contractors, BAC and Hawker Siddeley, were forced to re-examine their existing transport aircraft lines, while Shorts had now given up designs for larger based airliners, and instead turned their attention to larger developments of their Skyvan light aircraft.

For BAC, this now meant a far heavier dependency on the One-Eleven and its new variants, the series 475 and 500. Sadly, the aircraft was already losing out in the big new orders to Boeing and McDonnell Douglas, and only a trickle of small contracts were obtained during the seventies, despite numerous attempts to get new stretched variants launched, including the original series 700 with refanned Spey engines. At one time the line stopped altogether, and yet this was to be the project that kept BAC's Commercial Aircraft Division afloat. The Concorde programme, now with some seventy-four options, had yet to see any of these intentions converted into firm orders, and clouds were already beginning to gather ominously.

BAC QSTOL
The cancellation of the Three-Eleven saw BAC turn their attention towards a smaller airliner, the result of which was QSTOL (quiet short take-off and landing), which was revealed at the 1971 Paris Air Show.
(BAE SYSTEMS)

For a short while in the early seventies, it appeared that the VC10 line might be resurrected. In 1971, BAC studied a new stretched twin RB211 variant with seating for over 200 passengers. The VC10 had already been used as a test bed for RB211 flight testing in 1970. Meanwhile, with China not wanting to purchase American jets, a proposal was made by BAC in early 1973, following discussions in late 1972 on recommencing production of the Super VC10. Under this offer, BAC proposed that twenty aircraft would be supplied complete from the British assembly line – the first of these, thirty-nine months from the start of the programme. The remaining nineteen aircraft would then follow, with one aircraft every two months. In addition to this, BAC would also supply ten sets of components for the remaining ten aircraft, which would be assembled in China, with the first flying sixty-seven months after the start of the project. Subsequently, BAC was willing to discuss further production of the Super VC10 in China beyond the original thirty aircraft. Sadly, neither the RB211 scheme or a licence production deal with China materialised, and CAAC did end up operating Boeing 707 aircraft. The failure of this deal saw the last indigenous attempt by a British company to continue production of a long-range jetliner.

Hawker Siddeley were faring little better. Its major commercial project, the Trident, was only being kept alive by production for BEA until China placed the first of what eventually became thirty-five orders for the type in 1971. This sustained production at Hatfield at a steady, if very low production rate until 1978. Meanwhile, at the smaller end of the scale, the company continued to try to launch a new feederliner, first with the HS144, and then, with the collapse of Rolls-Royce and cancellation of the Trent engine, the ALF502-powered HS146. In order to maintain existing production levels, turnover and staff, it was vital for both companies that new projects be launched.

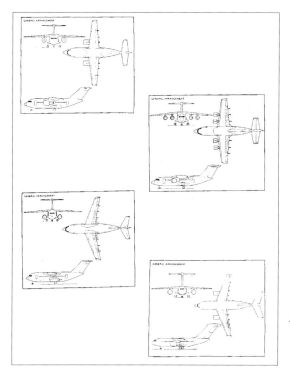

Europlane
Four of the early studies carried out by the Europlane consortium had capacities ranging from, from top to bottom: 60, 80, 118 to 173 seats, powered by either two or four engines. (BAE SYSTEMS – via Brooklands Museum Trust)

BAC Projects

QSTOL

At the Paris Air Show in May 1971, BAC revealed details of what was hoped would be its new commercial airliner, QSTOL (quiet short take-off and landing) which directly led on from the company's STOL project. QSTOL was to be an all-new aircraft of simple design with an AUW of 126,530lb, an unswept wing with high-efficiency flap systems with no blown flaps, a swept fin, and high-mounted tailplane. Accommodation was provided for a maximum of 140 passengers in a widebody, eight-abreast fuselage with 30in-pitch in a 2+3+2 layout, (or 108 seats at 34in pitch at 2+2+2), with an in-service date of 1977/78.

Power was to be provided by four Rolls-Royce/SNECMA M45S (RB410) turbofan engines of 14,525lb thrust, with variable pitch, mounted in pylons beneath the wing-leading edge. The airliner was designed to offer high standards of performance combined with passenger attractions for sophisticated markets. The high unswept wing design, with full-span leading edge slats and 75 per cent semi-span multi-slotted trailing edge flaps, enabled good operating capabilities. QSTOL could carry 108 passengers over a range of 500 nautical miles, or two successive 200 nautical-mile sectors without refuelling, with take-off-and-landing field lengths of 2,000ft, and an estimated cruising speed of 500mph. For STOL operation, BAC paid particular attention to landing with a shock absorber stroke of up to 36in enabling the higher rate of descent to be cushioned for passengers. BAC, however, now realised that any new project would require government funding and, in the climate permeating at that time, collaboration with companies from other countries would be required, so discussions were opened up with potential partners.

Length 110ft 4in, Span 114ft 6in, Height 38ft 6in

Europlane

Superseding BAC's solo effort was the establishment of Europlane between MBB of Germany, Saab-Scania of Sweden and BAC, at Weybridge in February 1972. It was set up to investigate future studies for the development of a quiet take-off and landing airliner. The studies that emanated from these discussions resulted in a number of different schemes being proposed, from earlier independent projects from the partner companies of 70- to 100-seater aircraft, to larger projects seating up to 200, with varying engine configurations. Later in September 1972, CASA of Spain joined the group, with each company then holding a 25 per cent stake in the new concern. At the Farnborough Air Show of 1972, four different design studies were revealed which showed various sized aircraft, from 60 to 180 seats, all featuring a high-wing layout. Many engine options were considered, including twin- and four-engine studies using the Rolls-Royce RB211, RB220 and M45S (RB410 and 415) to the CF34, ALF502 and T55. Studies were also undertaken on possible freighter variants. Presentations were made to the four respective governments, with the definitive Europlane project being revealed at the 1973 Paris Air Show. The new design was a 180- to 200-seater at seven-abreast, low-wing widebody with a two-lobe fuselage, rear-mounted engines and a T-tail. The aircraft would have been powered by either Rolls-Royce RB211 engines or General Electric CF6 engines of 40,000lb thrust for

Europlane
An artist's impression of the definitive Europlane airliner as proposed by BAC, with Saab, MBB and CASA.
(BAE SYSTEMS – via Brooklands Museum Trust)

short-/medium-range routes, over a range of 500 miles, from 4,000ft runways, with an AUW of 242,500lb. The option was also made for a range of up to 2,300 miles from a runway of 5,600ft. The engines were mounted high on the rear fuselage, giving maximum advantage of vortex shielding, with underwing, overwing and rear-mounted engines, and low tailplane designs ruled out. Forward noise was shielded by the wing (which used aerodynamics derived from the Three-Eleven) while rearward arc noise was reduced by the use of a full-length cowl and acoustic treatment. At all three measuring points, Europlane was designed to be at least 10 EPNdN below FAR Part 36. The engines chosen were designed for future growth and, combined with the rear-engined high-tailplane layout, this would have enabled Europlane to grow in both range and size. It was anticipated that a full go-ahead, given in 1974, would have enabled a first flight in 1977, and entry into service in 1978/79. Launch costs were put at £200 million.

For a number of reasons, Europlane never quite seemed real. MBB was already heavily involved in the A300B Airbus project (as were CASA), and Aerospatiale, the other major Airbus partner, could see that the Europlane project had, in the design, stretch potential, which would find it competing with the Airbus. The latter part of 1973 was also not a good time to be launching any new airliner, with rising fuel costs, spiralling inflation and

impending recession. The enormous cost of launching any new airliner, especially a completely new large transport such as Europlane, could not be justified, so, at the end of 1973, the project was put into abeyance for six months. However, as history records, the project was not revived during 1974, when Europe's thoughts turned to the Group of Six.
Length 157ft 4in, Span 124ft 6in, Height 42ft, Wing Area 2,066sq.ft

Hawker Siddeley

HS147

Alongside the HS141 VTOL project were studies undertaken at Hatfield on STOL airliners, under the type HS147. These were studies for a 100-seater fan-lift aircraft travelling at 530mph, and able to operate from 2,000ft field lengths, with a range of 610 miles. Many configurations were studied, including low wing and high wings, with two- and four-propulsion engines using the HS141 fuselage. One such study was powered by two Rolls-Royce RB202 fan-lift engines installed in semi-sponsons at the wing trailing edge to give optimum lift augmentation, with a further two quiet propulsion units mounted on underwing pylons. Other STOL studies included similar sized projects with high wings and mechanical flaps powered by RB410s, externally blown flap aircraft powered by four Rolls-Royce engines of 16,180lb thrust, an augmentor wing powered by four Rolls-Royce RB419s and a low-wing fan-lift design with rear-mounted engines.
Length 120ft 10in, Span 106ft 10in, Height 37ft 3in

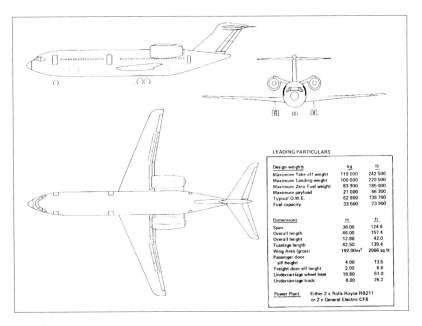

LEADING PARTICULARS

Design weights	kg	lb
Maximum Take-off weight	110 000	242 500
Maximum Landing weight	100 000	220 500
Maximum Zero Fuel weight	83 900	185 000
Maximum payload	21 000	46 300
Typical O.W.E.	62 900	138 700
Fuel capacity	33 500	73 900

Dimensions	m	ft
Span	38.00	124.6
Overall length	48.00	157.4
Overall height	12.80	42.0
Fuselage length	42.50	139.4
Wing Area (gross)	192.00m^2	2066 sq ft
Passenger door sill height	4.00	13.5
Freight door sill height	2.00	6.6
Undercarriage wheel base	18.60	61.0
Undercarriage track	8.00	26.2

Power Plant   Either 2 x Rolls-Royce RB211
or 2 x General Electric CF6

Europlane
Europlane owed a lot to BAC's earlier rear-engined Three-Eleven project, although the engines were now mounted high on the rear fuselage. (BAE SYSTEMS – via Brooklands Museum Trust)

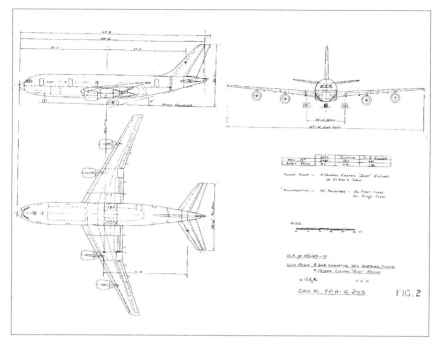

Hawker Siddeley HS149
Hawker Siddeley proposed the HS149 in 1971, a four-engined derivative of the A300B.
(BAE SYSTEMS)

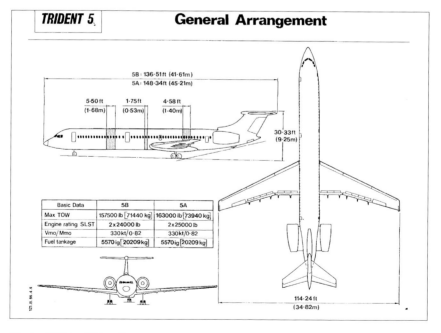

Hawker Siddeley Trident 5
With a redesigned wing, stretched fuselage and two CFM56 engines, the Trident 5 was Hawker
Siddeley's proposal to meet the Type B Specification of the Group of Six. (BAE SYSTEMS)

Airbus Derivatives

Although no longer a main partner in the Airbus consortium, Hawker Siddeley put considerable effort into various developments of the main A300B. As probably the most experienced commercial aircraft builder associated with the programme this was hardly surprising, and many of the company's schemes proved invaluable to Airbus with later projects. The first designs, the HS142 and HS143, were, respectively, short- and long-range A300B variants.

The HS148 was a RTOL (reduced take-off and landing) A300B development put forward in 1971 for a BEA specification for a 200-seater airliner with an in-service date of 1978. The HS148 had a range of 1,000-1,200 miles, with an AUW of 250,000lb. Power was to be provided by two Rolls-Royce RB211-24 engines of 45,000lb thrust. The design featured a modified wing of reduced sweepback with new high-lift devices, as well as increased thickness and aspect ratio to improve low speed performance, although it was noted that this created a penalty in cruise speed.
Length 167ft 11in, Span 144ft, Height 42ft 9in, Wing Area 2,600sq.ft

A further A300B derivative was the 1971 HS149 long-range jetliner, powered by four General Electric 'quiet' engines of 27,500lb thrust. Two main design proposals emerged: the HS149-06 provided seating for 195 mixed-class passengers, or 261 in an inclusive-tour layout at eight abreast, while the HS149-07 accommodated 181 in mixed layout and 237 in inclusive-tour configuration. Main differences between the project and the A300B were a shortened nose and main gear with an increased main gear tyre size, combined with the wing of the proposed A300B7 variant. The wing structural box was increased by one frame pitch with an 8ft 6in wing root insert. Outer flaps were deleted and the inboard leading edge modified with a 1ft 6in wing tip extension.
(HS149-06) Length 170ft 8in, Span 167ft, Height 52ft, Wing Area 3,485sq.ft

None of the above Hawker Siddeley projects were ever intended to be undertaken solely by the company. Instead, they were to be incorporated into future studies by Airbus Industries and, indeed, much of the HS149 emerged through the TA11 project finally to fly as the A340.

Trident Projects

Throughout the early seventies, Hawker Siddeley continued to study VSTOL, RTOL and STOL derivatives of the Trident airliner, alongside the HS141. The STOL project included adapted Trident 2 designs seating 109 passengers over a range of 800 miles, with take-off and landing distances of between 3,500 and 4,000ft with an additional six RB202s in pods, or four RB162s in sponsons. A study was also made of a Trident 1C STOL demonstrator aircraft, with two GE lift-fans of 13,650lb thrust, Trident 2E wing tips and a low speed aileron based on the first prototype Trident design. The RTOL Trident was to be powered by two Rolls-Royce RB211 engines, and would operate from 3,000ft-runways, with accommodation for up to 200 passengers.

Alongside these developments were stretched and re-engined variants. Four Trident developments were looked at in detail: the 3B with two 10-ton engines (CFM56), a twinjet powered by CFM56s with a stretched fuselage and centre section, a stretched fuselage twin with new wing based on technology from the A300B and a tri-jet powered by re-fanned Speys with stretched fuselage and centre section.

In July 1975, a proposal was made to British Airways under the Trident 4 legend. This development featured two rear-mounted CFM 56 engines eliminating the centre engine intake, combined with a stretched fuselage. The model 4A was lengthened by 20in. Other changes included a wing of reduced sweep with increased area and span, with Fowler-type flaps. The Trident 1 rudder was utilised, and there was to be improved silencing of the RB162 booster engine. Further developments included the 4B, which was stretched by an additional 13ft 6in, with leading edge slats and centre section fuel, and the double-bubble 4E seating up to 155 passengers.
(Trident 4B) Length 146ft, Span 125ft 2in, Height 31ft

CAST And The Group Of Six

As a response to the BAC Europlane consortium, Hawker Siddeley, under the guise of CAST (Civil Aircraft Study Team), with VFW-Fokker and Dornier, set up a rival grouping in 1972 to investigate a family of future quiet airliners, with bases at Hatfield and Bremen. The design groups studied airliners with many different configurations, from narrowbody to widebody,

BAC One-Eleven 800
BAC's series 800 development of the One-Eleven saw the Spey engines replaced by CFM56s, and the fuselage stretched by over 32ft, to accommodate up to 161 passengers. (BAE SYSTEMS – via Brooklands Museum Trust)

and powered by two, three or four engines, including 10 'tonners', and the M45H to replace the 737 and DC9, and be available by the early eighties. Although no definitive design ever emerged from the grouping, unlike Europlane, one proposal from 1974 showed a low-wing narrowbody design powered by two underwing 10-ton engines.

The setting up of EURAC, more commonly known as the Group of Six, was announced at the 1974 Farnborough Air Show. This was a European study team consisting of the major European aircraft companies – BAC and Hawker Siddeley from Britain, Aerospatiale of France, Dornier and MBB from Germany and the Dutch/German combination, VFW-Fokker. These companies announced that they had signed an agreement to 'work together in order to meet the European airline requirements for the 1980s. The new group encompassed earlier project work undertaken by these companies through Europlane and CAST. These efforts became more apparent after the three major European airlines, British Airways, Air France and Lufthansa, issued a common specification for a new 200-seater airliner. The new grouping identified two major market slots, the Type A for a 170- to 210-seater and Type B for more than 110 seats. In 1975 it was decided that the best course for both projects was for them to be derivatives of an existing aircraft. In the case of the 200-seater needed by the three major carriers, the only option was for a cutback A300, while for the smaller type variants of the Trident and One-Eleven alongside a new design, the Aerospatiale A200, were looked at. When the group finally embraced the French company Dassault, becoming the Group of Seven, it brought with it the Mercure programme, a derivative of which, the series 200, had already been proposed, with Aerospatiale as prime contractor.

British Type B Studies for the Group Of Six

Trident 5

Submitted to the Group of Six by Hawker Siddeley in April 1976, the Trident 5 utilised the earlier Trident 4 tail and stretched fuselage, again modified to accommodate two CFM 56 engines with an AUW of 163,000lb (5A). These were married to a redesigned wing using A300B and 146 design principles, with a sweep of 25 degrees (against the Trident 3 of 35 degrees), with a cockpit section based on the HS146 structure. The Trident 5A could accommodate 160 passengers, with a maximum take-off weight of 163,00lb, and the 5B up to 137 passengers, with a maximum take-off weight of 157,500lb. Its first flight was envisaged for 1980, with certification in 1981, and entry into service at the beginning of 1982. The Trident 5 project appears never to have been taken too seriously and, indeed, shortly after making its proposal, Hawker Siddeley withdrew the design, citing that it considered an all-new project as the best avenue to take for the type B-150 seater transport.
(Trident 5A) Length 148ft 34in, Span 114ft 24in, Height 30ft 33in

BAC One-Eleven 700, 800 and X-Eleven

BAC had studied a number of One-Eleven developments in the sixties. These included the series 600 Mk1, a major development which featured a fuselage stretched by 12ft 2in to accommodate up to 130 passengers, powered by uprated aft-fan Spey engines. Other major changes included a more aerodynamic rear fuselage and increased wing, tailplane and fin area. This was superseded by the series 600 Mk2 with a fuselage stretched by 80in, powered by aft-fan Spey engines and a stub fin above the tailplane.

By the mid-seventies, BAC were proposing the series 700 powered by re-fanned Spey 606 engines of 16,900lb thrust. This maintained the series 500 wing combined with a fuselage stretched by some 12ft, with the maximum take-off weight increased to 117,000lb, and accommodation for up to 134 passengers. Studies were also undertaken on a collaborative venture with the Japanese to replace their NAMC-YS11 turboprops. One design featured a Japanese manufactured wing, stretched fuselage and aft-fan Spey engines. None of these designs came to anything, nor did even more adventurous studies including a series 700, with an additional RB162 booster similar to the Trident 3B, or even a four 8,000lb Rolls-Royce/Snecma M-56-engined variant, with a stretched fuselage by 12ft to accommodate up to 129 passengers.

The series 800 design submitted to the Group of Six in 1975 was a more ambitious proposal than the series 700 and, in many ways, harked back to the original series 600 Mk1. This saw the fuselage stretched by nearly 32ft 6in to provide accommodation for up to 161 passengers, and the wing span increased by 10ft over the series 500, with a new centre section and an enlarged tail. Power was to be provided by two CFM56 engines of 22,000lb thrust, giving a range of 2,400 miles and an AUW of 137,000lb.

While these British projects were being proposed, it had been announced in France that the Mercure 200 was to be financed, and that other countries would be invited to join the programme, if they wished, but that this would be under French control and terms. BAC agreed to make an objective study of the project, which revealed that although the design was promising, it lacked the One-Eleven's customer base. The French, however, were intent on leading their own project and were seeking collaboration with the Americans – proposing Dassault to take a 5 per cent share, Aerospatiale 40 per cent and McDonnell Douglas 15 per cent. The balance was open for other partners (namely the Germans and British). The Mercure was not, in fact, developed, and French proposals returned to the all-new Aerospatiale A200.

In 1976, BAC decided that any new future airliner should have a wider fuselage with seating at six abreast, as against the five abreast of the series 800, and so put forward the ultimate One-Eleven development, the X-Eleven short-/medium-range airliner. Firmly based around the One-Eleven, the X-Eleven utilised around 40 per cent of common components to the series 500, including nose section, mainplane and rear fuselage. Major changes included a new fuselage with an internal width of 12ft 3in, some 4in wider than the 727/737, an extended wing centre section, strengthened undercarriage, and extended tailplane and fin. As with the series 800, power was to be provided by two rear-mounted CFM56 engines, now of 24,000lb thrust. Initially studied in three variants, it was eventually decided to offer the 140-seater series 100, with derated thrust engines, and the 179-seater, series 300. Maximum take-off weight was put at 145,000lb for the series 300, with a maximum range approaching 2,000 miles. Future growth potential was planned with increased capacity, higher thrust engines and greater fuel tank capacity.

With the reorganisation of the British Industries in 1977, and the formation of the new nationalised British Aerospace Corporation, the X-Eleven became one of the cornerstones of the new corporation's future airliner strategy. During 1977 the project was pushed firmly

BAC X-Eleven
The BAC X-Eleven from 1976 combined a new six-abreast fuselage and twin CFM56 engines, with components
of the One-Eleven. (BAE SYSTEMS – via Brooklands Museum Trust)

to become the new European 150-seater, and was incorporated into the new Joint European Transport studies (JET) being undertaken between Airbus and BAe. Development costs were put at $300 million, with a break-even of 400 aircraft, with BAe hoping that as a joint venture the UK would take a 50 per cent share, with France and Germany 25 per cent each. Despite all the efforts put in by the company, with the design reaching a very advanced stage, and major airliner interest, it was decided late in 1977 to abandon the project, when it was felt that an all-new airliner would serve the market better. After this, further One-Eleven developments returned to more straightforward projects. The Scries 600 of 1978 put forward to British Airways saw the Series 500 fuselage allied to the 670 wing (developed for the Japanese market) with engine silencers. It was envisaged that these could later be rebuilt with an extended fuselage, and re-engined with the proposed RB432 engine of 18,000lb thrust, becoming the Series 700. Sadly the British government allowed British Airways to order Boeing 737s at a greater cost, precluding any further One-Eleven developments.
(X-Eleven Series 300) Length 139ft 8in, Span 106ft 2in, Height 28ft 4in

JET

The Joint Engineering Team or Joint European Transport study was set up in June 1977 by British Aerospace (BAC/Hawker Siddeley), MBB, Fokker-VFW and Aerospatiale, to undertake studies of a new 130- to 170-seater airliner. At this time it has to be remembered that BAe was still not within the Airbus organisation. The largest of the team's engineering was based at Weybridge under Hawker Siddeley's Derek Brown, and was to become the last occasion that a British-based organisation investigated a new large airliner. The team's brief was to study a family of aircraft based around a pair of CFM56 engines.

The new team investigated the BAe X-Eleven and Aerospatiale AS.200, together with proposals for a new twin jetliner family. In March 1978 a Memorandum of Understanding was signed for a specification of a JET1 136-seater and JET2 163-seater airliner, with a range of 1,600 nautical miles with a full load. It was decided that an entirely new aircraft would be developed. It would be similar in design to the A200, which benefited from research carried out at Weybridge on new wing designs under the UK RSTOL (reduced short take-off and landing) studies. The basic design of JET was a short-/medium-range airliner powered by two CFM56 engines, mounted in pylons beneath a low wing of 24¾-degree sweep. A circular fuselage of 12ft 10in diameter was proposed, being wider than that of the Boeing 727 and new 757. After much discussion with the airlines, the smaller JET1 was dropped, and attention concentrated on the JET2, with a possible stretch to a 190-seater JET3, with more powerful engines. Maximum take-off weight of the JET2 was put at 156,525lb, with a 1,700 mile range carrying 163 passengers.

Development costs of the project were estimated to be in the region of £400 million (1978 prices), and it was envisaged that BAe would take between a 30 and 35 per cent share of the programme, with the team being UK-led, based at Weybridge rather than at Toulouse, but linked with Airbus Industries. It was also hoped that the UK would also be responsible for

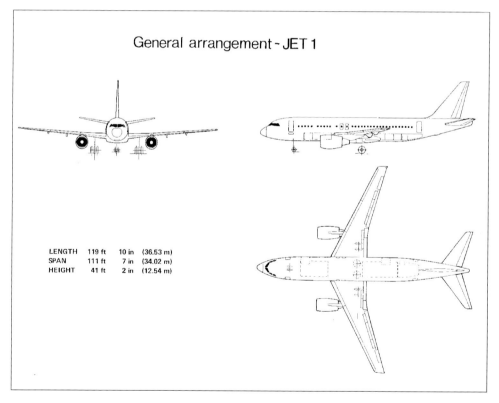

General arrangement - JET 1

LENGTH	119 ft	10 in	(36.53 m)
SPAN	111 ft	7 in	(34.02 m)
HEIGHT	41 ft	2 in	(12.54 m)

JET
The Joint Engineering Team or Joint European Transport, JET, was a collaborative study undertaken by British Aerospace, Aerospatiale, MBB and Fokker-VFW for a new CFM56-powered 130/170-seat jetliner.
(BAE SYSTEMS)

final assembly and flight testing. Its first flight was scheduled for late 1981 or early 1982, with certification and first deliveries by 1983.

After Britain rejoined Airbus Industries in 1979, the JET team was relocated to Toulouse, which took over all narrowbody studies. JET re-emerged in 1980 as the shortlived S.A1, S.A2 and S.A3 (Single Aisle) series, before evolving into the A320, which was finally launched in 1984. For a short while, it seemed as if the A320 would be assembled and flight tested in Britain, probably at Filton. However, the extra funds required for this were not forthcoming, despite intense Union lobbying, and so the A320 carried on the Airbus tradition of all their transports having final assembly at Toulouse, until Germany gained the derivative A321, A319 and A318 at Hamburg.
(Jet2) Length 133ft 10in, Span 111ft 7in, Height 41ft, Wing Area 1,384sq.ft

Nationalisation and Big Decisions

When the decision was taken to nationalise the British Industries, bringing together the design and production facilities of Hawker Siddeley Aviation, Hawker Siddeley Dynamics, British Aircraft Corporation and Scottish Aviation into the new British Aerospace Corporation, one of the most important decisions to be taken was on future commercial aircraft.

Work had been proceeding on the X-Eleven by BAC, and later under JET studies. Meanwhile, on the issue of larger types, the UK government and British Aerospace were approached by all the major Western manufacturers, with regards to becoming risk-sharing partners in their new programmes.

Boeing made proposals on a number of projects, including the original 737-300, 7N7 and 757. For a short time, the latter included manufacture of the wing, plus, possibly, final assembly and flight testing. Later, this became merely a subcontractoral role under Boeing leadership. Lockheed offered twin and tri-jet developments of the Tristar, while McDonnell Douglas projects included DC10 developments, plus the new ATMR. Getting Britain on board was seen as very important, as it brought possible major orders from the state-owned British Airways, engines supplied by Rolls-Royce and major government financial backing. However, none of the transports offered were to be British-based.

In the event, Britain opted for the European option and rejoined Airbus Industrie, albeit with a drastically reduced shareholding of only 20 per cent compared to its original 37 1/2 per cent, and the A300-B10 was launched filling the original Group of Six Type A proposal. All future British airliner projects would now be with capacities below the 150-seater bracket (that was eventually met by the A320). However, design centres at Weybridge, Woodford, Hatfield and Filton continued to investigate preliminary studies on aircraft, with capacities from small turboprops, up to 1,000-seater 747 replacements and Supersonic Transports. With the widebody future now being planned through A300 developments, and the narrowbody A320 launched, new aircraft design activity quietened.

In 1988 Shorts proposed to build a new small forty- to fifty-seater feederliner, the FJX. This promising design was sadly dropped when Shorts was taken over by the Canadian Bombardier company, with Shorts instead becoming partners on the Canadair Regional Jet. Shorts had also intended to become 5 per cent partners on the proposed mid-eighties Boeing 7J7 propfan airliner.

BAe RJX
Impression of the British Aerospace RJX twin-engined development of the BAe 146. (BAE SYSTEMS)

British Aerospace 146NRA

Following proposals for propfan and stretched developments of the 146 in the mid-eighties, in 1990 British Aerospace revealed the 146NRA, which featured two underwing-mounted CFM56-F5 engines of 21,000lb thrust, beneath a new wing of 25-degrees sweep, with winglets and trailing edge double-slotted flaps. The stretched fuselage could accommodate up to 136 passengers at 29/30in-pitch at six abreast, or 126 passengers at 32in pitch at five abreast. A maximum take-off weight was put at 123,000lb with an initial range of 1,750 nautical miles, while the advanced cockpit featured flat screen displays, sidestick controls and fly-by wire controls. For a short time, discussions were held with Tupolev about possible collaboration, but these talks came to nothing. The first flight was proposed for early 1995, with certification and first airline deliveries in 1996. Major interest was shown in the programme, including interest from US carrier Northwest Airlines. However, the airliner market was entering recession and this programme was dropped. There was also, the later follow-up Avro RJX (which was originally a twinjet development of the 146 NRA) to be developed with Taiwan, a radically different 90- to 110-seater powered by two BR700, at a cost of £1 billion, was dropped.

(146NRA) Length 119ft 6in, Span 106ft 2in, Height 31ft 3in, Wing Area 1,100sq.ft

Aero International (Regional)

Two further programmes, initially outside the Airbus sphere, opened up to British Aerospace in the mid-nineties. The short-lived formation of Aero International (Regional) in 1996 combined the Jetstream and Avro divisions of BAe with the French/Italian ATR group. This was expected to give renewed emphasis to the British Aerospace Jetstream 41 and Avro RJ range of regional aircraft, with all sales and marketing in the new venture being moved to new Toulouse headquarters. It was also intended to launch a new family of regional jets based around the ATR72 fuselage (later modified to provide underfloor baggage space), with a new low wing and rear-mounted jet engines. The AI(R) 58 would have fifty-eight seats, and the AI(R) 70, up to seventy seats at four abreast, with a maximum take-off weight of 67,769lb. It was originally envisaged that BAe would manufacture the wing, probably at Prestwick. However, the ever cautious British Aerospace were reluctant to commit funding to yet another new jet programme with a total development cost of around $1 billion, at the same time as having to make a substantial investment in the A340-600, so was ruled out as becoming a shareholder in the project. Seeing a lack of unity, BAe left the AI(R) group shortly after and, despite further efforts by ATR, the AirJet appears to have faded away.

(AI(R) 70) Length 96ft 1in, Span 84ft 2in

A further proposal from AI(R) was the 1996 Aero International Asia AIA220. This was to meet the AE-100 programme, which was for a new 100-seater jetliner to be built by China, with Singapore and a foreign partner. The project later become encompassed into the Airbus fold as the AE31X (AE316 and AE317), to be built by Airbus Industrie Asia (62 per cent Airbus, with Italian company Alenia holding 38 per cent) with a 39 per cent share, AVIC of China as majority shareholder with 46 per cent, and Singapore Technologies, the balance of 15 per cent. The programme would have seen the AE31X series assembled in China in two variants, with seating for between 95 and 125, powered by CFM56-9, BR715 or PW6000 engines. However, despite much effort, the programme was cancelled in 1998, due to high costs and low potential returns, and Airbus elected to produce the cheaper A318 100-seater derivative of the A320 series.

The Final Chapter

The final chapter in British commercial aircraft development came with the decision in 2000 to launch what would probably have been the final 146 development, the Avro RJX, a re-engined derivative of the Avro RJ. The tragic events of September 11, with the terrorist attack on the World Trade Centre, and the economic gloom and military repercussions that followed, severely hit the air transport sector, and saw BAE SYSTEMS take the sad, and possibly short-sighted decision, to cancel the programme in November 2001.

It is interesting that when British Aerospace was set up, it was to provide a full capability in designing and producing a range of commercial and military aircraft. The objectives of the former were initially achieved through the launch of the collaborative A310, and national 146 and Jetstream 31 projects.

However, the 1990s saw a new objective within BAe, with the company becoming more defence-based and later a systems integration organisation, and it began exiting the indigenous transport aircraft sector. The ATP-developed Jetstream 61 was axed when BAe joined AI(R), the Jetstream 41 line was closed in 1997 and, bizarrely, the successful 125 Corporate jet line was sold to Raytheon.

The 146/RJ line continued as the only British transport aircraft, and even showed a small profit, and the new RJX should have maintained the series success, with anticipated sales of 200. It should be noted that when the RJX was cancelled in November 2001, it was nearing certification with two aircraft (later three) engaged in flight testing, and had achieved

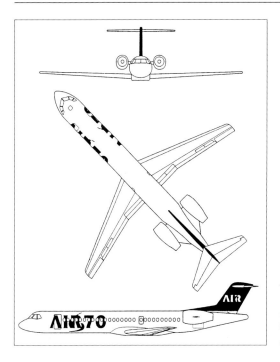

AI(R) 70
When BAe became part of the short-lived Aero
International (Regional) Group, the AI(R) 70, a
twinjet development of the ATR42, was proposed.
(BAE SYSTEMS)

commitments to twenty-eight aircraft. How many other projects have been cancelled so close to fruition?

The RJX cancellation thus probably brings to an end the manufacture and design of transport aircraft in Britain. When the last Avro RJ made its maiden flight in 2002, it signalled the end of fifty-three continuous years of UK jetliner manufacture, during which time over 900 jetliners (not counting the 125 business jet) have been produced. All future UK-produced interest in major commercial aircraft is now tied up in collaborative projects. The largest of these is BAE SYSTEMS' minority 20 per cent stake (compared to the 80 per cent stake held by EADS) in the new Airbus company. Britain still retains wing design and production at Broughton and Filton – this continuing probably as long as BAe's stake is held, and includes the massive wings for the new Airbus A380. Should this shareholding be sold to EADS then this high technology element may well be ceded to France or Germany. BAE SYSTEMS is also still a major subcontractor to Raytheon on the Hawker business jet line, manufacturing major components at Broughton.

At Belfast, fuselage barrels and other smaller components are manufactured by Shorts for parent company Bombardier's range of regional and executive jets. B-N Group (formerly Britten-Norman) have recommenced Islander production in Romania (for completion in the UK) and are to undertake the manufacture of the first new Trislander, for nearly twenty years, at Bembridge, in order to test the market. Sadly, it seems that the magical figure of 1,000 British jetliners is now forever beyond the reach of this once great and proud industry, as is maybe any future UK-produced transport aircraft.

Of the small executive aircraft currently on drawing boards, such as the six-seater Leopard 6, Farnborough F1 air taxi and Warrior Centaur amphibian aircraft, only time will tell if any of these ever reach production or if they too, will remain stuck on the drawing board.

Chapter 11

Project Lists

(Bold text denotes further information in specified chapter)

Airspeed

Specification 6/45	Preliminary designs for a forty-seater **Brabazon 3** Atlantic/Empire airliner.
AS.59	Initially a study of the Ambassador fitted with different engine options – four Dart, four Naiad or two Bristol Theseus engines to the Ambassador. The Rolls-Royce Dart study was chosen for what became known as the Ambassador II with a 6ft fuselage stretch, enabling an additional eight passengers to be carried, and the fitting of slotted flaps and additional fuel tanks. The maximum cruising speed was increased to 255 knots. The project was dropped in 1951 when the Ambassador programme was wrapped up. Length 87ft, Span 115ft, Height 18ft 4in
AS.64	Proposed Ambassador derivative to **Brabazon 5B** Specification.
AS.66	Civil Freighter variant of the proposed AS.60 put forward in 1947, featuring a new redesigned square section fuselage with a side-loading double door on the port side.
AS.67	A Civil Freighter variant of the Ambassador from 1950, which saw a new fuselage of pod and boom type married to the Ambassador's empennage, wings and systems. The design featured a full rear-loading door under the aperture. Provision was also made in the design for a quick change for up to sixty-five passengers. It was envisaged that the powerplant would be Bristol Centaurus 661, although consideration was given for retrospective installation of four Dart or two Armstrong Siddeley Double Mambas. The fuselage was designed to carry a maximum payload of 16,000lb. Length 83ft 4in, Span 115ft, Height 20ft 3in, Wing Span 1,200sq.ft
AS.68	Originally a proposal to re-engine the Ambassador with Bristol Proteus engines. The same designation was later applied to a four-engined Dart Ambassador derivative from 1950, with a stretched fuselage fore and aft of wing frames, enabling an additional two seat rows to accommodate sixty passengers, plus increased fuel tanks with a maximum weight of 60,000lb. Length 87ft 10½in, Span 115ft, Height 18ft 3in, Wing Area 1,200sq.ft

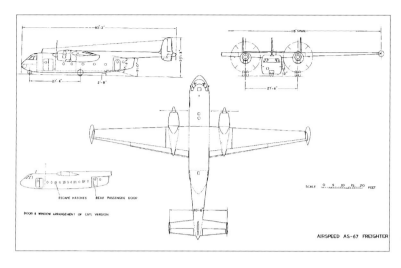

*Airspeed AS.67
A civil freighter
development of the
Ambassador, the
Airspeed AS.67
could accommodate
up to sixty-five
passengers. (BAE
SYSTEMS)*

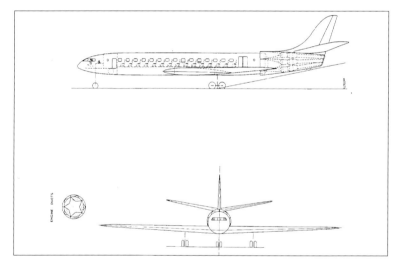

*Armstrong
Whitworth AW.167
The Armstrong
Whitworth AW.167
was a swept-wing
North Atlantic
jetliner powered by
five Armstrong
Siddeley Sapphires,
mounted annularly
around the rear
fuselage. (BAE
SYSTEMS – via
Ray Williams)*

Armstrong Whitworth

Specification 6/45   Design submitted for **Brabazon 3** – no further details.
Specification 18/44   Design submitted for **Brabazon Type V** – no further details.
AW.55 – Apollo II   Jet derivative of the AW.55 Apollo, powered by four Derwent engines,
for which a new wing would have been required to deal with added
stress of the new engines and additional fuel, with an AUW of 50,000lb.
BSAAC did express an interest in the project.
AW.57   Low-wing four Centaurus-engined design to the **MRE** Specification.
AW.65/66   Also called the 'Freightliner', for which the AW.65 was the civil variant, and the AW.66 a military transport. The design was of high wing
and was powered by two turboprop engines with a rear freight door
power operated and hinged downwards. Accommodation was provided
for up to sixty-five passengers at five abreast in a pressurised cabin, with
an operating range of between 2,000 and 2,200 nautical miles.

A number of powerplants were studied, including two Napier Eland, two Rolls-Royce Tyne, two Bristol Centaurus or four Rolls-Royce Dart with 16ft diameter propellers.
Length 88ft 4in, Span 112ft, Height 28ft 8in

AW.167   Swept wing North Atlantic turbojet project from April 1953, powered by five Armstrong Siddeley Sapphire S.A7 engines mounted annularly around the rear fuselage, with an AUW of 220,000lb. Up to 126 passengers could be accommodated at six abreast, which was envisaged flying from London–New York at 550mph. A model of proposed design was exhibited at the Farnborough Air Show in 1955. However, two main design problems surfaced due to the position of the engines, which meant that the rear fuselage took a high concentration of weight and that the lower engines would be susceptible to debris ingestion.
Length 152ft, Span 135ft, Wing Area 3,650sq.ft

AW.174   1956 Conway or Olympus design to meet BOAC 1964 **Long-range jetliner**, seating 110.

AW.175   1957 design for **BEA's short/medium jetliner** specification, powered by four Bristol–Siddeley BE47Cs.

AW.176   Proposal for BEA's **VTOL** airliner to seat sixty-three, powered by twenty ducted fans plus two Napier Elands.

AW.670   **Car Ferry** development of the AW.660 featuring a new upper deck and seating thirty passengers.

AW.671   All-passenger development of AW.670 **Car Ferry**, to seat 126 passengers.

Armstrong Whitworth AW.167
A model of the AW.167, which would have flown from London–New York at 550mph. (BAE SYSTEMS – via Ray Williams)

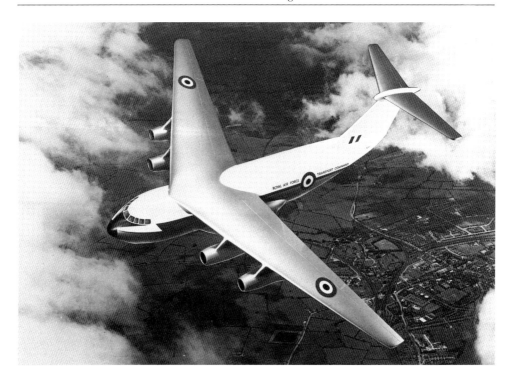

AW.682	Civil Freighter development of AW.681, powered by four Bristol–Siddeley BS53/5 (developed) engines featuring a new raised floor (by 1ft 2in), undercarriage structure and rear door. Other changes included a smaller bulkhead aft and loading ramp pressure-sealed. The control surface blowing was deleted and there were smaller high pressure tyres. Schemes were laid for a lengthened fuselage of 14ft 6in and strengthened wing variants. The Stage 3 variant could carry a payload of 70,000lb, and included further wing strengthening. The project was given a low priority over its military sister, and was dropped altogether when AW.681 was cancelled in 1964. **Length 108ft 9in, Span 130ft, Height 40ft**
Aerobus	Conventional designs put forward to the all-wing transport panel in 1962/63 pre-**Airbus** studies. **Length 109ft, Span 102ft, Height 28ft, Wing Area 1,482sq.ft**

Armstrong Whitworth Initial Projects

AW.P2	VTOL study.
AW.P8	December 1957 **VTOL** study for BEA, to seat fifty-two, powered by four Bristol Orpheus BOr 12.
AW.P13	M-wing planform **SST** to carry 100 passengers at Mach 1.2.
AW.P14	**SST** featuring a highly tapered and swept back wing planform with high tailplane.
AW.P18	Forty-seater **VTOL** aircraft featuring a straight wing.
AW.P20	Similar **VTOL** airliner to AW.P18, but with a different wing design and 12 RB147 fan-lift engines.

| AW.P22 | A further M-wing **SST**, seating 126 and cruising at Mach 1.2. |
| AW.P23 | **Car Ferry** design. |

Auster

| A7 | 1949 design for high-wing twin-boom light twin pusher-engined aircraft powered by two Blackburn Bombardiers. A mock-up was built at Rearsby, showing accommodation for up to seven passengers within a fuselage pod. The project proceeded no further than the mock-up stage. |

Aviation Traders (Engineering)

ATL95	Low-wing double-deck development of Accountant, also proposed as a **Car Ferry**.
Carvair 7	Design studies undertaken on Carvair **Car Ferry** variants of the DC6 and DC7.
Freighter	Two early seventies designs undertaken for Safe Air of New Zealand, for a Bristol Freighter replacement. The high-wing designs were powered by two wing-mounted Rolls-Royce Dart engines. Nose loading through split doors was incorporated with freight holds of 40 and 46ft 6in long, 9ft 6in wide and 6ft 10in high, and a range of 400 nautical miles was predicted.

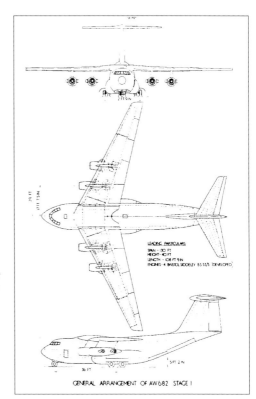

Opposite: *Armstrong Whitworth AW.681*
The Armstrong Whitworth AW.681, designed against OR351 for a short-/medium-range short take-off and landing freighter, was cancelled in 1964. (BAE SYSTEMS)

Right: *Armstrong Whitworth AW.682*
The AW.682 was the commercial variant of the AW.681 and was powered by four Bristol–Siddeley BS53/5 engines. (BAE SYSTEMS)

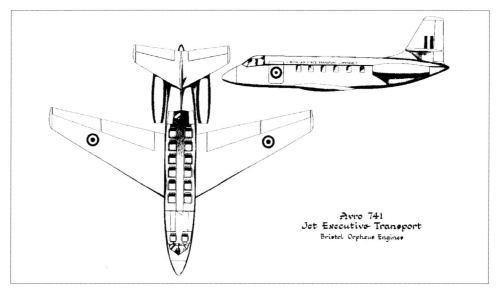

Avro 741
The Avro 741, a twelve-seater executive aircraft powered by two Bristol Orpheus engines. (BAE SYSTEMS)

Avro

690	Original thoughts for the Brabazon Type 3 requirement from 1944 – powered by six Rolls-Royce Merlin engines – also called the Avro 22 (XXII).
692	Avro 23 (XXIII) was a further design put forward for the **Brabazon Type 3** requirement, again powered by six Rolls-Royce Merlin engines.
693	Avro's official proposal for the **Brabazon 3**, the 693, was originally powered by contra-rotating Rolls-Royce Clyde turboprops and, later, Armstrong Siddeley Pythons, before the final design emerged with four Rolls-Royce Avon engines mounted within the wing. The aircraft was cancelled in July 1947.
697	A low-wing forty-eight-seater design, put forward in 1947 for the **MRE S**pecification.
700	January 1945 design for a low-wing twelve-eater feederliner/executive transport powered by Armstrong Siddeley Cheetahs.
703	January 1947 turbojet studied for Trans-Canada Airlines, to accommodate thirty-five passengers.
705	Low-wing transport aircraft powered by four Rolls-Royce Nene engines. **Length 86ft 6in, Span 120ft**
708	Put forward in three variants for the **LRE** Aircraft Specification.
709	Variant of the Avro Tudor II studied for the Long-range Empire Aircraft.
711	A tricycle undercarriage development of the Tudor IV.
715	Low-wing design possibly proposed as a Dove replacement, to seat up to ten passengers, powered by four wing-mounted propeller engines.

722	Avro Atlantic long-range delta wing four-turbojet design, powered by Bristol Olympus or Rolls-Royce Conway engines of 15,000lb thrust. Based around the Vulcan bomber, the December 1952 airliner was proposed for transatlantic operation, to carry up to 131 passengers at six abreast in a fuselage of 12ft 6in diameter. In a luxury layout, seventy-six passengers could be carried within three compartments, seating four abreast, with a bar and bunks for eleven passengers. A cruising speed of 600mph was projected, with an AUW of 200,000lb. Until 1955, the design utilised the Vulcan delta wing and straight leading edge but, as a result of transonic buffeting, the Phase 2 wing introduced a kinked leading edge. The fin and rudder were also adapted from the Vulcan, with a new four-wheel bogie undercarriage. **Length 145ft, Span 121ft**
723	May 1953 design for a DC3 replacement, powered by four Alvis Leonides.
735	1956 **Supersonic airliner** derived from the Avro 730 bomber.
736	Transport aircraft proposed in January 1957, powered by four Armstrong Siddeley P1.82 or Napier E223 engines.
737	Another January 1957 design for a STOL transport, again powered by either four P1.82 or E223 engines.
740	Proposal to meet **BEA** specification for a short-/medium-range jetliner.
741	Low-wing twin rear-engined Bristol Orpheus executive or feeder aircraft proposed in July 1957, seating twelve passengers.
742	Three Bristol BE53-engined Jet Flap Transport aircraft from 1957.
743	Long-range high-wing military freighter proposal powered by four Bristol Orion engines which may have had a commercial freighter potential for large payloads. Its all-up weight was 241,000lb with a payload of 40,000lb being carried over a range of 3,750 nautical miles. **Length 127ft, Span 148ft 4in, Height 43ft 6in, Wing Area 2,200sq.ft**
747	A high-wing twin Rolls-Royce Dart-engined transport, proposed in 1957 to carry either passengers or freight.
749	February 1958 study for a BEA **VTOL** airliner powered by eight RB145 engines.
750	A low-wing rear-engined **feederliner** with T-tail and either two or four jet engines, proposed in February 1958. Design features incorporated into joint Avro/Bristol jetliner study.
751	March 1958 study for a low-wing tri-jet with the third engine mounted in the tail, as with the 121. Up to fifty-six passengers could be carried at four abreast. **Fuselage Length 83ft, Span 86ft 5in, Height 28ft**
753	1958 freighter design utilising the wing of the Avro 745 Maritime Reconnaissance Aircraft.
754	Low-wing twin turboprop **feederliner** design from 1958 utilising the wing of the proposed Avro 745 MRA design.
755	1958 study for a deflected slipstream STOL aircraft.
756	Long-range military transport powered by four Rolls-Royce Tynes, that may have had potential as a commercial freighter.
760	November 1958 design for a **supersonic** airliner.
761	Jet Viscount replacement proposed in 1958. The low-wing **feederliner** design of 35-degree sweepback was powered by two rear-mounted

	Rolls-Royce RB163 engines, and could carry up to sixty-five passengers.
766	Large four-engined military transport that may have had commercial freighter potential.
767	Joint study with Bristol for a four-engined transport.
771	A further Jet Viscount replacement, the sixty-seater feederliner 771 proposed in March 1960 featured a low-swept wing with two rear-mounted Bristol–Siddeley BS75 engines.
772	A January 1960 **Car Ferry** project studied with a number of fuselage options that could seat twenty-five passengers and five cars.
778	**Feederliner** Jet utilising the 748 fuselage and wing.
779	Freighter development of 748 with STOL capability.
781	Further **feederliner** twin turbofan development of 748.

Beagle

208	Development of Beagle 206.
220	Further development of 206 which featured an extended fuselage by 40in, allowing seating for up to eight passengers, with a large entrance door aft of the wings. Power was to be provided by two Rolls-Royce Continental GTSIO-520C engines of 340hp. The 220 was hoped to be available for delivery in the spring of 1966, and was proposed for an Air Staff requirement for a VIP communications aircraft.
222	The 'Treble Two' was yet another development of the 206 and, like the 220, was powered by GTSIO-520C engines. The redesigned fuselage

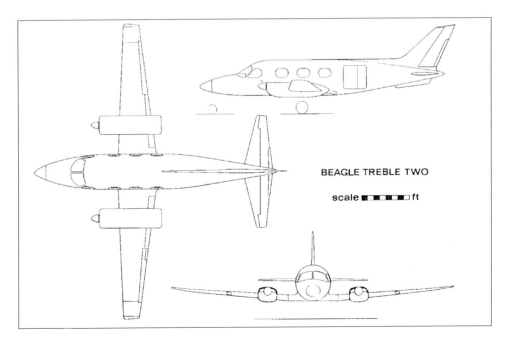

BEAGLE TREBLE TWO

scale ▪▪▪▪▪▪ft

Beagle 222
A development of the Beagle 206, the 222, or Treble Two, could accommodate up to eight passengers. (BAE Systems – via Alan Greenhalgh)

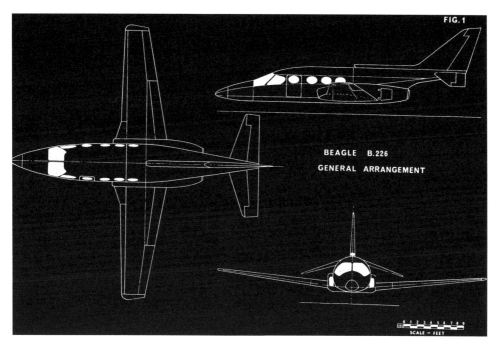

Beagle 226
The rear jet-engined Beagle 226 executive aircraft for May 1966. (BAE Systems – via Alan Greenhalgh)

may have been pressurised on future developments and could accommodate up to eight passengers with access via a large door, incorporating built in airstairs situated at the rear of the cabin aft of the wings, with an AUW of 7,850lb. A mock-up of the fuselage was built at Shoreham. The 222 was proposed as a short-range transport, VIP transport, navigational trainer, aerial survey, freighter and air ambulance. With a maximum payload of 2,050lb a range of 410 nautical miles was quoted, while with maximum fuel a range of up to 1,430 nautical miles was predicted. Maximum continuous cruise speed at 10,000ft was 218 knots.

224   A small four- to six-seater utilising components from the Bulldog, including the outer wings.

226   One of Beagle's most interesting designs, the 226, from May 1966, was a rear-engined twin Rolls-Royce RB188 turbofan executive aircraft. It had a range of 1,000 nautical miles and a maximum gross weight of 9,000lb, with a cruising speed of 300 knots. Accommodation was for up to eight passengers in a fuselage with an internal width of 61in. The low-wing design saw the wing torsion box running continuously through the fuselage, with the top skin forming the rear bench seat base and the front spar web forming the lower half of the pressure bulkhead. Length 38ft 6in, Span 40ft, Height 13ft, Wing Area 220sq.ft

228   A 1968 design for a six-seater executive aircraft featuring front canards with a high wing, and powered by two Pratt & Whitney PT6A-20s.

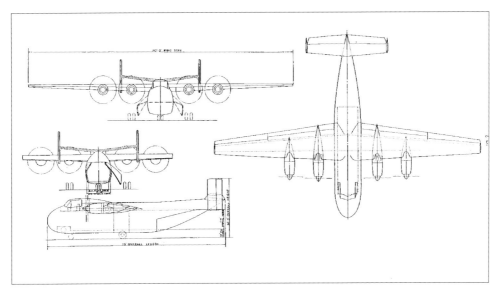

Blackburn B-104D
The smallest of the Blackburn B-104 models was the Type 'D', a medium-range high-wing transport.
(BAE SYSTEMS)

Blackburn

B-49	The Clydesman, a 1945 **flying boat** project, powered by six engines and able to accommodate up to 160 passengers.
B-51	A Rolls-Royce Merlin-powered five-seater aircraft from 1945.
B-55	The first Blackburn proposal for the Brabazon 2 Specification to seat twenty-four, powered by Rolls-Royce Dart engines.
B-60	A twin Armstrong Siddeley Cheetah transport from 1946.
B-63	A 1946 high-speed transport design.
B-65	The second proposal put forward for the **Brabazon 2** Specification, the B-65 was powered by two Armstrong Siddeley Mamba engines and could seat twenty passengers.
B-69	A 1946 study for a sixty-four-seater transport, powered by four Armstrong Siddeley Mambas.
B-70	A four-engined design put forward for the **MRE** Specification.
B-72	A 1947 short-range transport design for BEA.
B-73	Twin-engined single- and double-deck designs submitted to meet the **LRE** requirement.
B-75A	A four- to five-seater design from 1947, powered by two Cirrus Majors or Cirrus Bombardiers.
B-75B	An eight- to ten- seater-design powered by two Cirrus Bombardiers or Majors.
B-76	Commercial Freighter from 1948.
B-77	Rapide replacement feederliner aircraft of low-wing configuration to seat up to fourteen passengers, proposed in A, B and C variants, powered by four Cirrus Major X engines. The B Variant had an AUW of 8800lb.
	(B-77b) Length 39ft, Span 61ft 6in, Height 16ft 2in, Wing Area 419sq.ft

B-84A	A four-engined low-wing Gypsy Major X feederliner transport from 1949, again to replace the Rapide. The B-84 superseded the B-77, and could accommodate up to twenty passengers. The B-84B was a fourteen-seater variant, with reduced wing span and all-up weight of 9060lb, while the B-84C could accommodate seventeen passengers. **Length 47ft 2in, Span 64ft 6in, Height 17ft 6in**
B-93	The low-wing Highlander five-seater powered by two Cirrus Bombardiers. A later study was powered by four Cirrus Bombardiers, and had an increased wing span. **Length 31ft, Span 49ft 6in, Height 13ft 11in**
B-98	1952 study of a passenger/freighter transport powered by either Wright turbo-compound or Napier Nomad engines.
B-104	Medium-range high-wing aircraft proposed for the RAF's OR323 Specification, but with commercial freighter possibilities, powered by two Rolls-Royce Tyne engines with a freight compartment 38ft-long. **Length 90ft 9in, Span 125ft 10in, Height 34ft 6in**
B-105	The Baronet low-wing eighteen-seater **feederliner** powered by four Bombardier engines.
B-106	A four Turbomeca Marcadau-engined low-wing **feederliner** airliner to seat twenty-six passengers at three abreast.
B-107	A high-wing freighter study using the Beverley wing and tail, with new fuselage powered by four Bristol Orion or Rolls-Royce Tyne engines. A freight hold of 60ft with a width of 12ft could accommodate a

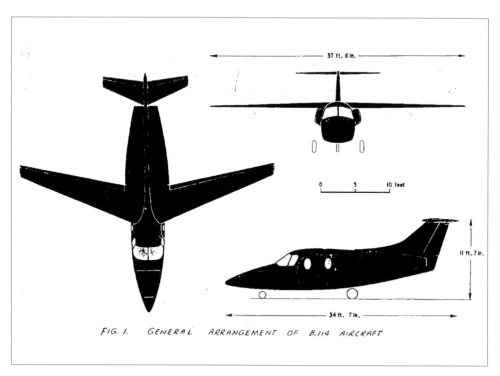

FIG. 1. GENERAL ARRANGEMENT OF B.114 AIRCRAFT

Blackburn B-114
Although designed to replace the Anson in RAF service, the Blackburn B-114 was also proposed as an executive aircraft to seat between four and nine passengers. (BAE SYSTEMS)

payload of 58,000lb. Accommodation could be provided for up to 200 passengers, although in a commercial role this would probably have been limited to 150. The project was dropped when Shorts were awarded a Belfast contract.

Length 120ft, Span 166ft, Height 31ft 6in

B-110   1958 project for a twenty-eight-seater **feederliner**. The low-wing design with two rear engines, proposed as Rolls-Royce RB150s, which could travel over a range of 250 miles at 340mph.

B-114   Designed to replace the Anson RAF communications aircraft, the 7,000lb all-up weight 114 was also proposed as a civilian executive and personnel transport. Proposed powerplants were either the Bristol–Siddeley BS85/2 or Blackburn A204J. The unique performance of the aircraft was to be achieved by using a jet flap wing supplied with air from the by-pass side of its two ducted engines. The high-wing design of 20-degree sweepback could accommodate four passengers and baggage over 600 nautical miles, nine passengers in bench seats, or 1,650lb of freight over 100 nautical miles. With a cruising speed of 400 knots, it would have the ability to take-off and land in fields of 900ft or fewer.

Length 34ft 7in, Span 37ft 6in, Height 11ft 7in, Wing Area 140sq.ft

B-120   Further development of the 114.

B-122   A cold jet flap aircraft with a freight compartment 31ft-long, with rear loading doors that could accommodate a payload of 10,000lb. It was powered by two Bristol–Siddeley BS75s of 7,350lb thrust mounted above the wing of 30-degree sweepback, and could cruise at 480mph.

Length 65ft, Span 70ft, Height 23ft 3in, Wing Area 600sq.ft

B-125   An enlarged version of the 122, powered by two underwing-mounted Rolls-Royce Speys that could accommodate a payload of 12,000lb over 1,600 miles at a cruising speed of 460mph.

Length 78ft, Span 80ft, Height 23ft 9in, Wing Area 750sq.ft

SP60   A large-diameter six-bladed rotor helicopter proposed under Hawker Siddeley's Advanced Projects Group, with six vertically-mounted gas turbines in the rotor head able to lift a gross weight of 135,000lb, with loads including a 250-seater passenger pod, or eighteen cars and a ninety-passenger container.

Boulton Paul

P138   **VTOL** Transport seating thirty-two passengers, powered by four Bristol Orpheus engines.

P140   October 1957 eighty-seater **VTOL** transport.

P141   January 1960 air-driven fan-lift **VTOL**.

P143   Fifty-two-seater VTOL transport powered by ten Rolls-Royce RB144s.

P145   Twin-boom VTOL design seating up to sixty passengers.

P146   November 1960 private venture design for a ninety-six-seater **VTOL** airliner.

Bristol

Project Y	Bristol development of Lockheed Constellation, powered by Bristol Centaurus engines.
179	1951 Bristol Freighter replacement high-wing twin-boom design, also with **Car Ferry** capabilities.
179A	1953 new freighter design with upswept rear fuselage and possible use as **Car Ferry**.
179B	Further new Freighter replacement design, powered by Centaurus, Hercules or Eland engines, with a first flight for 1957, and entry to service in 1960.
181	1953 Twin Proteus helicopter designed against the BEAline **VTOL** requirement to seat eighty passengers.
187	1953 Britannia replacement aircraft proposed for **BOAC**, also called the Britannia 600, powered by Bristol Orion engines. Later variants seated up to 170 passengers.
Bristol/Convair/ Canadair	Double-deck transport derived from 187, also proposed for **BOAC**.
192C	A twenty-three-seater commercial development of twin rotor 192, powered by two Napier Gazelle engines with an AUW of 20,000lb, and a cruise range of 500 miles. **Fuselage Length 54ft 4in, Height 18ft 4in**
194	Large compound six-bladed tandem helicopter with stub wings design, first proposed in 1955 (see **VTOL**).

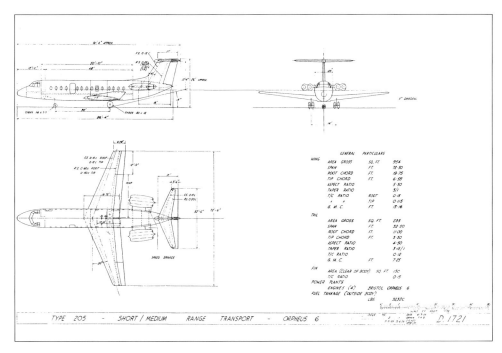

Bristol 205
Developed from the Bristol 200, the Type 205 was first discussed with BEA, and then as a joint proposal by Bristol and Avro as the 'Jetliner', for BOAC medium-range routes. (BAE SYSTEMS)

195	High-wing rear-leading freighter powered by Bristol Proteus engines. Bristol later joined with Shorts to build Britannia wings for the Britannic (later Belfast) freighter.
197	1956 boundary layer control transport powered by four Orions 198.
198	Studies from 1956 onwards for **Supersonic** Transports including STOL and VTOL variants.
199	1956 tilt-wing convertiplane proposal, powered by four Rolls-Royce Tyne or Proteus engines (see **VTOL**).
200	Low-wing short-/medium-range jetliner for **BEA** which evolved from a four jet to a tri-jet, Bristol later joined with Hawker Siddeley on the programme, but lost out to the de Havilland 121.
201	Proposed long-range variant of 200 for one-stop North Atlantic or Commonwealth routes. Fuselage stretched to accommodate up to 117 passengers with a cruising speed of 609mph, and a range, with a pay-load of 25,000lb, of 4,000 miles. It had a gross weight of 170,000lb and was originally powered by four Olympus 551 or Rolls-Royce RA50 engines of 10,500lb thrust.

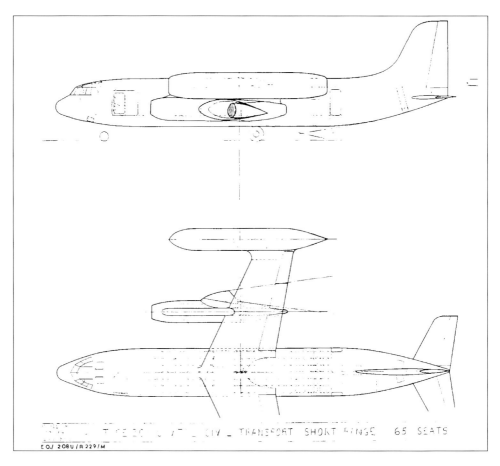

Bristol 208U
The Bristol 208U was a sixty-five-seater commercial transport development of the 208 V/STOL jet lift freighter.
(BAE SYSTEMS)

205	An April 1958 development of the low-wing Bristol 200, with a wing sweep of 20 degrees, to seat up to seventy-six passengers. Originally proposed as a Viscount replacement and discussed with BEA, it was then put forward as a joint project with Avro, as the 'Jetliner' to meet BOAC's medium-range routes, such as London–Kano and Johannesburg. The project was also discussed with BWIA and MEA. Initial power came from two BE58s, and later four Bristol Orpheus, BE61 or RB140 engines. The AUW was 97,000lb, with a range of 1,520 nautical miles. If the go-ahead had been given in mid-1959, the first flight was scheduled for early 1962. When Bristol became part of the new BAC group, input from the 205 was provided for the new 107/One-Eleven project. **Length 102ft, Span 80ft, Height 23ft 10in, Wing Area 1,070sq.ft**
208U	A civil derivative of the 208 VSTOL jet lift freighter, to accommodate up to sixty-five passengers and be powered by four BE53/6 Pegasus and twelve BR59/7 engines.
211	A 1958 study of a four-wing-mounted BE47 development of the Bristol 205.
213	Mach 3 **SST** powered by Olympus engines from 1959.
214	Eighteen-seater utility helicopter powered by two de Havilland Gnome engines developed from the 203 Sycamore replacement.
216	1959 **Car Ferry** proposed for Silver City Airways, powered by Rolls-Royce Darts.
218	Twin Continental IO-470 four-seater executive aircraft.
219	Single-engined executive aircraft to seat five passengers, powered by IO-470s. The design was sold to Beagle.
220	Twin-engined executive five-seater, powered by IO-470 engines. The design formed the basis of the Beagle model 206.
223	A four Olympus-engined Mach 2.2 **SST** proposed in 1961. The design combined with Super Caravelle to become Concorde.
Aerobus	Design studies to Lighthill Committee forerunner of **Airbus** for 100- and 200-seater all-wing delta jetliners.

British Aerospace

Filton

AST	BAe studies of advanced **SST** designs from the seventies onwards.

Hatfield

225	Internal project number for projected 125-700 development, powered by RB401 engines.
146DEV	At Farnborough in 1986, BAe exhibited a twin propfan 146 with engines mounted underslung from the wing, and featuring streamlined spinners. Other studies included an open rotor, and a design with a low-wing, with engines mounted at the rear. Rear-loading freighter variants were proposed from the 146 relaunch in 1978, which should have flown in 1982, and been produced at Woodford. The 1984 146-300, in its original form, featured winglets and a fuselage stretched by

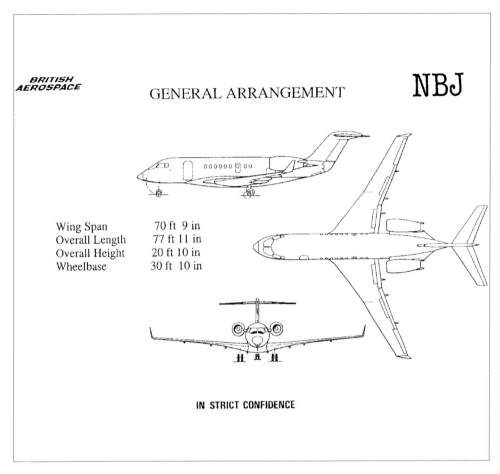

British Aerospace BAe NBJ
One of many studies undertaken at Hatfield for a future executive aircraft was this New Business Jet (NBJ),
which looks like the Challenger. (BAE SYSTEMS)

over 10ft from the series 200, to accommodate a standard load of 120 passengers, or more than 130 in high density configuration. In 1987, a further rear-loading transport was mentioned, while the Model 350 featured a 5ft stretch, allowing up to eight or nine standard pallets to be carried. Further 146 studies included re-engined developments with RB580 engines.

146NRA   Announced in 1990, the NRA development (also called the RJX) featured a stretched fuselage with a new wing, powered by two wing-mounted CFM56 engines (see **seventies**).

NBJ   Hatfield undertook many studies of future business jets during the eighties. The NBJ that emerged looked not unlike the Canadair Challenger, with a low-swept wing, wing tips and T-tail, with two rear-mounted engines, either PW305 or CFE378, with a wider fuselage than the 125. The NBJ had transatlantic capability, with a range of 8,800km.
Length 77ft 11in, Span 70ft 9in, Height 20ft 10in

Hatfield/Filton

SST BIZ JET   Joint project study undertaken between Hatfield and Filton for a small twelve-seater **supersonic** business jet powered by three engines – two over the wing and the third mounted in the tail.

Prestwick

Jetstream 51   Originally proposed to be a stretched Jetstream 41. The Jetstream 51 later emerged as a smaller fifty-two-passenger variant of the 1993 Jetstream 71 **feederliner**.

Jetstream 71   Announced at Paris 1993, the seventy-eight-seater Jetstream 71 turbo-prop **feederliner** featured new technology, wings and T-tail.

Weybridge

JET   Last major new airliner study to be proposed in Britain, JET, based at Weybridge, was a joint European study for a new 150-seater jetliner. The project was later incorporated into Airbus Industries, and emerged through the S.A1 into the A320 (see **seventies**).

Woodford

839   September 1979 design for a 100-seater airliner.

840   748 replacement aircraft, designed against FEAT (Fuel Efficient Aircraft Technology) specification from January 1982.

848   A further FEAT design from November 1983 to seat up to eighty passengers.

850   April 1987 twenty- to thirty-six-seater business/commuter design.

851   High-speed commuter aircraft from September 1988.

852   December 1988 long-term commuter aircraft system.

853   Seventy-five-seater twin or tri-jet, proposed in May 1989.

854   June 1989 fifty-seater jet hub by-pass design.

855   600-to 1,500-seater 747 replacement study from August 1989.

856   Jetstream 41 replacement from March 1990.

857   Avro RJX twin BR715 design to seat between 90 and 120 seats, proposed as a joint venture with Taiwan in March 1993 (see **seventies**).

Aero International (Regional)

Aerospatiale/Alenia/British Aerospace

AIA220   Put forward by AI(R) as a family of new 100-seater jetliners for collaboration with China and Singapore, and later incorporated into Airbus as the AE316 and AE317, before being dropped and replaced by the A318 (see **seventies**).

AIRJET   A projected low-wing jet development of the ATR42, to accommodate between fifty-eight and seventy seats (see **seventies**).

British Aircraft Corporation

BAC 107	Developed from the Percival P107, this fifty-nine-seater rear jet feeder-liner formed the basis for what became the BAC One-Eleven.
VC10 DB265	Double-deck 260-seater development of the VC10, put forward for BOAC in 1965, and powered by four Rolls-Royce RB178 engines.
Type 1199	A BAC all-rounder project from November 1966, featuring a new wide body fuselage with raised cockpit like the 747, combined with the VC10 tail unit, powerplant and slightly redesigned wing. Up to 284 passengers could be accommodated in a cabin of 16ft 2in diameter. **Length 185ft 6in, Span 141ft 2in, Height 44ft 6in, Wing Area 2,742sq.ft**
SUPER One-Eleven	1966 One-Eleven development put forward for BEA, with new six-abreast fuselage, powered by Rolls-Royce Conway engines to seat up to 179. The design was later incorporated into Two-Eleven (see **Airbus**).
BAC 201	Announced at the Paris Air Show in 1967, the 201 high-wing design was a low-cost aerial truck of robust structure, mainly for developing countries. The wing was of simple design with high aspect ratio. Power was from two Rolls-Royce Dart R Da 7 engines, with the large fuselage able to be used for carrying fifty passengers at five abreast, or freight through a rear-loading door, which could include up to two vehicles, or three pallets of 9ft by 7ft 4in diameter. The maximum take-off

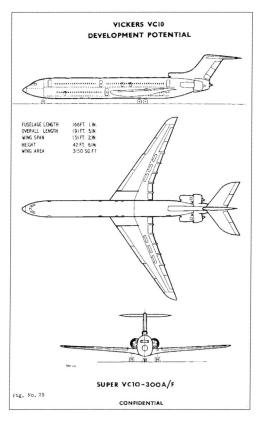

BAC Super VC10 300
Many VC10 proposals were made during the sixties, including the tri-jet double-decker series 300A/F. (BAE SYSTEMS – via Brooklands Museum Trust)

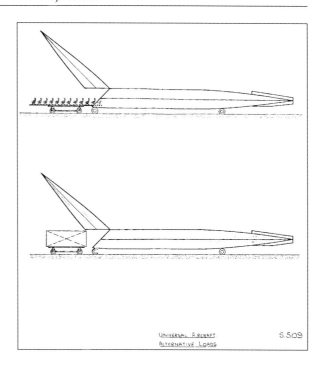

*BAC (Barnes Wallis) Universal
A 1970 study undertaken by Barnes
Wallis at Weybridge, the Universal
would have travelled at Mach 6.
(BAE SYSTEMS – via Brooklands
Museum Trust)*

weight was put at 38,000lb, with the ability to carry a maximum pay-load of 11,950lb. The design continued to be evolved by BAC, and became the 401.
Length 67ft 8in, Span 95ft, Height 27ft 8in, Wing Area 750sq.ft

Two-Eleven   A twin RB211 low-wing airliner announced in 1967, initially to meet BEA's interim **Airbus** requirement, seating up to 219 passengers at six abreast.

Biz Jet   Long-range business jet proposed in the late sixties, designed to meet the requirements of Pan–American Business Jets. The low-wing design with an AUW of 47,000lb was powered by two rear-mounted Rolls-Royce Trent engines, with a range of 2,600 nautical miles, and a maximum cruise speed of Mach 0.9. Up to fifteen passengers could be accommodated within a cabin of 8ft 5in maximum width, at three abreast. The design with a T-tail was very similar to the later Canadair Challenger, with planned certification for 1970.
Length 70ft 6in, Span 68ft 4in, Height 23ft 4in

Three-Eleven   A 1968 270-seater widebody **Airbus** jetliner proposed to BEA, powered by two rear-mounted RB211 engines.

B. Wallis Universal 1970 study by Sir Barnes Wallis at Weybridge for a Mach 6 combined passenger/freighter that could use conventional airfields, powered by four jet engines. Up to 153 passengers could be accommodated at eight abreast in special passenger containers.
Span 52ft

STOL   Design studies undertaken of STOL aircraft under a TARC requirement from the late sixties (see **VTOL**).

QSTOL   High-wing 108-140-seater widebody jetliner to be powered by four Rolls-Royce/Snecma M45S. (see **seventies**).

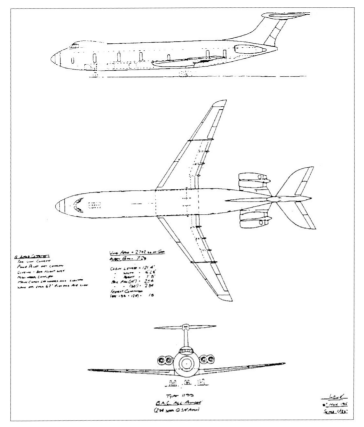

Left: *BAC 1199*
The BAC Weybridge Type 1199 from 1966 was developed from the Super VC10, and could seat up to 284 passengers in a widebody fuselage with a raised cockpit. (BAE SYSTEMS – via Brooklands Museum Trust)

Below: *BAC 201*
A low-cost aerial truck, the Dart-powered BAC 201 could also seat fifty passengers. (BAE SYSTEMS – via Brooklands Museum Trust)

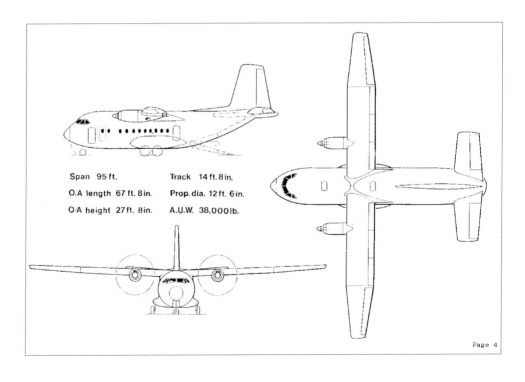

Span 95 ft.   Track 14 ft. 8 in.

O/A length 67 ft. 8 in.   Prop. dia. 12 ft. 6 in.

O/A height 27 ft. 8 in.   A.U.W. 38,000 lb.

Page 4

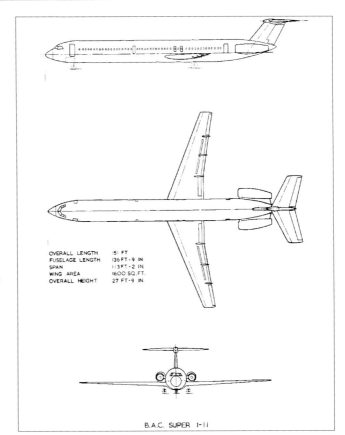

Right: *BAC Super One-Eleven*
The original Super One-Eleven
featured a new six-abreast fuselage
with Rolls-Royce Conway
engines. (BAE SYSTEMS – via
Brooklands Museum Trust)

Below: *BAC Business Jet*
This BAC low-wing Trent-
powered business jet was proposed
to Pan–American Business Jets.
(BAE SYSTEMS – via
Brooklands Museum Trust)

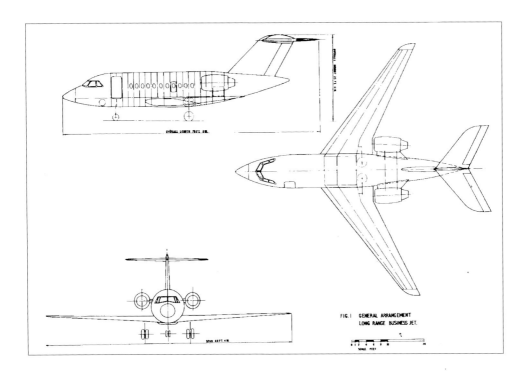

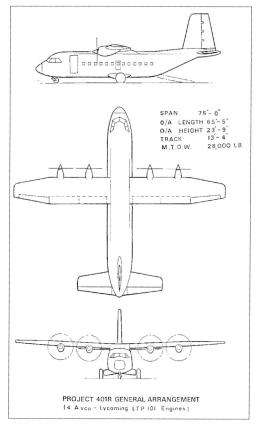

SPAN   75'- 0"
O/A LENGTH 65'- 5"
O/A HEIGHT 23'- 9"
TRACK   13'- 4"
M.T.O.W.   28,000 LB.

PROJECT 401R GENERAL ARRANGEMENT
(4 Avco - Lycoming LTP 101 Engines)

BAC 401
The BAC 401, developed from the 201 aerial
truck, would have been powered by four Avco
Lycoming LTP101s. (BAE SYSTEMS – via
Brooklands Museum Trust)

Europlane	1972 study with MBB, Saab-Scania and later CASA, for a quiet short take-off and landing jetliner powered by two Rolls-Royce RB211, based at Weybridge (see **seventies**).
RSTOL	Joint British government/BAC study for development of a reduced short take-off and landing airliner, undertaken between 1972 and 1976. It was then continued into the CTOL (conventional take-off and landing) study. Numerous designs were studied of two, three and four CFM56 powered-aircraft, including high wing and low wing. One study which emerged was a 146-seater with a low wing and double-bubble fuselage, the wing of which formed the basis for the A320.
RTOL	Design studies undertaken looking at various aircraft configurations. These included widebody RB211-24 high- and low-wing projects and 12 ton-CFM 56 powered projects – with rear engines, low underwing-mounted engines, tri-jets and high wings with four engines.
BAC 401	Further development of the BAC 201 produced the 401, a high-wing design powered by four Avco Lycoming LTP101 engines, again featuring a rear-loading door and a maximum take-off weight of 28,000lb. **Length 65ft 5in, Span 75ft, Height 23ft 9in**
One-Eleven Japan	A 100- to 120-seater short field twinjet proposed for joint development with Japan, based around the One-Eleven new wing (see **seventies**).
X-Eleven	Proposal to the Group of Seven of a new six-abreast fuselage development of the One-Eleven, powered by CFM 56 engines (see **seventies**).

AST   Numerous design studies undertaken by BAC for a new **supersonic** airliner during the seventies.

Britten-Norman (Fairey Britten–Norman)

Mainlander   A 1972 design for a short-/medium-range STOL aircraft to accommodate either freight, or up to 101 passengers at six abreast. Adopting the same three-engine layout as the Trislander, the key to the project was simplicity. Powered by reliable Rolls-Royce Dart RDa7 engines, the undercarriage was fixed, and the aircraft non-pressurised, with mechanical flying controls. In freight configuration, up to eight cars could be accommodated, with a maximum take-off weight of 62,500lb, and maximum cruising speed of 225mph. In 1973 Fairey Britten-Norman announced that the project would require a launch aid of £25 million, and required a risk-sharing partner. The company did not approach the British government for finance and, although British Air Ferries were interested, the company elected to devote resources to the Islander/Trislander family. Had the project gone ahead, it would probably have been built at Fairey Britten-Norman's Belgian factory.
                             Length 82ft 6in, Span 130ft, Height 31ft 9in

BN4   A follow-on project from the BN2 series, the BN4 was a twin turbo-prop high-wing all-metal aircraft with fixed undercarriage and T-tail. The tailplane, elevator, trim tabs and systems were those common to

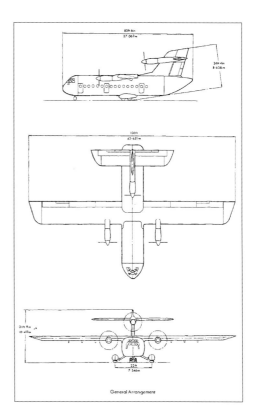

Britten-Norman Mainlander
Powered by three Rolls-Royce Dart engines, Fairey
Britten-Norman's Mainlander project would probably
have been built at the company's factory in Belgium.
(Britten-Norman)

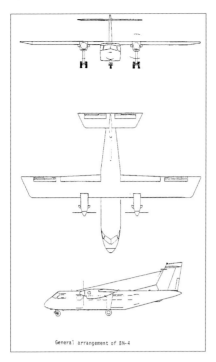

General arrangement of BN-4

Britten-Norrman BN4
A larger three-abreast fuselage was featured on the Britten-
Norman BN4, an Islander follow-on project.
(Britten-Norman)

the Trislander, combined with a new unpressurised fuselage to seat up to a maximum of twenty-one passengers at three abreast, although further growth was also predicted. Power was to be provided by two Pratt & Whitney PT6A-27 engines, with a maximum take-off weight of 11,500lb.
Length 46ft 3in, Span 60ft, Height 17ft 2in, Wing Area 402sq.ft

Cierva

W11T   Three-rotor helicopter powered by derated Merlin 502 engines with an enlarged fuselage over the W11, with strengthened undercarriage and longer blades. The design also featured a cleaner and simpler outrigger boom structure, enlarged freight compartment with strengthened floor and engines mounted on the outside of fuselage. Up to twenty-four to thirty-two passengers could be accommodated, or $2\frac{1}{2}$ to $4\frac{1}{2}$ tons of freight. The all-up weight was put at 25,000lb, with an estimated maximum speed of 137mph and range of 440 miles. A Rolls-Royce Dart variant was also studied. At one time the Colonial Office were interested in taking one aircraft.
Fuselage Length 56ft 6in

W12   Smaller variant of the W11 powered by two Alvis Leonides of 500hp, with seating for twelve passengers, or $1\frac{1}{2}$ tons of freight, with a three-rotor arrangement. The powerplant was divided into two units each mounted on the side of the fuselage to be readily accessible from the ground. In the freighter variant, two large double-hinged doors were provided in the rear of the fuselage with a built-in folding ramp.

Clarke–Norman

Triloader

A 3-ton-loader air freighter proposed in 1995. The high-wing design was powered by three Pratt & Whitney Canada PT6A-114 engines, two on the wing, and the third, like the Trislander, on the fin, with an AUW of 18,000lb. The hold, which was 30ft-long, 7ft 8in-wide and 6ft 6in high, could accommodate up to five LD3 IATA containers, with front loading for containers and side loading for palletised cargo. A maximum range with full payload was put at 315 nautical miles, with a high cruise speed of 186 knots. Proposals were made for the prototype aircraft to be manufactured at Sandown on the Isle of Wight, with series production to be undertaken by a European manufacturer. In the event, no production ever ensued.
Length 62ft 6in, Span 80ft, Height 23ft 9in

De Havilland

Comet 5

Stretched development of Comet 4 proposed to **BOAC**, with swept back fin.

DH118

Further development of Comet 5 for **BOAC**, powered by four under-wing-mounted Rolls-Royce Conway engines for transatlantic operations.

DH119

Study for a **BEA** jetliner from 1956, with swept wing, powered by four Rolls-Royce Avons.

DH120

Joint study to meet both **BEA** and BOAC jetliner requirement, powered by four Avon or Conway engines.

DH122

Christchurch design study for a eight- to eleven-seater turboprop transport.

DH122

Derivative of Trident 121 for BOAC.

DH123

Small executive aircraft based on Vampire trainer, able to seat up to six passengers. A similar project was later taken up by the US company,

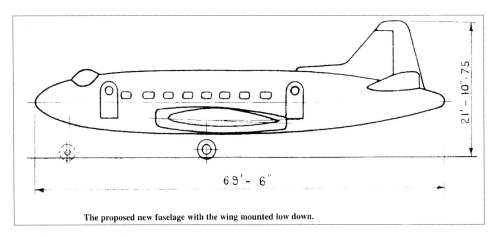

The proposed new fuselage with the wing mounted low down.

English Electric Civil Canberra
The civil development of the Canberra would have accommodated thirty-four passengers and been powered by two Rolls-Royce AJ65 jet engines. (BAE SYSTEMS)

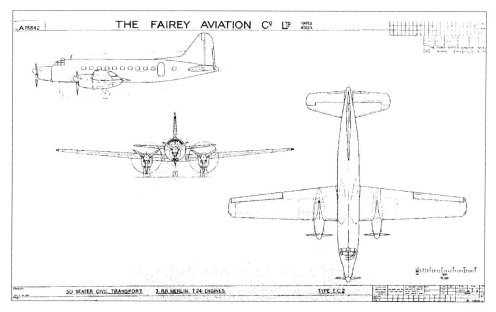

Fairey FC2
Fairey's FC2 was a thirty-seater transport powered by three Rolls-Royce Merlin engines. (Westland Helicopters – via RAF Museum Hendon)

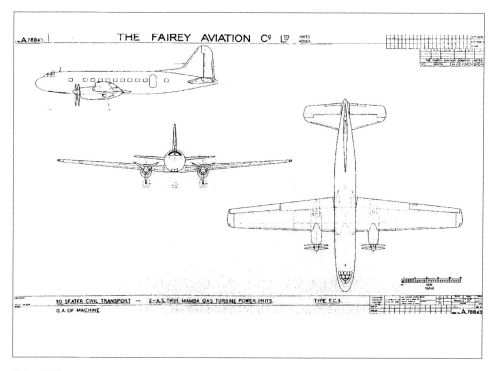

Fairey FC3
Similar in design to the Fairey FC2, the FC3 was powered by two Armstrong Siddeley Twin Mambas mounted on the wing. (Westland Helicopters – via RAF Museum Hendon)

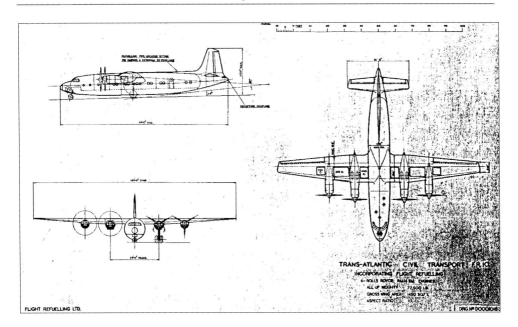

Flight Refuelling FR10
The long-range Flight Refuelling FR10 could travel 2,400 miles, with seating for up to sixty passengers.
(Flight Refuelling)

	Jetcraft, with the MJ11, a mock-up of which was built at Aviation Traders' Southend factory.
DH123	1959 design, originally from Christchurch, for a high-wing turboprop **feederliner** to seat up to forty passengers, powered by two de Havilland Gnome engines.
DH124	Forty-seater rear-mounted jet (see **feederliners**).
DH126	1960 proposal for a twenty-six- to thirty-seater jet feederliner, similar in design to the 125.
DH130	**Supersonic** airliner proposal, later incorporated into the HS APG 1011 design.

English Electric

Civil Canberra	October 1946 airliner proposal based on the Canberra, able to accommodate thirty-four passengers in a pressurised circular fuselage of 10ft diameter and low wing. Range with full payload was put at 930 miles, with power provided by two Rolls-Royce AJ.65 engines of 6,500lb thrust, with a cruising speed of 450mph. The design would not have been available until 1949 and there were doubts about the small size of the fuselage. **Length 69ft 6in, Span 67ft 56in, Height 21ft 10in**
Transport	1947 design with wing-mounted Napier Nomad or Bristol Proteus engines.
Rapide Rep	March 1948 study for a low-wing Rapide replacement to seat up to eight passengers, with twin engines geared to a single propeller. Various engine proposals were put forward, including Gipsy Major and Gipsy Queen.

P7	Single-engined DC3 **feederliner** replacement from June 1953.
P17F	Design for VTOL launcher platform incorporated into the P20 study.
P20	Series of studies of **VTOL** airliners.
P24	**VTOL** projects from April 1958 incorporating P20 studies.
P29	Viscount **feederliner** replacement from November 1958, to seat up to fifty-two passengers.
P30	A series of studies of **Supersonic** Transports, including variable geometry studies.
P32	Medium-range low-wing rear-engined **feederliner** from 1959, powered by either Bristol–Siddeley BS75 or Rolls–Royce Spey engines.
P40	Low-wing **feederliner** from 1962, powered by two rear-mounted Bristol–Siddeley BS75 engines.

Fairey

FC1	Designed against Specification 15/38 for a short-/medium-range transport, With the mock-up already complete, the FC1 was cancelled in 1939, at the advent of the Second World War. However, it was reported that late in 1945 Fairey did reconsider building the aircraft powered by Bristol Hercules engines. In the end the project was not relaunched.
FC2	Short-haul airliner of low-wing design powered by three Rolls-Royce Merlin T24 engines, two wing-mounted and the third at the front of the fuselage. Up to thirty passengers could be accommodated.
FC3	Similar design to the FC2, except it was powered by two wing-mounted Armstrong Siddeley Twin Mambas.
FC4	One of three proposals for the BOAC **LRE** contract, the FC4 was a low-wing airliner seating up to fifty-six passengers, powered by four Bristol Proteus engines.
FC5	Second Fairey study using FC4 wing and shortened fuselage for the BOAC **LRE** contract, but powered by four Napier Nomad engines.
FC6	Third BOAC **LRE** submission based on the FC4, with a reduced wing span and shorter fuselage than the FC5. Power was to be from four Bristol Proteus engines.
Project X91	**Supersonic** design proposed in 1958 to seat 120 passengers.
Rotodyne FA1	Proposed production variant of Rotodyne, powered by Rolls-Royce Tyne engines and seating for up to fifty-four passengers.

Flight Refuelling

FR10	Long-range double-deck airliner with flight refuelling capability for transatlantic operations, powered by four Rolls-Royce Merlin 14 SM engines. Accommodation was for up to forty day passengers or twenty sleepers. The maximum range was to be 2,400 miles, with a top speed of 322mph and gross weight of 72,500lb. Length 99ft, Span 120ft, Height 27ft, Wing Area 1,450sq.ft
FR11	Larger flight refuelling airliner of mid-wing design, powered by six Rolls-Royce Merlin 14Sm engines, with a gross weight of 117,000lb. It had provisions for 100 day or 50 night passengers, with a maximum range of 2,400 miles, and maximum speed of 310 miles. Length 129ft, Span 150ft, Wing Area 2,340sq.ft

FR12	1945 study for a large capacity double-deck, mid-wing, long-range flight-refuelled airliner powered by six Bristol Centaurus 57 engines with contra-rotating propellers. Provision was made for up to 134 day or 100 night passengers. Passengers were accommodated in cabins with eight seats designed for conversion to six bunks. The lower deck also made provision for a lounge and freight compartment. The gross weight was 185,200lb, with a maximum range of 2,320 miles at 242mph. **Length 146ft, Span 195ft, Height 48ft, Wing Area 3,800sq.ft**
FR13-16	Four designs from 1948 all featuring the same fuselage length and wing span, and providing accommodation for up to fifty-one passengers with different engine configurations and flight refuelling capacity.
FR13	Powered by four Bristol Centaurus 663 engines with a maximum speed of 360mph, a range of 3,180 statute miles and an AUW of 95,190lb.
FR14	The FR14 saw an increase in AUW to 101,450lb, and was to be powered by four gas turbines in two coupled pairs. The range was increased to 3,340 statute miles, with a constant cruising speed of 365mph.
FR15	The most interesting of the quartet, the FR15, with an AUW of 109,500lb, was to be powered by four unspecified jet engines, two in each nacelle mounted beneath the wing. A constant cruising speed of 460mph was projected.

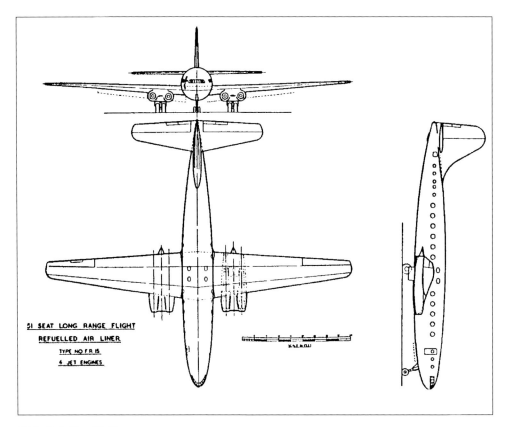

Flight Refuelling FR15
The most interesting of the four proposals from Flight Refuelling in 1948 for a fifty-one seater transport was the
FR15, powered by four unspecified jet engines. (Flight Refuelling – via Colin Cruddas)

| FR16 | Powered by four compound engines, the FR16 had an AUW of 94,000lb and a range of 3,450 statute miles, with a maximum speed of 418 mph.
(FR13-16) Length 105ft, Span 126ft 4in |

Folland

FO 122	March 1946 design for a five-seater personnel aircraft powered by Gipsy Queen 71s.
FO 127	The 'Fiona' Three Gipsy Major 10-powered high-wing design from September 1947. One engine was located in the aircraft's nose while two pusher engines were located on the wing. Up to eight people could be accommodated with an AUW of 10,000lb. **Length 37ft 3in, Span 55ft**
FO 129	Later 'Fiona' high-wing design to seat up to ten passengers put forward in April 1947, powered by three Gipsy Queens. A mock-up of the cabin, cockpit and test rig was built. Like the 127, the third engine was mounted in the nose, with the two pusher engines situated on the wing. **Length 44ft 2in, Span 55ft, Height 13ft 4in, Wing Area 375sq.ft**
FO 130	Small feederliner design proposed in four variants between November 1947 and March 1948.
FO 130/1	Eight-seater low wing powered by three Cirrus Major III engines, two on the wing and one in the nose. **Length 38ft, Span 54ft 6in, Height 10ft 3in**
FO 130/2	Eight-seater three-engined design powered by Cirrus Major III engines. **Length 38ft**

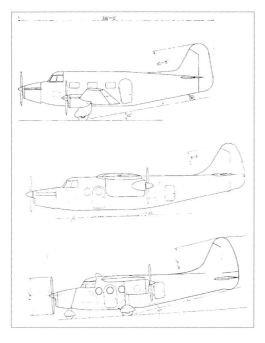

Folland
Folland undertook a number of small feederliner studies. From top to bottom: the FO130, FO129 'Fiona' and FO127, also called 'Fiona', with accommodation from eight to ten passengers. (BAE SYSTEMS – via Southampton Hall of Aviation)

FO 130/3	Five- to eight-seater low-wing design powered by two wing-mounted Armstrong Siddeley Cheetah 25 engines. **Length 40ft**
FO 130/4	Eight- to ten-seater twin Cheetah-engined low-wing design from March 1958 **Length 42ft 8in, Span 58ft 6in, Height 14ft 3in, Wing Area 380sq.ft**
FO 134	Rapide replacement from October 1949, built to Specification 26/49. It was to be powered by four Gipsy Major 10 or Blackburn Bombardier engines. Studies were undertaken with Saunders Roe under their model number P132 for an eleven-seater low-wing design, with twin fins and an AUW of 8,500lb. This evolved into a seventeen-seater powered by four Gipsy Queen II with an AUW of 12,500lb. **(Eleven-seater) Length 42ft, Span 60ft, Height 13ft 3in, Wing Area 425sq.ft** **(Seventeen-seater) Length 48ft, Span 70ft, Height 15ft 3in, Wing Area 595sq.ft**
Utility Freighter	Exhibited at the 1954 Farnborough Air Show, this high-wing monoplane of box-car design, with an all-up weight of 17,000lb, had high-tail booms and was powered by four Gipsy Queen 30 or Queen 70 engines. Up to 2½ tons of freight or thirty-two passengers could be accommodated, with a cruising speed of up to 147mph. The fixed undercarriage design had rear doors and could also accommodate two Land Rover type vehicles, and would have been able to operate from a 1,400-yard grass runway in tropical conditions.
FO 145	January 1958 study of an intercity transport or military freighter. Power would have been provided by turboprop engines, either two Napier Gazelle IVs or Armstrong Siddeley Mamba 6s, powering 15in propellers. Two different configurations were studied, either slipstream lift with multi-flap non-tilting wings or a simple flap tilting wing – during the design stages there was no clear preference for either design. The high-wing monoplane had a fixed undercarriage and slabsided fuselage with aft loading for a jeep or other small vehicles. The aircraft was designed as a simple structure and was conventional throughout, with normal controls for cruising flight and a special system for low speed flight. Accommodation was provided for two crew and ten passengers or a Land Rover loaded through rear clamshell doors, with an AUW of 15,000lb. **Span 36ft**
OTHER VSTOL STUDIES	Folland studied a number of other commercial STOL and VSTOL projects, including the tilt wing SK1761H with an AUW of 29,400lb, and the SK1836 with an AUW of 44,000lb, powered by six engines. The SK1761B high-wing transport with twin fins and rudders at the tips of the tailplane would have been powered by four Napier Gazelle engines, and would accommodate thirty-three passengers. The 1767 could seat up to fifty and propulsion was by four Rolls-Royce Dart engines. Each engine would have driven a separate propeller, and these would be coupled together by means of high-speed shafts in the leading edge of the wing. **(SK1767) Length 46ft, Span 80ft, Height 20ft, Wing Area 960sq.ft**

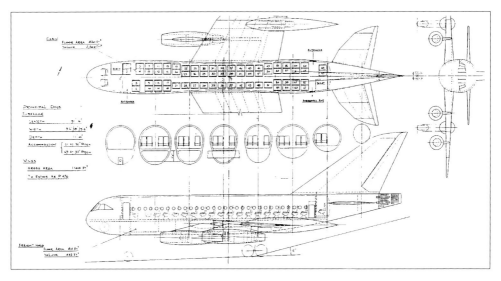

Gloster 479
Area-ruled fuselage Gloster 479 with accommodation for sixty-nine passengers. (BAE SYSTEMS – via Ray Williams)

Gloster

392	1958 study for a thirty-seater transport powered by two or four paired Orpheus engines.
393	A low-wing T-tail Tri-jet powered by rear-mounted Orpheus engines to seat thirty passengers was also studied, and included twin- and four-engine designs with an AUW of 40,000lb.
394	A four Orpheus-engined thirty-seater design.
398	High-wing, thirty-nine-seater, area-ruled fuselage transport with T-tail from April 1958, powered by four podded Orpheus engines with an AUW of 40,000lb.
404	1958 study for a double-bubble fifty-six seater.
405	Area-ruled fuselage transport with seating for fifty-six passengers, again from 1958.
409	A 1958 fifty-two-seater airliner of conventional fuselage design.
411	Twin BE53/2-powered high-wing VTOL transport with T-tail to seat up to fourteen passengers.
414	Area-ruled fuselage study from 1958 with accommodation for eighty passengers.
418	Area-ruled fuselage transport seating 160.
454	Further 1958 development of the Gloster 418.
458	1958 study of Gloster 418 with the trailing edge of wing now accommodating the landing gear.
459	1958 scheme for a twin BE61-engined thirty-six-seater transport.
460	Twin derated BE61-powered thirty-six-seater transport.
462	Gloster 458 development with STOL capability.
463	Elliptical wing development of 458.
464	Further STOL development of 458 from 1958.
465	Elliptical wing transport to seat up to fifty-four passengers.

467	STOL variant of 458 from 1958.
471	Development of 465 from 1959, to seat eighty passengers.
473	1959 design for fifty-four-seater Gloster 458.
474	1959 fifty-four-seater transport.
475	Study of fifty-four-seater transport.
476	Further development of Gloster 475.
479	1959 study for a low-wing design with area-ruled fuselage, powered by four underwing-mounted engines. It seated sixty-nine passengers at three and four abreast at 32in-pitch, with an underfloor freight compartment. **Fuselage Length 91ft 6in, Wing Area 1,100sq.ft**
480	Studies in 1959 of a double-deck transport to seat 141 passengers with area-ruled fuselage and elliptical wing, powered by four BE50 engines mounted underwing.
486	Double-deck design accommodating 144 passengers from 1959.
492	1959 transport powered by six Olympus 591 engines.
493	Development of the 492 with a different engine layout. The Bristol–Siddeley Olympus engines were mounted four around the rear fuselage/tail unit, and two beneath the low wing. The January 1960 design could accommodate up to sixty passengers, with access gained by a ventral airstair.
494	1960 high-wing twin Orpheus jet study to seat eighteen passengers with an AUW of 17,000lb.
496	High-wing light twin-engined aircraft to seat six passengers powered by Continental engines.
499	1960 six-seater light twin design.
500	Seven-seater twin-engined light aircraft from 1960.
501	Four- to five-seater light aircraft of high-wing design with pusher Continental engines.

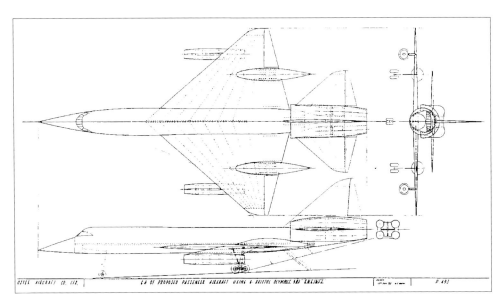

Gloster 493
The Bristol Olympus-powered Gloster 493. (BAE SYSTEMS – via Ray Williams)

511	Forty-seater VTOL transport from 1960
.512	1960 scheme for VTOL aircraft powered by four Orpheus and ten BE59 engines.
514	VTOL transport accommodating sixty passengers from 1960.
515	Hinged rear fuselage development of 514.
516	VTOL transport from 1960 seating eighty passengers.
520	VTOL transport of T-tail design, powered by four wing-mounted Bristol–Siddeley BS75s for forward thrust, and ten BE 59/7s mounted alongside the fuselage for vertical lift. The fuselage of waisted design could accommodate up to eighty-two passengers at four and five abreast. **Length 112ft, Span 80ft, Height 33ft, Wing Area 1,150sq.ft**
529	1961 medium-range STOL transport.
533	Further STOL development of 529.
534	Twin-boom transport from 1961, with STOL capability.

Handley Page

HP.76	Low-wing monoplane submitted for **Brabazon 2** Specification.
HP.77	Twin Bristol Theseus design for **Brabazon 2**.
HP.78	Four Armstrong Siddeley Mamba-engined design for **Brabazon 2**, from 1946.
HP.79	1947 Hermes III powered by four Bristol Theseus engines.
HP.83	Proposed for the BOAC **MRE** Specification Bristol Centaurus development of Hermes.

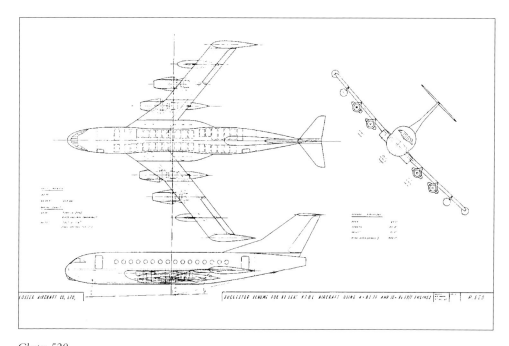

Gloster 520
The Gloster 520 was a vertical take-off and landing transport powered by four Bristol–Siddeley BS75s, with an additional ten BE 59/7s for vertical lift. (BAE SYSTEMS – via Ray Williams)

HP.84	Bristol Proteus development of the Hermes BOAC **MRE**.
HP.85	Twin-coupled Bristol Proteus Hermes with single spar for BOAC **MRE**.
HP.86	Final design for BOAC **MRE** with HP.85 wing and Bristol Centaurus engines.
HP.90	Civil Freighter project based on Hermes IA, powered by Bristol Hercules 630.
HP.91	Hermes VI powered by Four Bristol Hercules 783.
HP.92	Hermes VII study from 1948, powered by four Rolls-Royce Griffon engines.
HP.97	Commercial four-Conway development of Victor bomber for **BOAC**.
HP.102	Study for **BOAC** Empire routes, this jet transport had boundary layer control.
HP.108	Boundary layer-control Rolls-Royce Avon design for **BOAC** for transatlantic routes.
HP.109	Mach 2.2 **SST**.
HP.110	Mach 1.2 **SST**.
HP.111C	The 'Treble One' four Conway-powered Victor development for **BOAC** from 1958.
HP.113	This was originally based on a Canberra bomber to be a boundary layer-control test aeroplane, but interest was so great that a long-range executive design was also proposed. It was powered by two Bristol Orpheus BOr 12 turbojets mounted on the rear of the fuselage, with a swept wing and seating for up to twelve passengers. The original design featured the Canberra's front fuselage and nosewheel assembly. Typical routes were put at London–New York direct, carrying twelve passengers at 528mph, with a take-off weight of 36,500lb. Later designs featured a T-tail. **Length 71ft, Span 71ft 3in, Height 19ft, Wing Area 775sq.ft**
HP.117	All-wing airliner study in two variants, a 200-seater powered by three Rolls-Royce Speys, and a 300-seater powered by four Rolls-Royce RB963s, with a take-off weight of 250,000lb and a range greater than 4,500 nautical miles. The designs closely integrated the wings and cabins, both aerodynamically and structurally, with fins and rudders attached at each wing of conventional design. Proposals were also made of military variants, including troop transports and long-range anti-submarine patrol aircraft. The design would have had a number of problems to overcome, not least passenger accommodation and emergency exits in an all-wing airliner. However, against these were weighed the estimates of half the direct operating costs of conventional transports. **(200-seater) Length 121ft, Span 125ft, Height 32ft 6in, Wing Area 5,860sq.ft** **(300 seater) Length 101ft, Span 125ft, Height 36ft, Wing Area 5,820sq.ft**
HP.126	100-seater all-wing design put forward to Lighthill Committee, which led to **Airbus** studies.
HP.127	1962 Jet Herald **Feederliner** powered by two wing-mounted RB183 Spey Juniors.
HP.128	1962 Mach 1.15 short-range **SST**.
HP.129	A 'Mini Jet Herald' **feederliner** to seat thirty passengers.
HP.134	Ogee Aerobus with integrated thick wing, evolved from the HP.126

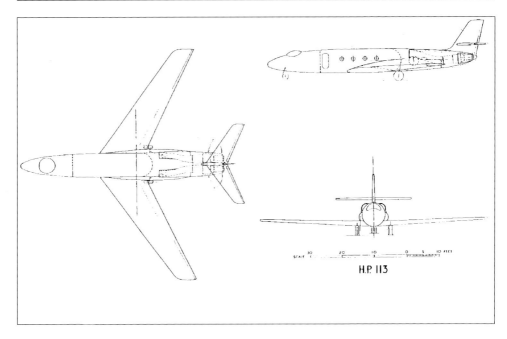

Handley Page 113
The original Handley Page HP.113 was to have been a boundary layer control test aeroplane, utilising the Canberra's front fuselage. (Handley Page Association)

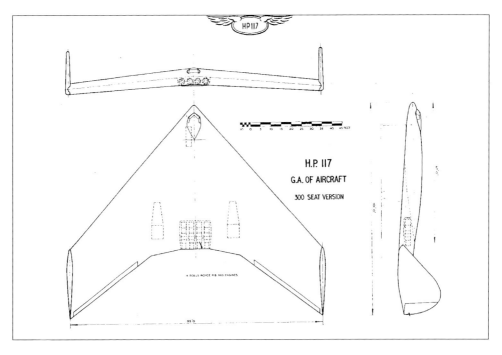

Handley Page 117
Handley Page's 300-seater HP.117 all-wing airliner study, powered by four Rolls-Royce RB 963 engines. (Handley Page Association)

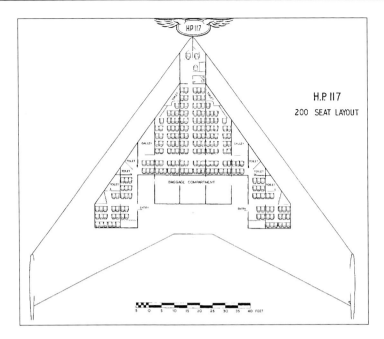

Handley Page 117
Interior layout of the 200-seater variant of the Handley Page HP.117. (Handley
Page Association)

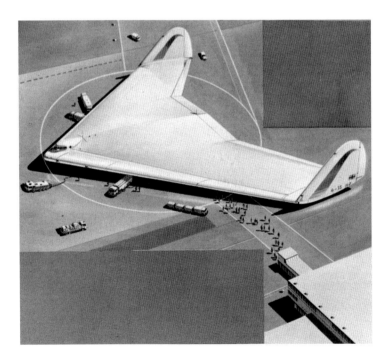

Handley Page 117
An artist's impression of the HP.117. (Imperial War Museum London: Negative
No. HP.358)

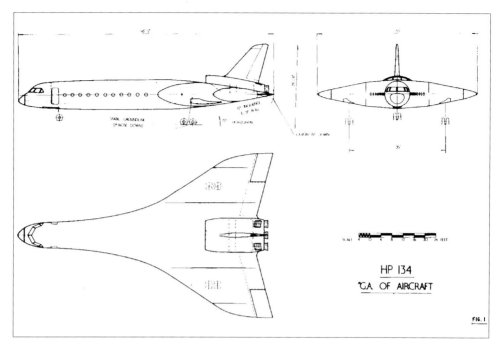

Handley Page 134
The HP.134 Ogee Aerobus with integrated thick wing. (Handley Page Association)

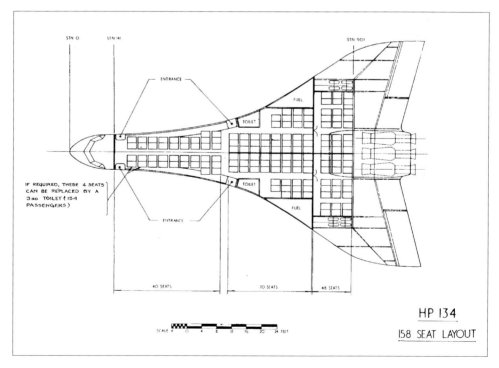

Handley Page 134
Laid out for 158 seats, the interior plan of the HP.134. (Handley Page Association)

with smoother ogival plan and a central fin and rudder. It was to carry up to 154 passengers, and be powered by three by-pass turbojets, with a maximum weight of 103,000lb and a range of 500 miles.
Length 95ft, Span 55ft, Wing Area 2,350sq.ft

HP.135 — 200-seater T-tail high-wing laminar flow design controlled by suction, a model of which was exhibited at the Paris Air Show 1965. Proposed as either a civil or military transport with a maximum range of 13,700 nautical miles, an AUW of 475,000lb and a cruising speed of Mach 0.875.

HP./SAAB Biz Jet — April 1965 study for the Saab 105's wings and tail unit to be fitted to a new fuselage and centre wing accommodating ten passengers, with an AUW of 11,000lb. The new fuselage would have had a similar cross-section to that of Miles Century, but with more headroom. The engine intakes were close to the fuselage under the high wing, with the undercarriage retracting into engine nacelles. The powerplant was to be two Turbomeca Aubisque fan engines, giving a maximum cruising speed of 385mph, and a range of 2,200 miles with six passengers.
Fuselage Length 39ft, Span 40ft, Wing Area 235sq.ft

Biz Jet — February 1970 study for a Mach 1.1 executive jet with quasi-subsonic wings of 45-degree sweep, and a fuselage waisted at the wing root. Up to six passengers could have been accommodated in a cabin 17ft-long.
Length 65ft, Span 37ft 6in, Wing Area 400sq.ft

Slewed Wing Airliner — A Mach 2 design study, which began in 1959, for a transport aircraft for up to 150 passengers carried in a cabin within the wing, and pilots accommodated in a small cabin at the forward tip, which would rotate in flight as the flight angle of yaw changed. Designs were studied for up to Mach 5. However, it was found that potential gains from the yawed wing of 72-degree sweepback while cruising, and 25 degrees when landing, did not seem very large, and there were also concerns for stability and control. The design would have been powered by four podded engines mounted under the wing, and would have had a gross weight of 350,000lb.
Length 320ft, Span 270ft

Intercity Transport Aircraft Study — A study in 1963/64 for a 125-seater tri-jet with a 500 mile range, which was used as a conventional airliner study against the HP.128.

Global Range Airliner — A number of projects were studied for a laminar flow airliner powered by four Rolls-Royce Conway engines, with laminar flow wing, fin and tailplane. One such study could accommodate 120 passengers and travel non-stop from Britain–Australia via Central Africa.
Span 198ft, Height 46ft

Handley Page (Reading)

HP.R3 — Original HP.R3 design, similar to the Miles M73 of high wing with triple fins and rudders, the thirty-six-seater was powered by four Alvis Leonide Major engines. The design was replaced by a 'new' HP.R3 which became the Herald.
Length 67ft 6in, Span 95ft, Height 17ft 6in

HP.R4 — October 1953 project for twin Napier Eland Herald. Designation was later given to a Dart-powered Herald, which became the HP.R7.

HP.R6   1955 study for high density transport for **BEA** with RB109 engines.
HP.R8   Herald-based **Car Ferry** carrying six cars and twenty-five passengers,
                or 100 passengers.

Hawker

P1055   A 1946 scheme for a high-wing seven- to eight-seater light aircraft
                Length 37ft 10in, Span 47ft 6in

P1058   Designed in 1947 as a low-wing four- to five-seater private aircraft,
                powered by two wing-mounted Lycoming/Continental engines.
                Length 27ft 6in

P1098   A high-wing design which featured fuel in wing tanks, and a rear fuse-
                lage with swing tail for loading bulky cargoes. It was put forward for the
                Dakota replacement in 1953. However, Hawker had no intention of
                building the aircraft themselves. The aircraft, powered by two Alvis
                Leonide engines, could accommodate up to sixteen passengers.
                Length 49ft 2in, Span 67ft 6in, Height 18ft 2in

P1128   A commercial five- to six-seater executive transport development of the
                Hunter, powered by two rear-mounted Orpheus engines from 1957.
                The design utilised the Hunter's wings, main undercarriage and tail.
                Span 33ft 8in, Wing Area 349sq.ft

P1131   High-wing transport powered by four Rolls-Royce Tynes, similar in
                design to Shorts Belfast, with an AUW of 230,000lb, which may have
                presented commercial freighter opportunities.
                Length 143ft 5in, Span 170ft, Wing Area 3,400sq.ft

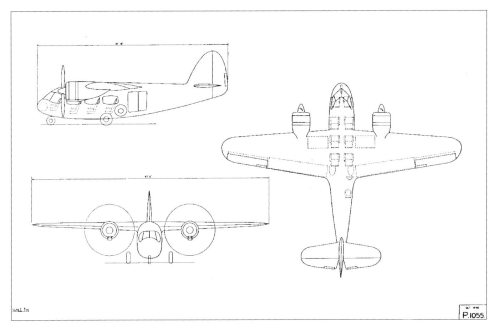

Hawker 1055
The Hawker 1055 seven/eight-seater light aircraft. (BAE SYSTEMS – via Brooklands Museum Trust)

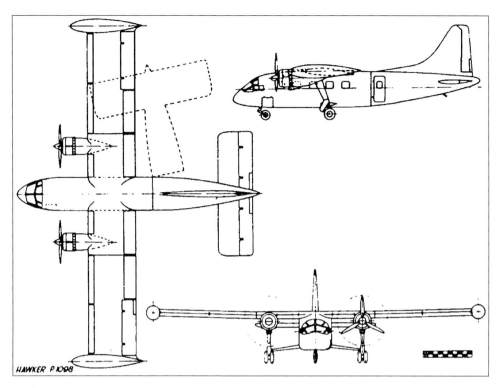

Hawker 1098
The swing-tail Hawker 1098 was proposed as a Dakota replacement. (BAE SYSTEMS – via Brooklands Museum Trust)

Hawker Siddeley (Hatfield)

HS131	748-based thirty-two-seater jet **feederliner** powered by two Rolls-Royce RB172 engines.
Double-deck Trident	Twin-decked Trident derivative (see **Airbus**).
HS132	Twin-engined RB178 development of Trident for **Airbus**.
HS133	Delta fan-lift VTOL transport.
HS134	Further Trident development with two RB178 engines mounted under the wing (see **Airbus**).
Modified Circular Integrated Wing	1965 design for a 238-seater with an integrated circular wing, with a domed circular pressure cabin giving a biconvex sectioned wing of circular planform, with added swept wing extensions giving a higher aspect ratio than gothic or slender wings. Three engines of 26,000lb thrust were sited above the rear part of the wing, with an AUW of 180,000lb. Launch costs were estimated at £74 million, with further studies of military aircraft, VTOL and freighters. Length 109ft 3in, Height 35ft 3in, Wing Area 3,660sq.ft
HS135	Six-seater executive aircraft of low-wing design with T-tail and twin jets mounted on the rear fuselage. It was to have a take-off weight of 13,350lb, and fuselage of 5ft 8in diameter. Length 46ft, Span 40ft 7in, Height 13ft 7in

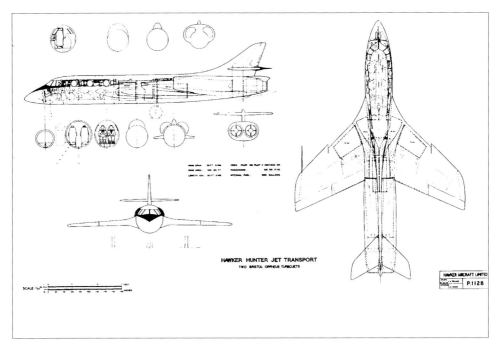

Hawker 1128
Developed from the Hunter, the Hawker 1128 executive transport seated six passengers. (BAE SYSTEMS – via Brooklands Museum Trust)

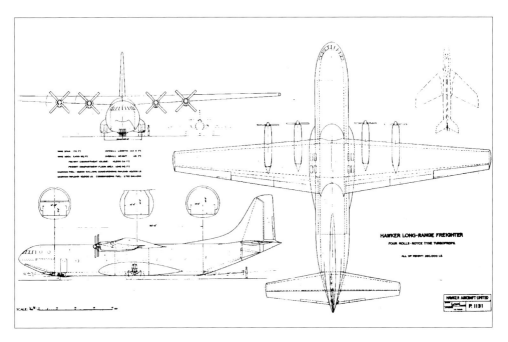

Hawker 1131
Long-range Rolls-Royce Tyne-powered Hawker 1131 freighter. (BAE SYSTEMS – via Brooklands Museum Trust)

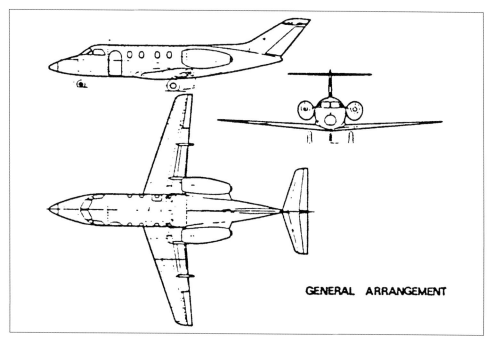

Hawker Siddeley HS135
Hawker Siddeley HS135 executive aircraft. (BAE SYSTEMS)

HS136	Originally rear-engined, later two-underwing-mounted, RB172-powered **feederliner**.
HS137	Mid-wing six-seater executive aircraft proposed in 1967, powered by two rear-mounted Bristol–Siddeley BS358 engines, with a range of 1,500 miles, a cruising speed of 540mph and a maximum take-off weight of 9,350lb. **Length 33ft, Span 33ft, Height 9ft**
HS139	Fan-lift **VTOL** transport.
HS140	1969 design for a fan-lift communications aircraft powered by a single Rolls-Royce RB202 for lift, plus a 4,000lb turbofan engine for propulsion. A maximum speed of 530mph and a range of 880 miles was proposed, with accommodation for five people. The high-wing design had the lift engine mounted in the rear of fuselage between the wings. **Length 33ft 3in, Span 22ft, Height 10ft 1in**
HS141	100-seater **VTOL** transport.
HS142	Short-range development of A300B.
HS143	Long-range development of A300B.
HS144	Joint Hatfield/Manchester eighty-seater Trent-powered **feederliner**.
HS145	VTOL low-wing civil executive aircraft seating eight passengers, powered by two Rolls-Royce RB153-61s mounted over the wing for propulsion, and four RB202-25s buried in large fuselage-mounted sponsons for lift. A cruising speed of 610mph at 28,000ft was predicted. **Length 52ft, Span 36ft 3in**

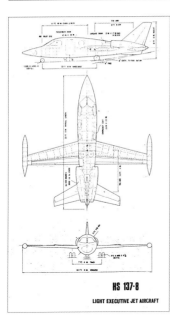

HS 137-8

LIGHT EXECUTIVE JET AIRCRAFT

Hawker Siddeley HS137
Twin Bristol–Siddeley BS358-
powered Hawker Siddeley
HS137. (BAE SYSTEMS)

HS147	Series of design studies for a fan-lift STOL airliner conducted in the early **seventies**.
HS148	RTOL development of the A300B put forward to BEA, with an in-service date of 1978 (see **seventies**).
HS149	Four-engined A300B development (see **seventies**).
Trident 4	July 1975 study for BEA for a twin CFM-powered Trident (see seventies).
Trident 5	Submitted to the Group of Six twin CFM 56-powered Trident with redesigned wing (see **seventies**).
Tri-Jet Commuter	1972 study for a three JT-15D-1-engined commuter jet, seating up to twenty-one passengers, or ten passengers in an executive layout. The low-wing design with small T-tail had two engines mounted on the rear fuselage, with the third mounted above the fuselage, similar to the Trident. Length 55ft, Span 45ft, Height 16ft 5in, Wing Area 290sq.ft

Beechcraft/Hawker Siddeley Hatfield

BH200	1970 joint study undertaken by Beechcraft and Hawker Siddeley for a new small executive jet, which could also serve as a military transport, mission support and crew trainer. The low-wing design with T-tail could accommodate up to six passengers, and was expected to fly in early 1973, with manufacture by Hawker and sales undertaken by Beechcraft. Further developments included a seventeen-seater commuter jet variant. The basic BH200 was powered by two rear-mounted ALF 301B engines, while the 'B' and 'C' commuter models were proposed with TFE-731-2 engines. (BH200) Length 47ft 6.2in, Span 43ft, Height 14ft 2in, Wing Area 253sq.ft (BH200C) Length 56ft 102in, Span 43ft, Height 14ft 8in, Wing Area 253sq.ft

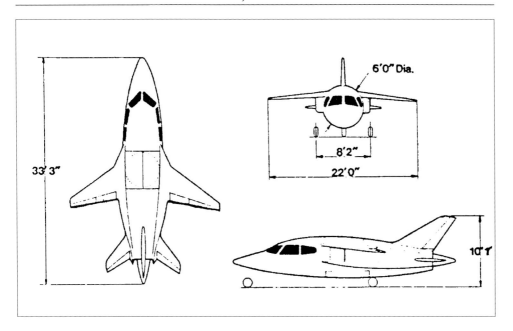

Above: *Hawker Siddeley HS140*
Hawker Siddeley HS140 fan-lift
communications aircraft. (BAE
SYSTEMS)

Right: *Hawker Siddeley HS145*
Hatfield's VTOL executive aircraft,
the Hawker Siddeley HS145.
(BAE SYSTEMS)

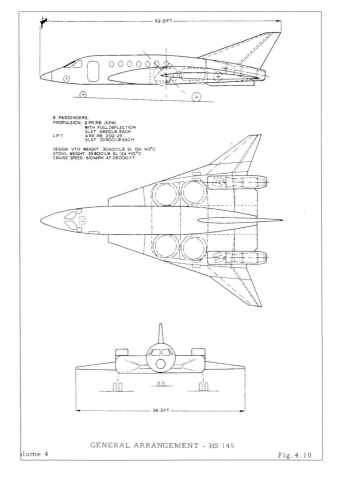

GENERAL ARRANGEMENT - HS 145

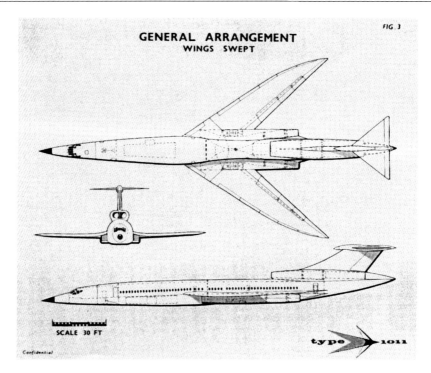

Hawker Siddeley HS1011
The variable swing-wing Hawker Siddeley HS1011 with wings swept, was designed as a 'no-boom' Mach 1.15 airliner. (BAE SYSTEMS – via British Airways Archives)

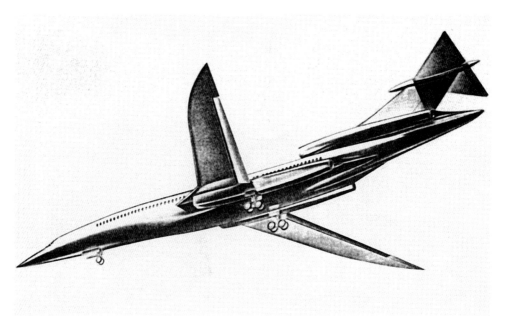

Hawker Siddeley HS1011
An artist's impression of the HS1011, with wings extended. (BAE SYSTEMS – via British Airways Archives)

Hawker Siddeley (Kingston – Advanced Projects Group)

HS1000   Six-engined **supersonic** airliner study.

HS1011   A commercial derivative of the design submitted for the Maritime Reconnaissance contract based on de Havilland's DH130 proposal. The Mach 1.15 four-jet airliner with a variable swing wing could accommodate 160 passengers over a 2,500 nautical mile range, with an AUW of 269,000lb. Designed as a 'no boom' airliner, the HS1011 could travel at an altitude of 40,000ft with no shock waves reaching the ground, thereby allowing unrestricted supersonic operations. The waisted fuselage saw seating at four-, five- and six-abreast, with an underfloor cargo hold.

Hawker Siddeley (Manchester)

HS803   **VTOL** transport with folding circulation control rotors (CCR) October 1966.

HS804   October 1966 tilt-wing short-range transport (see **VTOL**).

HS805A   Deflected slipstream transport, January 1967 (see **VTOL**).

HS805B   January 1967 Mechanical flap transport (see **VTOL**).

HS805C   Blown flap transport (see VTOL).

HS806   August 1967 twin-jet **feederliner** based on the 748.

HS807   October 1967 VTOL civil executive/wide speed range/aircrew rescue aircraft, with circulation control rotors and RB162 lift engines applied to a HS125 type design.

HS810   Twin-CCR design **VTOL** intercity airliner.

HS816   Mach 1.1 transport from February 1970.

HS817   April 1970 smaller variant of HS144, powered by two M45H engines.

HS821   Feederliner to seat between twenty-six and forty, powered by two ALF502, T55, T53 or ATF3 engines.

HS823   Smaller HS146-derived forty to sixty-five-seater powered by three ALF502 engines, December 1971.

HS824   January 1972 feederliner powered by two scaled ALF502 or M45H engines.

HS827   April 1974 Jet 748 derivative powered by two ALF502 engines.

HS831   November 1975 advanced turboprop feederliner.

HS832   HS748 series 5 **feederliner** twin-turbofan development.

HS833   February 1976 study of an advanced turboprop variant of A300B.

HS834   February 1976 development of the HS125.

HS835   September 1976 high-wing advanced feederliner powered by turboprops.

HS860   April 1968 Jet 748 development **feederliner**.

Hawker Siddeley/Breguet/Nord

HBN 100   261-seater widebody **Airbus** study from 1966, powered by two RB178 engines.

HBN 101   High-wing **Airbus** study with sideways double-bubble fuselage.

HBN 102   Double-deck mid-wing **Airbus** study.

HBN 103   Double-deck mid-wing **Airbus** study.

HBN 104   Double-deck low-wing **Airbus** study with rear-mounted engines.

Hawker Siddeley/Fokker–VFW/Dornier

CAST

Joint study to look at new quiet jetliners for the **seventies**, with two, three or four engines.

Hurel–Dubois/Miles

HDM 106

Also called the 'Caravan', the HDM 106 was to be the production development of the HDM 105, a Freighter/Transport with a Hurel Dubois high-aspect ratio wing, with larger all-metal fuselage, powered by two Lycoming GSO480s or Turbomeca Astazous. Capable of accommodating up to fifteen passengers or cargo in a hold of 565cu.ft, with a rear-loading cargo door. A gross weight of 8,000lb and cruising speed of 129mph was predicted. Interest in the project was shown by NATO. However, F.G. Miles, being a small company, were not able to undertake manufacture and the design was eventually purchased by Shorts, later being incorporated into that company's SC7 Skyvan.
Length 37ft 10in, Span 75ft 4in, Wing Area 279sq.ft

HDM 108

Larger twenty-five-seater/freighter variant of the HDM106, undertaken mostly by Hurel Dubois, with high-aspect ratio wing powered by Turbomeca Bastan turboprops.

Miles

X11

Miles' unsolicited proposal to meet the **Brabazon 1** Specification.

X14

1943 design for one-stop Transatlantic operation or Empire routes. It was based on the X11, but was powered by four 2,400hp Bristol Centaurus engines, with reduced fuel capacity and weight to accommodate sixty-four passengers, with a range of 2,500 miles at a cruising speed of 260mph and AUW of 120,000lb.
Length 110ft, Span 150ft, Wing Area 2,350sq.ft

X15

A six Napier Sabre variant of the X11, with an increased wing span, a range of 5,100 miles at 300mph, and an AUW of 165,000lb.
Length 110ft, Span 170ft, Wing Area 2,500sq.ft

M.56

Miles' proposal for a Dakota replacement for a small feederliner. The M.56 was a high-wing all-metal monoplane to seat up to twenty-four passengers at three-abreast. It would have been powered by two Rolls-Royce Merlin 24 engines. The tailplane featured endplate fins and rudders. Alternative powerplants considered were the Bristol Perseus or, if a four-engined design, the Armstrong Siddeley Cheetapard. The M.56 had a range of 1,500 to 1,600 miles, estimated cruising speed of 194mph, and an AUW of 25,600lb. The design, not taken up by the Ministry, was originally talked about as a possible competitor against the AW.55 in early documentation for the Brabazon 2 contract.

Length 66ft, Span 80ft, Wing Area 800sq.ft

M.59

Seeing that the M.56 was too large, Miles turned their attention to a smaller variant, the M.59, which was, in many ways, a scaled-down variant of the 1943 M.54. The high-wing design of an all-metal construction could accommodate thirteen passengers, with power being provided by two Armstrong Siddeley Cheetapards. It had a range of 1,000 miles and an AUW of 12,000lb. The design was submitted to

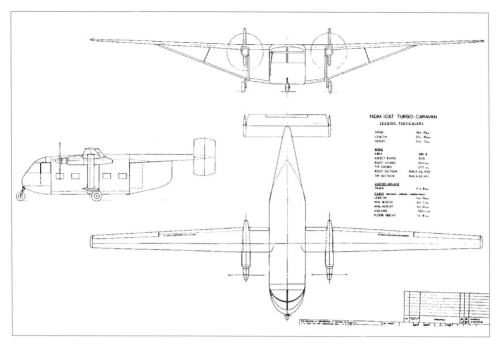

Hurel Dubois Miles HDM 106
The HDM 106 'Caravan' was to be the larger production variant of the HDM 105. (Miles – via British
Airways Archives)

the Ministry at the beginning of 1944. However, it was felt that the aircraft was now too small. In 1947, when the Navy needed a communications aircraft, the M.59 design was again looked at, combining components of the new Marathon project such as the tail and undercarriage, plus the fuselage jigs. In this new form, the project was re-designated the M.59A, with a potential variant on offer to civil operators. The order for the communications aircraft, however, went to Percival with the Sea Prince, and the M.59A was shelved.
(M.59) Span 57ft, Length 50ft, Wing Area 400sq.ft

M.62 — A twin-engined high-wing all-metal freighter with fore and aft loading and a hold some 30ft long, with the cockpit located in line with the wing and tail boom. Powered by two Wright Cyclone GR-2600 A5B or Bristol Hercules engines, the M.62 had a range of 1,100 miles and an AUW of 45,120lb, and could be operated from small areas of unprepared ground.
Span 110ft, Length 69ft, Wing Area 1,500sq.ft

M.63 — The M.63 Libellula was a project for a jet-propelled mailplane in 1944. Based on the M.39 Libellula bomber, the M.63's three jet engines were mounted at the back of the aircraft, two under the wing, which was itself positioned at the back of the aircraft, with a small wing at the front by the cockpit. The powerplant was either Power Jets W2/700 or Rolls-Royce B37s (a derivative of the W2/700) – the design being in effect the first rear-engined aircraft. The M.63 would have cruised at

500mph, with a range of 1,600 miles. At the time it was considered that a dedicated aircraft for carrying mail was required. It was greeted with enthusiasm by BOAC and the Postmaster General – the ministry however, decided that the aircraft would not be made available.

Span (Forward Wing) 39ft 3in, (Rear Wing) 55ft, Length 35ft 9in

M.67   A 1945 proposal to meet American Airlines' specification for a DC3 replacement with increased performance. The M.67, unlike most Miles designs, was of low wing, and powered by four Rolls-Royce Dart engines. To be un-pressurised, the aircraft could accommodate a maximum of thirty-two passengers, although twenty-four would be more common, with underfloor freight compartments. The all-metal tricycle undercarriage design with adjustable fins was very similar to that of the M.56.

Span 80ft, Length 66ft, Wing Area 800sq.ft

M.72   A four-engined development of the Aerovan, the M.72 did actually enter production, but was never completed after Miles collapsed.

M.73   This project began life as a larger development of the Marathon, and featured a new centre fuselage and centre section. The design, a high-wing monoplane, was powered by four Alvis Leonides of 500hp, while utilising the Marathon's nose and tail units plus outer wings. One of its major drawbacks was the fact that it was not pressurised. The aircraft should have flown in 1948 but, due to the financial state of Miles, the project never proceeded. The M.73 design was, however, developed into the HP.R3 Herald, after Handley Page took over Miles.

F.G. Miles

Surrey 1   Put forward for the Rapide Replacement, the Surrey 1 could accommodate fifteen to seventeen passengers or, on short runs, up to twenty-two, and was powered by four Gipsy Queen II engines, with an all-up weight of 10,000lb. The design was not unlike that of the Aerovan/Merchantman series. In fact, it was stated that BEA might even have been interested in the Merchantman, had it still been in production. The Surrey 1 featured a tail unit carried on the boom, with the fuselage suspended beneath the wing/boom structure. The project, if built, would have seen F.G. Miles building the prototype at Redhill, while discussions on production were held with Portsmouth Aviation, British Air Transport and Cornercraft Ltd. As with the Aerovan/ Gemini, the flap had a permanently extended surface of variable angle. The design was considered a little on the light side and there were still problems with the takeover of the original Miles company.

M.101   A **Car Ferry** designed for Silver City Airways, powered by four Rolls-Royce Dart engines. The large box fuselage could accommodate up to six cars.

M.102   Renumbered M.101 **Car Ferry**, due to the numbers connection with the tragic R101.

M.103   Twin-engined 3-ton high-wing freighter, with fuselage similar to Aerovan, and with rear-loading capability. The Hurel Dubois HD31 high-aspect ratio wing was utilised, and power was provided by two Alvis Leonides and one Rolls-Royce Soar RSr2 booster, mounted

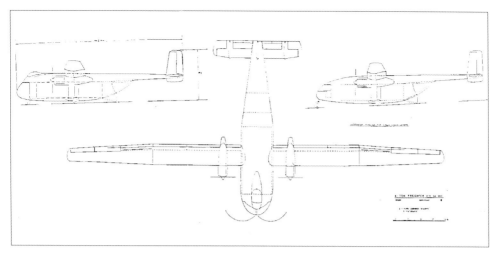

Miles 103
Utilising the wing of the Hurel Dubois HD31, the Miles 103 was a 3 ton-freighter (an alternative layout is also shown). (Miles – via Grahame Gates)

	between the two tail fins. The maximum speed was 205mph, and a maximum payload could be carried over a range of 765 miles with an AUW of 20,330lb. **Length 65ft, Span 152ft, Height 19ft, Wing Area 1,100sq.ft**
M.104	Larger high-wing 6-ton freighter with three fins and Aerovan-type fuselage and Hurel Dubois HD32 wing. Powered by two Alvis Leonide Majors and two Rolls-Royce Soar RSr2s, with a maximum speed of 255mph, a range with capacity payload of 658 miles was projected with an AUW of 56,000lb. Loading was through both front clamshell doors and it had rear loading. **Length 69ft, Span 152ft, Height 19ft, Wing Area 1,100sqft**
M.109	A small six-seater with a high wing of 'semi' H-D design with an aspect ratio of 12.5. The light utility aircraft was powered by two Lycoming 0-320 engines. The maximum speed was 154mph with an AUW of 4,000lb. All the fuel would be carried in the 'bullets' at the wing/strut junction. **Length 50ft, Span 27ft 9in, Wing Area 200sq.ft**
M.111	Six-seater aircraft utilising the outer wing of the crashed HDM 105 prototype, and powered by a single Turbomeca Astazou.
Centurion	Development of the M.100 Student powered by Rolls-Royce RB108, Turbomeca Gourdon or Arbizon engines, the latter being proposed as a four-seater liaison aircraft/business jet, with an AUW of 4,000lb. A variant with a larger fuselage was known as the Graduate, and would have been powered by a Turbomeca Aubisque.
Century	A new design, the Century was put forward in 1963 after a commission from Col. J. Scott of Johannesburg, and was to be a six- to seven-seater executive twinjet able to travel over 1,600 miles at 450mph. In 1964 a mock-up was built at Shoreham, and Scottish Aviation were invited to partner the project. Power would have been provided by two

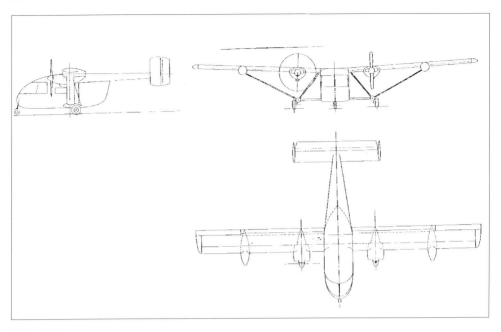

Miles 109
The light utility Miles 109, powered by two Lycoming 0-320 engines. (Miles – via Grahame Gates)

Turbomeca Aubisques of 1,540lb thrust. The design, of high-wing layout with single fin and mid tailplane, attracted interest of joint funding from the government, and studies were made as a joint venture with France, but the company was unable to fund its share of the project.
Span 40ft

ML Aviation

26/49   A design put forward for the Rapide replacement, Specification 26/49. The high-wing design with a large wing area of 640sq.ft was to be powered by either four Queen 2 or Queen 30 engines, and could accommodate up to seventeen passengers, with an AUW of 13,500lb (Queen 30 variant). The simple design had no aircraft hydraulic or pneumatic systems incorporated. Should the design have been chosen, it would have been built at ML's White Waltham factory. The project was deemed too large and too heavy, being the largest submitted against the Rapide replacement specification.

Percival/Hunting Percival/Hunting

P41   High-wing twin Perseus-engined design for the **Brabazon 5** proposal.
P42   Four Leonides-engined high-wing development of P41 for **Brabazon 5**.
P51   Low-wing twin-engined five-seater executive aircraft.
P60   Five-seater twin-engined low-wing executive aircraft.
P64   This was proposed for the Rapide replacement, based on the Prince design, with seating for fourteen passengers, boosted Leonide engines

and a low drag 'V' windscreen. Modifications were made to the Prince's wing to give a slight increase in span, and chord, giving a more efficient flap.
Length 42ft 10in, Span 60ft, Height 16ft 1in, Wing Area 435sq.ft

P65   A four-engined Gipsy Major X transport using outer wings of the new Prentice trainer, with new centre wing and engine nacelles. The fuselage had a 5in increase in internal width, allowing three-abreast-seating for up to fifteen. The fin, rudder and tailplane were taken from the Prince aircraft. A further development with Gipsy Queen 30 engines, would have given a higher cruising speed with the same payload, with a split flap added to the wing. This variant would have had an AUW of 10,650lb. A further composite design study married the P64 wing and tail with the fuselage and undercarriage of the P65.
Length 41ft 9in, Span 63ft, Height 16ft, Wing Area 417sq.ft

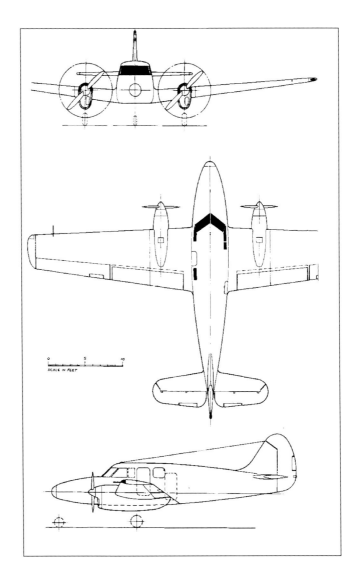

Percival P51
Percival P51, a five-seater light executive aircraft. (BAE SYSTEMS)

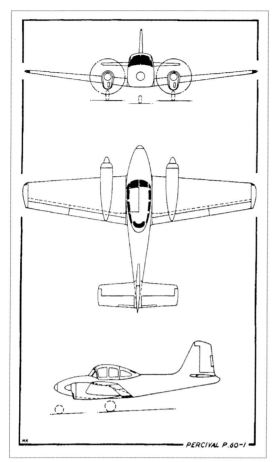

PERCIVAL P.60-1

Left: *Percival P60*
Twin-engined Percival P60 executive aircraft.
(BAE SYSTEMS)

Below: *Percival P64*
The Percival P64 was designed as a Rapide
replacement. (BAE SYSTEMS – via RAF
Museum Hendon)

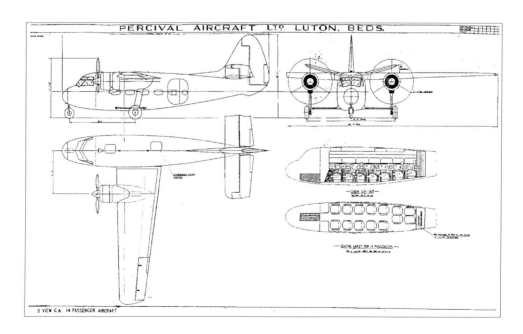

P85	BEA large helicopter study for BEAline transport (see **VTOL**).
P86	Sixty-seater compound helicopter for BEAline specification (see **VTOL**).
P87	DC3 replacement **feederliner** powered by two pusher turboprops.
P92	Twin pressurised Rolls-Royce Dart **feederliner**.
P95	Twin pressurised Napier Gazelle **feederliner**.
P99	Eighteen- to twenty-seater Pembroke development.
P100	Eighteen- to twenty-seater Twin Alvis Major development of the Pembroke.
P101	Thirty- to thirty-two seater four Alvis-engined transport.
P105	Multi-purpose helicopter to seat up to ten passengers, or as a flying crane developed from P74, with a range of 150/160 miles, powered by two Oryx Nor4s, with a rotor of 63ft diameter. (Transport variant) Length (blades folded) 44ft, Height 14ft 3in
P106	Twenty-seater transport powered by four Marcadau engines.
P107	Jet transport developed into BAC 107 **feederliner**.
P108	Fourteen-seater helicopter proposed to BEA, powered by two Napier Nor5s, with a cruising speed of 100 mph.
P110	Twenty-seater twin Oryx transport.
P113	Single RB108 and single rotor-powered helicopter developed from the P74.
P116	Twenty-seater transport powered by two rear-mounted Viper engines, or alternatively, Orpheus engines. The low-wing design featured a T-tail arrangement.
P117	Orpheus-powered executive aircraft.
P118	Stretched President development.
P119	Eighteen-seater transport.
P122	Twenty-six-seater jet flap transport with an AUW of 18,000lb.
P124	Twin T-58-powered eighteen- to twenty-four-seater turboprop transport of twin-boom design, and rear clamshell door similar to the Armstrong Whitworth Argosy.
H129	Gnome-powered stretched President.
H134	Twinjet transport.
H151	Twinjet transport.
H152	Small feederliner powered by four overwing jet engines.
H154	Jet flap transport.
H172	Twin turboprop light transport.
PFH1	Single-rotor feeder helicopter with an AUW of 19,800lb, accommodating thirty passengers.
PFH2	Further study of single-rotor feeder helicopter with an AUW of 19,800lb, and rotor diameter of 88ft 6in. Power was to be provided by four twin Turbomeca engines, with accommodation for thirty passengers at three abreast. Fuselage Length 46ft, Height 18ft 3in

Edgar Percival/Samlesbury/Lancashire

Prospector 4	Eight-seater development of Prospector Utility aircraft.

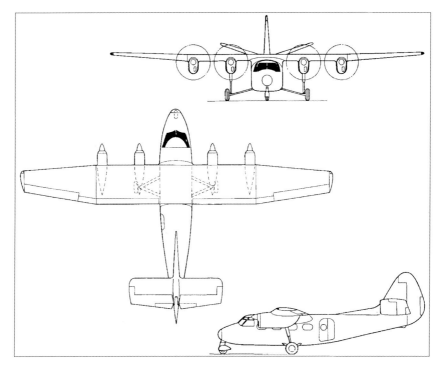

Percival P65
Powered by four Gipsy Major X engines, the Percival P65 provided seating for fifteen passengers
at three abreast. (BAE SYSTEMS – via RAF Museum Hendon)

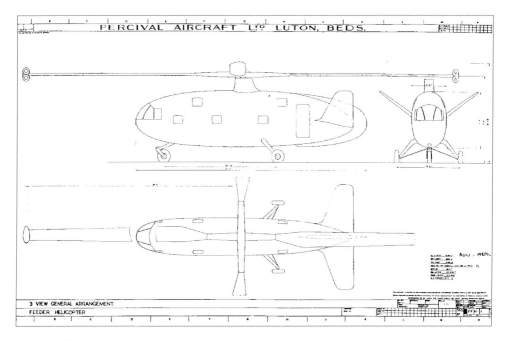

Percival PFH 2
Single-rotor Percival PFH 2 feeder helicopter seated thirty passengers. (BAE SYSTEMS)

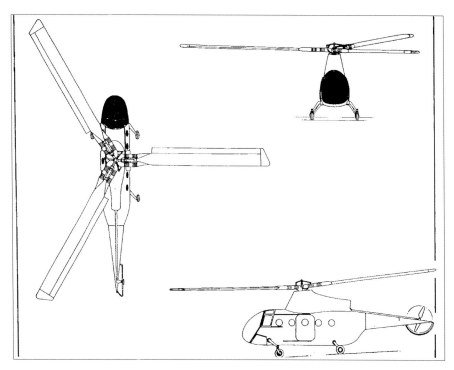

Hunting Percival P113
The Hunting Percival P113 was developed from the aborted Percival P74 helicopter. (BAE SYSTEMS)

Hunting Percival
P124
Side view of the
Hunting Percival
P124 twin-boom
transport. (BAE
SYSTEMS)

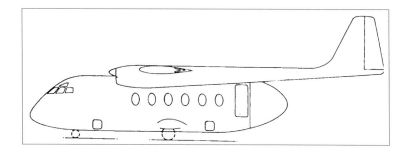

Hunting 152
The Hunting H 152
transport/executive
aircraft with four
overwing-mounted jet
engines. (BAE
SYSTEMS)

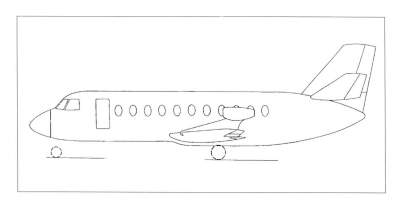

Saben-Hart

Freighter	**Flying boat** designed with a gross weight of 3,000,000lb.
Airliner	1,800-seater **flying boat** study from 1957.

Saunders Roe

P111 A 1954 study of an amphibian development of the Princess.

P112 A large 220,000lb flying boat powered by six contra-prop Napier Nomads.

P117 A V-tailed flying boat from 1949, powered by four Napier Nomad contra-props.

P123 Two flying boat studies, the first with an AUW of 120,000lb, powered by Bristol Proteus or Centaurus engines, and the second by four compound Rolls-Royce Griffons, with an AUW of 98,000lb.

P124 An amphibian aircraft to seat up to sixteen passengers with a V-tail, powered by two Armstrong Siddeley Mambas with an AUW of 27,380lb.
Length 68ft, Span 82ft, Height 10ft 9in

P125 A 1948 freight-carrying flying boat powered by four Bristol Centaurus in coupled pairs. Two variants were proposed, one with twin fuselages, the other a single hull with twin booms.

P126 A 160-seater stretched Princess with an AUW of 360,000lb.

P129 A 1949 study for a V-tailed Bristol Proteus flying boat seating up to 150 passengers.

P131 The Duchess flying boat with swept wings, powered by either six Rolls-Royce Avons jets or four Napier Nomads turboprops. It was replaced by the P135.

P132 A joint study from 1948 with Folland for a Rapide replacement aircraft of low-wing design, with four engines, either Gipsy Major or Blackburn

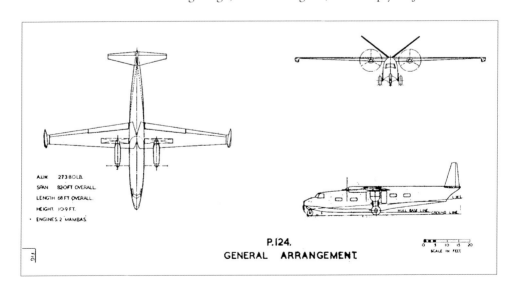

Saunders Roe P124
V-tailed amphibian Saunders Roe P124. (GKN Aerospace Services)

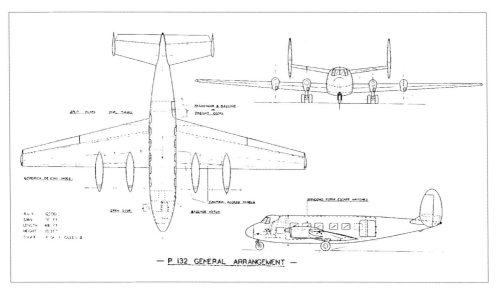

Saunders Roe P132
Studied jointly with Folland as the FO134, the Saunders Roe P132 was a prospective Rapide replacement
aircraft. (GKN Aerospace Services)

	Bombardier engines, seating up to eleven passengers. A further design to accommodate seventeen passengers had an AUW of 12,500lb, and was powered by four Gipsy Queen IIs. **Length 48ft, Span 70ft, Height 15ft 3in**
P133	Two projects were proposed under the P133 number. The first was a flying boat with a Comet wing, the second a development of the Comet with Sprite rocket motors between the jet engines.
P135	Based on the 131, the 135 became the definitive Duchess **flying boat**.
P136	1950 four-engined flying boat study with an AUW of 82,000lb.
P138	A jet derivative of the Princess with power from either twelve DH Ghosts or ten Rolls-Royce Avons with two RB93 jet packs.
P139	A 1950 study for a landplane to seat 200 passengers on two decks – ninety-six on the upper deck at four abreast and 104 on the lower deck at six abreast. The design was of low wing, with four Napier Sabre VII engines and twin tail fins, with an AUW of 130,000lb **Fuselage Length 125ft, Span 144ft, Height 25ft, Wing Area 2,600sq.ft.**
P145	Princess variant powered by eight Napier Nomads.
P152	A 1952 development of the Duchess, featuring a V-tail.
P160	1952 studies covering four versions of a Car Ferry amphibian/twin boom freighter, powered by Bristol Hercules engines.
P164	Princess powered by ten or twelve Napier Eland coupled engines.
P165	Various engine schemes on Princess, including Allison T38 and T40.
P166	A large 400-seater passenger transport or freighter flying boat schemed in 1953, with an AUW of 400,000lb.
P171	A low-wing landplane from 1952 with a straight wing, to seat up to fourteen passengers, with an AUW of 9,000lb, powered by two Armstrong Siddeley Viper jets. **Length 38ft 6in, Span 52ft**

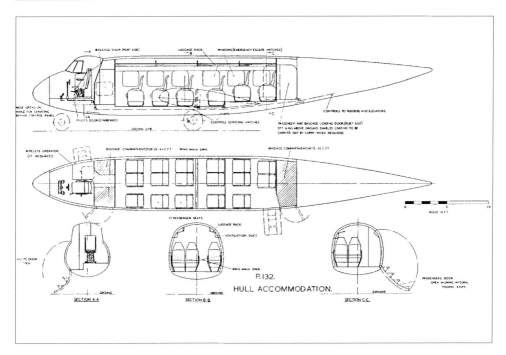

Saunders Roe P132
Interior layout of the P132, showing three-abreast seating for seventeen passengers. (GKN Aerospace Services)

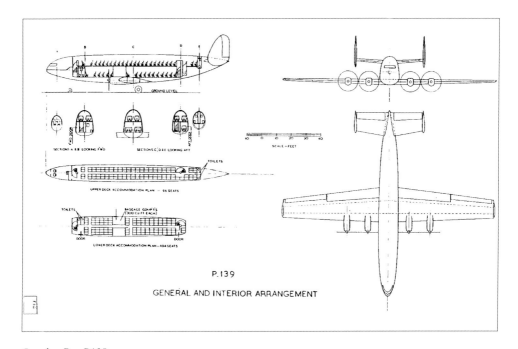

Saunders Roe P139
The 200-seater double-deck Saunders Roe P139 was powered by four Napier Sabre VIIs. (GKN Aerospace Services)

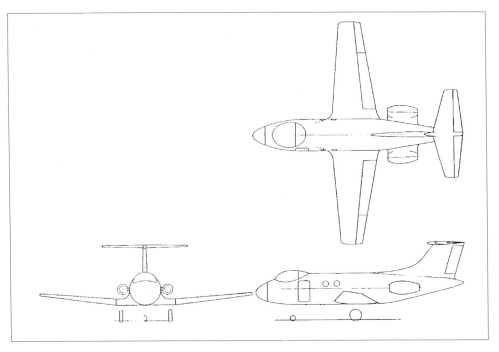

Saunders Roe P195
One of a number of schemes for a VIP transport, the Saunders Roe P195 had various engine positions and high-
and low-wing configurations. (GKN Aerospace Services)

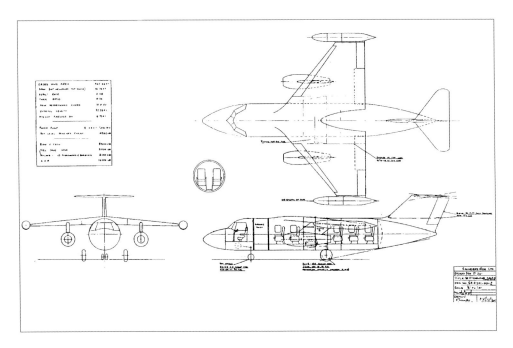

Saunders Roe P201
The Saunders Roe P201 was an executive aircraft development of the company's SR.177. (GKN Aerospace
Services)

P173	Numerous schemes for stretched re-engined Princess developments to seat up to 264 passengers. Among the powerplants studied were six Rolls-Royce RB109s or six Bristol BE25s.
P192	A 1956 study of a 1,000-seater **flying boat** powered by twenty-four Rolls-Royce Conway engines, with an AUW of 1,500,000lb and a range of 1,900 miles.
P195	A designation given to a number of schemes for a VIP transport to seat up to seven passengers in a fuselage of 7ft diameter, with an AUW of 12,000lb. Various engine positions included under the wings, rear-mounted and on the tips of the tailplanes, plus a tilt engine variant. Studies were made with both high and low wings, and were powered by either RB108 or Viper engines. **Fuselage Length 44ft, Span 45ft 5in, Height 16ft 7in**
P199	A 1957 study for a conversion to a landplane Princess, powered by Rolls-Royce Tynes.
P201	A ten-passenger executive aircraft based on the SR177, powered by either Bristol Orpheus or Armstrong Siddeley Viper engines, with an AUW of 16,000lb. Both high- or low-wing variants were studied, with engines mounted at the rear or beneath the wings. **Length 52ft 75in, Span 31ft 75in (not including wing tips), Wing Area 407sq.ft**
P202	A 1957 executive aircraft based on the SR177, to seat eight rearward-facing passengers, powered by three Bristol Orpheus BOr 12 engines. It would be able to travel at Mach 1.8, with a range of 2,500 nautical miles and an AUW of 50,000lb. **Length 81ft 10in, Span 36ft**
P203	Princess derivative powered by two Pratt & Whitney T57 and four Rolls-Royce Tynes.
P206	Floatplane and panto-based developments of HDM 106.
P207	A 1958 study for developing the HDM 106.
P220	Autogyro studies including a high stub wing single-rotor transport with an AUW of 8,000lb.

Saunders Roe Eastleigh

P508	Helicopter of light pod and boom design with a tail rotor with two gas turbines mounted on high stub wings, driving a three-bladed rotor.
P514	A fifty-passenger 1953 design to meet BEAline specification (see **VTOL**).
P539	1967 high-wing twin Gnome-powered VSTOL/STOL transport.
P541	A five-seater helicopter powered by Blackburn Turmo 603 engines.

Scottish Aviation

SAL 50 Concord	A proposal that originated before the end of the war for a new fuselage to be mated to a Consolidated Liberator aircraft, utilising the spare wings available. The low-wing, twin-tailed airliner would have been powered by four Rolls-Royce or Bristol engines. In October 1944, the company had decided to go-ahead with a prototype aircraft, and the name Concord was registered in October 1945, with registration number

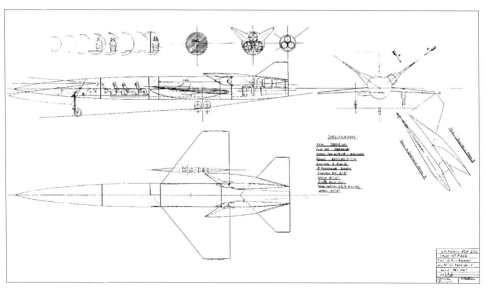

Saunders Roe P202
Developed from the SR177, the model 202 was an eight-seater executive aircraft. (GKN Aerospace Services)

G-AGTK allocated towards a prototype aircraft. Interest in the project was received from Iceland and the Netherlands. However, there was no official backing and, as time progressed, the Lockheed Constellation had arrived, and any advantage of the Concord was lost.

Twenty- to thirty-seater	A proposal originally put to the Ministry of Aircraft Production in December 1944, to build a prototype aircraft able to travel between 1,200–1,500 miles, carrying twenty to thirty passengers.
Spec 26/49	A proposal for a four-engined low-wing Rapide replacement airliner with circular fuselage and single slotted flaps. It would be powered by four Major 10 engines with an AUW of 9,030lb, to carry between ten and twelve passengers, looking not unlike the de Havilland Heron. **Wing Area 500sq.ft**
Turbo Pioneer	A January to April 1956 study for a large forty-seater aircraft, looking like an enlarged cleaned up Twin Pioneer. The high-wing twin Dart design also featured a rear-loading door. The design was superseded by the Super Twin Pioneer **Length 64ft 75in, Span 104ft**
Pioneer 4 (Clydesdale)	Under the General Purpose Light Transport Aircraft (GPLTA), studies were carried out between 1958 and 1960 on a number of schemes based on the Prestwick Pioneer. The Type 1 featured a new fuselage, while the Type 2 became the Pegasus. The Pioneer 3 was a ten-seater design powered by an Alvis Leonide 504, featuring a wider and deeper fuselage, while the type IV Clydesdale was an eight-seater with a redesigned fuselage, and Alvis Leonide Mk130 engines.
Super Twin Pioneer	Studied between 1958 and 1961, the Super Twin Pioneer Types 2 and 3 were stretched developments of the Twin Pioneer, seating up to twenty-two passengers, with a new straight cantilever wing, stretched

fuselage, retractable undercarriage and a lengthened and remodelled nose. Power was to be provided by two de Havilland Gnome P1200 turboprops.
(Scheme 2) Length 51ft 7in, Span 80ft

3 Tonner | 1959 study of a high-wing 3 ton-freighter with single fin, powered by twin Gnomes with rear-loading capability.
Length 62ft 6in, Height 27ft, Span 88ft

Gleneagle | A high-wing executive aircraft from 1961 to seat six to eight passengers, featuring a tailplane midway on the fin, and powered by either two Turbomeca Astazou or Continental engines.

Chieftain | A single-engined low-wing executive aircraft to be powered by a Lycoming IG30-480-A1A6 engine, with seating for up to six passengers.

Shorts

Specification 2/44 | Unsolicited proposal for a six Centaurus-powered design to meet **Brabazon 1** Specification.

Specification 2/44 | Tailless monoplane based on Pterodactyl VIII, to meet **Brabazon 1** Specification.

S.A5/S43 | A four-engined design to meet **Brabazon 2** Specification.

S.A7/S46 | Twin Cougar fifteen-seater flying boat.

S.A8/S47 | A twin-deck fifty-two passenger **flying boat** powered by four Napier Nomads.

LR Empire flying boat | 1946 design for a 106-seater long-range **flying boat**.

S.A8 Landplane | 1946 Landplane derivative of the S.A8 flying boat, submitted to the **LRE** Specification.

LRE1 | A 1948 low-wing four Nomad-engined submission for **LRE**.

Commonwealth | Similar to LRE1, this project from the Belfast office featured an increased wing span and was Shorts final submission to LRE.

26/49 | Low-wing design with seating for up to fifteen passengers to meet Rapide replacement (26/49). A number of engine options were studied, including Gipsy Queen II, Gipsy Major X and Blackburn Bombardier. The Queen II variant had an AUW of 11,250lb, and the Major X, 8,400lb. The design featured two emergency exits in the roof, and single slotted flaps.

PD14 | Twin Turbomeca Marcadau executive transport.

PD15 | 1954 design for a small high-wing freighter with twin tail booms extending from the outer nacelle, with rear-loading capability. The original powerplant was four Alvis Leonides, later twin Dart turboprops. The design was too small for would-be operators, only being able to carry a payload of 9,000lb over a range of 200 miles.
Length 64ft, Span 86ft 5in

PD16 | Large freighter/passenger transport/**Car Ferry**, powered by two Bristol Proteus engines.

PD18 | The predecessor to the Belfast, the original PD18 featured the Britannia flight deck with a nil dihedral thin wing and underslung Bristol Orion engines, with a 10ft hold cross-section. The design was replaced by the Britannic, later called the Belfast, with a 12ft hold cross-section. It would be powered by Rolls-Royce RB109 Tyne engines.

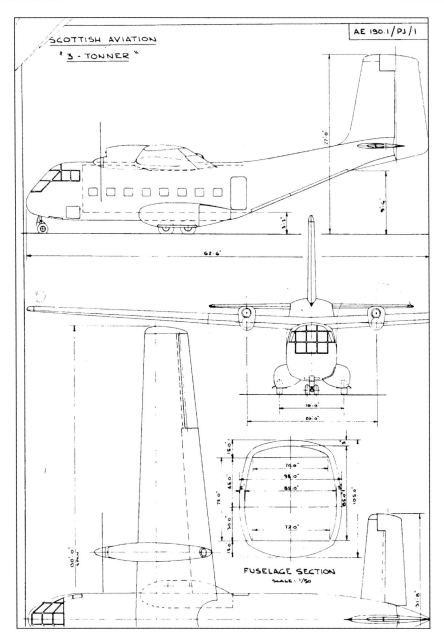

Scottish 3-Tonner
The Scottish Aviation 3-Tonner, a Gnome-powered freighter. (BAE SYSTEMS)

PD20	1957 transatlantic airliner study powered by either four Bristol Orion turboprops or four Bristol Olympus jets.
PD22	Mach 1.3 medium-range swept wing **supersonic** airliner.
PD24	Twin Rolls-Royce Tyne-powered Airbus study.
PD26	Short-range **feederliner**.
PD27	Short-range **feederliner**.

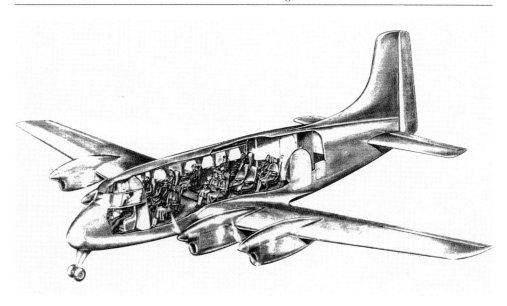

Short 26/49
An artist's impression of one of the Shorts proposals for the Rapide replacement Specification 26/49. (Courtesy of Bombardier Aerospace)

PD29	Mach 1.8 long-range **supersonic** airliner.
PD30	**Supersonic** airliner study to the STAC.
PD47	Derivative of the Belfast with STOL capability.
PD52	Five-passenger development of Beech Baron.
PD53	The issuing of the Air Staff Requirement in 1964, for a long-range jet-liner capable of carrying a payload of 100,000lb over 5,000 miles, saw Shorts propose a development of its Belfast freighter. The PD53 was to be powered by four Rolls-Royce RB178 engines of 25,000lb thrust, to cruise at Mach 0.75, and saw the existing SC5 forward fuselage mated to a new tail fuselage and a swept wing based on the Lockheed C141. The twin-decked fuselage could accommodate 140 passengers on the upper deck, or a maximum of 242. BOAC were interested in the design as a long-range freighter, although it could also have been used as a long-range jetliner. **Length 146ft 10in, Span 163ft 5in, Height 41ft 8in**
PD60	Short-range civil transport.
PD65	DC3 replacement **feederliner** powered by jet engines, later incorporated into joint VFW614 studies.
PD75	200-seater jet **Airbus** study.
PD80	Low-wing turboprop **feederliner**.
333/335	Early stretched 330 developments that led to the Short SD3-60.
450	Stretched 360 **feederliner** to seat up to forty-eight.
NRA90	Joint **feederliner** project with de Havilland Canada, to seat twenty-five passengers. There were two proposals – the NRA 90A conventional high-wing twin and the NRA90B, a low-wing pusher design.
FJX	1988 study for forty- to fifty-seater jet **feederliner**.

Vickers

VC3   Civil development of Varsity to seat twenty-seven passengers, powered by Bristol Hercules engines, with a maximum weight of 3,500lb. It was not proceeded with after the success of Viscount.

VC4   Schemes for a 1946 North Atlantic jet airliner under a number of configurations, including three Rolls-Royce Avons and four underwing engines. A design from November 1947 featured a pressurised fuselage to accommodate up to seventy passengers with a high wing, single fin rudder and swept back wings with double slotted flaps, and an AUW of 119,598lb, and a range of 3,000 miles. Power would have been provided by four Metropolitan Vickers Sapphire engines.
Length 114ft 6in, Span 147ft 3in, Height 30ft, Wing Area 3,300sq.ft

VC5   Early studies centred on a high-wing seventy- to ninety-nine-seater transport capable of flying from London–New York in eight hours, with a cruising speed of 468 knots, a range of 3,000 nautical miles, and an AUW of 179,000lb. Later proposals centred on a Valiant development for BOAC as a long-range jetliner, which was later incorporated into V1000/VC7 proposal.
Length 152ft, Span 130ft 6in, Wing Area 2,176sq.ft

VC6   Short-range Valiant-based airliner proposed for BEA, based on VC5 study.

VC7/V1000   Originally a transport aircraft based on the Valiant, this was later developed into a military transport for the RAF, and a commercial airliner for **BOAC**, cancelled in November 1955.

Type 870   Developments of Viscount, firstly with RB109, and later with jet engines (see **BEA**).

Vanjet   A number of studies carried out on jet developments of the Vanguard to meet **BEA** specification, also given Medium-Range Transport and VC10 monikers.

VC11   A Type 1400 1959 study for a short-/medium-range transport based on the VC10, and offered to **BEA**.

586/587   **Supersonic** airliner studies.

799   High-wing **Car Ferry**/OR323 proposal.

Project X   **Supersonic** airliner studies.

Westland

Specification 25/43   Thirty-seater design to meet **Brabazon 2A** Specification.

Specification 26/43   Twin-engined design against **Brabazon 5B** Specification.

Specification 18/44   Twelve-seater twin-engined and ten- to twelve-seater turbojet transports to **Brabazon 5A**.

Specification 20/44   Design submitted towards **Brabazon 4**.

Specification 15/46   Design study against **Brabazon 2B**.

26/49   Two studies undertaken, both of low-wing design: a twelve-seater powered by Gipsy Queen X, and a fifteen-seater with three-abreast seating, powered by four Gipsy Queen 30 engines, with an AUW of 12,500lb.
Length 47ft 6in, Span 80ft, Wing Area 580sq.ft

BEAline   A four Rolls-Royce Dart-engined design to BEAline specification (see VTOL).

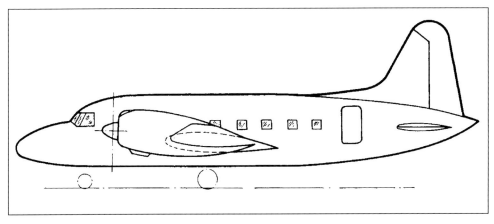

Vickers VC3
The civil variant of the Varsity was to be the Bristol Hercules-powered Vickers VC3. (BAE SYSTEMS – via Brooklands Museum Trust)

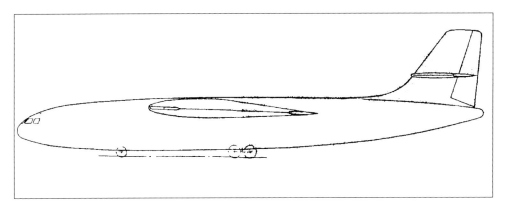

Vickers VC5
An early drawing of the proposed high-wing Vickers VC5, capable of travelling from London–New York. (BAE SYSTEMS – via Brooklands Museum Trust)

BEAline	A three Napier Eland-engined BEAline design (see VTOL).
Transport	A thirty-seater twin Armstrong Siddeley Double Mamba helicopter with a 75ft-main rotor.
Light Transport	A four-five-seater light transport and communications aircraft of high-wing design, powered by two Gipsy Queen 30 engines. This multi-purpose design could also convert to freighter or ambulance duties.
W80	Twenty-seater Twin Hercules-powered helicopter with a gross weight of 14,500lb, and a maximum cruising speed of 135mph, proposed in 1951. **Fuselage Length 60ft, Rotor Diameter 75ft**
W81	Thirty-seater Single Double Mamba helicopter with a gross weight of 18,000lb and a maximum speed of 187mph. **Fuselage Length 65ft, Rotor Diameter 75ft**

W85	A six Armstrong Siddeley Adder (three pair) mounted on the rotor blade tip, with seating for up to 102, a gross weight of 53,000lb, and a cruising speed 120mph, with a nose loading ramp. **Fuselage Length 64ft, Rotor Diameter 104ft**
WS61	Civil development of Sea King, powered by twin Gazelles, also called Wiltshire.
WG1	Twin-rotor helicopter similar to Chinook, powered by four Gnome H 1600 engines, grouped either side of the rear rotor pylon, with three blade rotors. The WG1 was designed for both military (ASW and heavy lifting) plus civil roles.
WG11C	Twin rotor sixty-seater large compound helicopter with four-abreast seating, a main rotor of 57ft, aft stub wings and forward sponsons, powered by four Gnome H1400 engines. Like the WG1, the WG11 was proposed for both military and civil roles. The latter featured a 12ft fuselage extension, and had an AUW of 35,000lb. **Fuselage Length 64ft 6in, Height 18ft 10in**

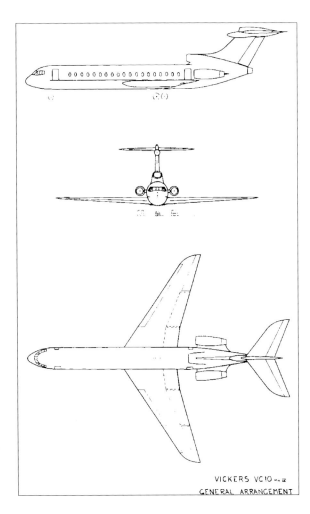

Vickers VC10 Mk4
One of the many schemes proposed under the VC10 designation, the Mk4 was a tri-jet design. (BAE SYSTEMS – via Brooklands Museum Trust)

WE01	A six-seater tilt-wing executive aircraft with four T63 engines, proposed as a research vehicle for **VTOL** studies.
WE02	Larger tilt rotor design to seat up to 100 passengers, with a gross weight of 100,000lb (see **VTOL**).
WG22	Convertible rotor aircraft proposed to TARC (see **VTOL**).
Compound	1971 design for a high-speed multi-purpose compound helicopter with high wing, to seat up to forty passengers, with a 60ft diameter.
606	Civil Lynx development to seat up to twelve passengers. The 606 kept the Lynx transmission and main rotor, but had an extended fuselage with either Rolls-Royce Gem or Pratt & Whitney PT6B engines. Lynx XW836 saw its cockpit area removed, and the cabin area was increased by the addition of a plug of wood and metal some 2ft long. The aircraft, however, did not fly. In 1974 the mock-up was exhibited in Disneyland at the twenty-seventh Helicopter Association of America Seminar and Exhibition. Later, a civil Lynx derivative emerged as the Westland 30.
656	Civil Sea King development put forward in September 1974 for offshore oil-drilling work. The 656 would have been powered by more powerful H-1400-1 engines, and had a greater fuel capacity. Up to twenty-four passengers could be carried over 345 miles. The 656 never entered production as operators did not consider its capabilities to benefit over the existing S61.

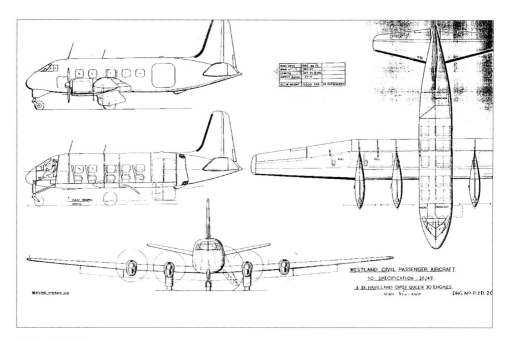

Westland 26/49
Westland's proposal to meet Specification 26/49 was this low-wing four Gipsy Queen 30-engined design.
(Westland Helicopters)

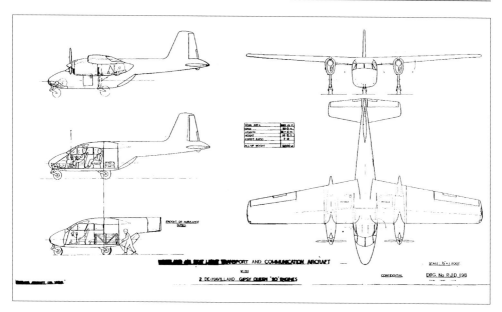

Westland Light Communications
The four/five-seater Westland Light transport powered by two de Havilland Gipsy Queen 30 engines. (Westland
Helicopters)

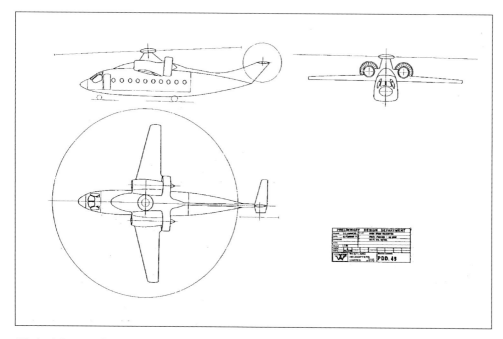

Westland Compound
A 1971 proposal from Westland for a forty-seater high-speed helicopter. (Westland Helicopters)

| Eurofar | The European Future advanced rotorcraft (Eurofar) was a thirty-seater civil tilt rotor proposed by a team of European companies, including Westland with Aérospatiale, Agusta, CASA and MBB in the mid-eighties. The basic design was of a high-wing layout with T-tail and tilting nacelles. |
| WG34 | Designed as a successor to the Sea King under Naval Staff Requirement 6646, issued in spring 1977, the WG34 was a triple-turbine helicopter powered by General Electric T700s, with a five-bladed main rotor, which was to be offered for both military and civil customers. Construction of a prototype was quite advanced when the decision was taken, due to costs, to amalgamate the programme with that of a European partner. In November 1979, a joint Anglo–Italian Memorandum of Understanding was set up to investigate a joint project. This resulted in the EH101, which was officially launched in 1984, and was heavily based on the WG34 design. |

Bibliography

Air Bridge, Paul Doyle, Forward Airfield Research, 2000

Airspeed Aircraft, H.A. Taylor, Putnam, 1970/91

Armstrong Whitworth Aircraft, Oliver Tapper, Putnam, 1973

Avro Aircraft, A.J. Jackson, Putnam, 1965/90

BAC One-Eleven, Stephen Skinner, Tempus, 2002

Blackburn Aircraft, A.J. Jackson, Putnam, 1968

Bristol Aerospace, Geoff Green, 1985

Bristol Aircraft, C.H. Barnes, Putnam, 1964/94

Bristol Britannia, Phil Lo Bao, Aviation Data Centre, 1996

Britain's Aircraft Industry – What went right, what went wrong, Arthur Reed, Dent, 1973

British Aircraft Corporation, Charles Gardner, Batsford, 1981

British Aircraft Specifications, K.J. Meekcoms and E.B. Morgan, Air Britain, 1994

British Independent Airlines, A.C. Merton Jones, LAAS International/Merseyside Aviation Society, 1976

British Military Helicopters, John Everett-Heath, Arms & Armour, 1986

British Secret Project – Fighters, Tony Butler, Midland Publishing, 2000

Concorde Affair, John Davis, Leslie Frewin, 1969

Concorde Story, Christopher Orlebar, Osprey, 1997

De Havilland Aircraft, A.J. Jackson, Putnam, 1962/78

De Havilland Comet, Phil Lo Bao, Aviation Data Centre

De Havilland Comet, Philip J. Birtles, Ian Allan, 1990

English Electric Aircraft, Stephen Ransom and Robert Fairclough, Putnam, 1987

Fairey Aircraft, H.A. Taylor, Putnam, 1974

Fairey Aviation, John W.R. Taylor, Chalford Publishing, 1997

First Jetliner – The Story of the Comet, Timothy Walker, Scoval, 2000

From Sea to Air, A.E. Tagg and R.L. Wheeler, Crossprint, 1989

From Spitfire to Eurofighter, Roy Boot, Airlife, 1990

Gloster Aircraft, Derek James, Putnam, 1971/87

Golden Age, Charles Woodley, Airlife, 1992

Handley Page Aircraft, C.H. Barnes, Putnam, 1976

Handley Page Herald, Graham Cowell, Janes, 1980

Hawker Aircraft, Frank K. Mason, Putnam, 1961

Hawker Siddeley Trident, Max Kingsley-Jones, Ian Allan, 1993

Hawker Siddeley Trident, Phil Lo Bao, Aviation Data Centre, 1992

Illustrated History of BEA, Phil Lo Bao, Browcom, 1989

In Cobham's Country, Colin Cruddas, Cobham, 1994

Lion Rampant and Winged, Alan Robertson, 1986

Modern Airliner, Peter W. Brooks, Putnam, 1961

Percival Aircraft, Norman Ellison, Chalford Publishing, 1997

Project Cancelled, Derek Wood, Bobbs Merrill, 1975

Shorts Aircraft, C.H. Barnes, Putnam, 1967/89

Silent, Swift, Superb – Vickers VC10, Scott Henderson, Scoval, 1998

Spirit of Folland, Derek N. James, Tempus, 2000

Vickers Aircraft, C.F. Andrews and E.B. Morgan, Putnam, 1969/88

Vickers VC10, Phil Lo Bao, Aviation Data Centre, 1993

Vickers Vanguard, Phil Lo Bao, Aviation Data Centre, 1994

Vickers Viscount, Alan J. Wright, Ian Allan, 1992

Westland Aircraft, Derek James, Putnam, 1991

Westland, David Mondey, Janes, 1982

Wings Across the World, Harald Penrose, Cassell, 1980

Wings over the Island, David L. Wiliams, Coachouse, 1999

Periodicals

Aeroplane

Air International

Air Pictorial

Air Enthusiast

Flight International

Index

If you are interested in purchasing
other books published by Tempus, or in case you have
difficulty finding any Tempus books in your local bookshop,
you can also place orders directly through our website

www.tempus-publishing.com